Cultural Memory
in
the
Present

Mieke Bal and Hent de Vries, Editors

SILENT URNS

Romanticism, Hellenism, Modernity

David S. Ferris

STANFORD UNIVERSITY PRESS

STANFORD, CALIFORNIA

2000

Stanford University Press
Stanford, California
© 2000 by the Board of Trustees of the
Leland Stanford Junior University

Printed in the United States of America

CIP data appear at the end of the book

Acknowledgments

I extend thanks to Yale University for Morse and Senior Faculty fellowships, which permitted much of the reading and research that helped define and focus the subject of this book. Special thanks go to Roger Blood, Susan Blood, and Haun Saussy for their intellectual company at a time when distance makes such company all the more valuable; to Paul Fry and Heinrich von Staden, for conversations in which the early direction of this project took shape; to Vincent Crapanzano, for his encouragement and unswerving sense of intellectual integrity; to Burton Pike, for his consistent helpfulness in supporting this and other projects; to Elizabeth Brown, for her invaluable help as my research assistant in the final stages of preparing the manuscript. Special thanks must also be extended to those students at the Graduate School whose participation in seminars on the material discussed here as well as related materials, provided a welcome oasis of collegiality and intellectual purpose. In a moment that reflects the influence of Winckelmann, thanks are also due to the climate. Without its help in the summer of 1996, the writing of the bulk of this book would have undoubtedly sweltered on to another year.

Chapter 2 first appeared in an earlier version that reflected the occasion of its publication in *The Lessons of Romanticism*, edited by Robert Gleckner and Thomas Pfau. Chapter 5 was first published in *Afterimages: A Festschrift in Honor of Irving Massey*, edited by William Kumbier and Ann Colley. These chapters are reprinted here by the kind permission of Duke University Press and the Shuffaloff Press, Toronto, respectively.

D.S.F.

Contents

Preface

In Book 12 of Homer's *Odyssey*, Odysseus sails toward the Sirens, about whose song Circe had warned him. Having blocked the ears of his men to prevent them from listening to the song, thus forgetting the purpose of their voyage, Odysseus, tightly bound to the mast of his ship, first hears the Sirens speak. They promise a song that will not only leave their listeners well pleased but will also give them a knowledge of "everything that the Argives and the Trojans did and suffered in wide Troy through the gods' despite." This, however, is only a part of what the Sirens can offer. They add, "Over all the generous earth we know everything that happens."[1] The lure of the Sirens is, in effect, the promise of a knowledge of history. In the case of Troy this is the promise of a history Odysseus already knows, which Demodokos, Alkinoös's singer, sang for him in Book 8. Why Odysseus should want to listen to this history must be due to some other quality in the version sung by the Sirens. Their voices are "honey-sweet"; they will give pleasure. Odysseus wants to listen to this aesthetic quality, rather than to what is said. The promise of a knowledge of history is offered up by an aesthetic beguilement, from which neither Odysseus nor his men would return if not forewarned.

The story of the Sirens in the *Odyssey* embodies much of what eighteenth-century Hellenism promised: a knowledge of history in a resolutely aesthetic form. But the similarity ends here, even before it has properly taken hold. Unlike Odysseus, we have no Circe to warn of the effects this aestheticization of history will have on modernity. Like so many before Odysseus, we will be trapped on the beach before the Sirens by this absence of a warning; an insatiable desire to know our history will detain us, listening until we can listen no longer. Unable to warn those who will come after and unable to negotiate this danger by lashing ourselves to the mast of a ship, we will be detained by a song whose promise of history has been coated with aesthetic pleasure. Our only hope of rescue from this fate seems to lie in an ability to expose the ideology at work in such an aesthetic experience. If we recognize ideology, then maybe we too can break free from the Sirens and the beauty of their song. But the recognition of such ideology offers us no safe voyage when its purpose is to realize the promise of history made by the Sirens. At this point, the recognition of ideology promises an understanding of history that threatens to become the Siren song of our modernity, because ideological criticism comes to repeat the promise it was meant to expose, the promise made by the Sirens. In this situation, rather than freeing ourselves, we run the risk of detaining ourselves further, precisely by being tempted with the promise of a history no longer subordinate to the aesthetic pleasures of Homer's Sirens. To escape such Sirens we must forget how they lure us into their song in the first place. When we attempt this feat, we are no longer like Homer's Odysseus, rather we are more like the Odysseus of Kafka who plugs his ears and, in so doing, believes he has avoided hearing the aesthetic seduction of their song. But what if, as Kafka suggests in his reflection on this scene, the Sirens have "a still more fatal weapon than their song, namely their silence"?[2] Faced by their silence, Odysseus, as Kafka notes, would never know that the Sirens had tricked him and would thus sail on elated by his false sense of victory. In this respect, Kafka's Odysseus emerges as the figure of a modernity that does not want to face the silence of the past, always capable of disassociating himself from the aesthetic seduction of the song sung in its place.

This introductory parable points to the predicament our modernity must face as it tries to come to terms with the Hellenism it inherits from Winckelmann's aesthetic account of the history of Greece. This legacy can be characterized as a Siren song whose aesthetic promise conceals the profound silence from which it arises, the profound silence of a past that can no longer speak for itself. If the Sirens are silent, as Kafka says, then they are silent because someone has decided to withstand their song. The Sirens entrap Odysseus in this silence, from which he can never escape. Refusing the Sirens' song, he is unable to know if he has in fact refused anything at all. Indeed, Kafka's Odysseus will never know whether or not they were silent. If, like Kafka's Odysseus, we are to refuse this song and plug our ears, then we will never know either. Escape from this predicament appears impossible: if we unplug our ears, we can only know what no one else will ever know, because we end up rotting on the beach like all the Sirens' victims. (Here, it should be remembered that Kafka's Sirens appear to sing only for those who do not plug their ears.) In these circumstances, the only option left appears to be that of Homer's Odysseus: to hear the song of the Sirens while lashed to the mast. Yet, this does not help much either. Even if Circe's advice is taken, no one else can hear this song because everyone must be made temporarily deaf if the stratagem is to succeed. Who then can know what Odysseus heard? Any attempt to confirm the song—or even that the Sirens sang—will be met with silence. This situation is complicated further. As even Homer's text reveals, it is unclear how long Odysseus listens to their song. Odysseus, in his narrative, states, "They sang, in sweet utterance, and the heart within me desired to listen, and I signalled to my companions to set me free."[3] Odysseus seems to indicate that to listen requires being set free to go to the Sirens. In this case, the song of the Sirens—the song of history that will steal away from Odysseus any prospect of coming home—remains a promise. Moreover, the promise extended by their song can be realized only when its listeners no longer have any need of history and can no longer participate in any history, least of all their own. The Sirens promise nothing more than the silence of a death, a promise whose realization absolves them of the need to fulfill any other promise. What Odysseus survives is the promise of this silence.

Hellenism is directed toward such silence, as if it had heard the song of the Sirens and was now able to sing of the Greek past that they had only promised. Even more than Odysseus, this Hellenism would have listened and survived. But if the situation present in both Homer and Kafka remains in force, then this Hellenism has written the history of a promise and not a history of Greece. If this is so, then the question of what Hellenism achieved becomes more important than what Greece achieved. Posing this question reveals that more is at stake than a mere idealization of the aesthetic productions of Greece. What Hellenism establishes for the first time is that such productions also express a history. This relation of the historical to the aesthetic forms the principal subject of inquiry in this book and, in particular, the poetic reflection on this relation in the work of Keats, Shelley, and Hölderlin.

To deal adequately with the historical as it arises in this period, one must first examine its origin in a discourse that is essentially aesthetic, rather than historical, in organization. Such a discourse occurs within Winckelmann's *History of Ancient Art.* In reading this text, the emphasis falls on how an aestheticization of history underlies the formation of a concept of culture in the image of a state. Since what is at stake for Winckelmann is an identity of nation and culture, his work seeks to overcome the relation of a concept to what has or can have material existence (that is, Greek art). From this, the history of art arises as a discipline that maps the representation of the different forms taken by culture. A refusal to account for the concept of culture lying behind this history sustains art history as a discipline in its own right: the analogy between how a discipline sustains itself and modernity's means of self-perpetuation is not an accident of history.

Keats isolates a crucial aspect of Winckelmann's legacy (and it *is* Winckelmann's legacy, rather than the legacy of Greece): the aesthetic. Ironically, this aspect has often been confused with Keats's poetry, as if his poetry were merely its exemplar. A poem that makes use of the aesthetic as both its subject matter and its means of reflection on that subject matter is not saying the same thing twice, particularly not when the reflection takes the form of granting speech to an object that can neither speak nor be seen except by reifying the language of the poem's description. Although the internal complexity of a poem such as Keats's "Ode on a Grecian Urn" may be aestheticized into the traditional history of our relation to Greece, this very complexity cautions against such a move. Keats's earlier sonnets on Grecian topics already reflect a more complex relation to Greece. As with the urn, his relation explores the discrepancy between conceptual understanding (in the form of knowledge and history) and the resources of poetic language. Out of this discrepancy, the question of Greece returns as the question of its freedom from a modernity that would espouse and also reject it for the same reason: its tyranny over subsequent history.

Although Keats, in the "Ode on a Grecian Urn," adopts, or rather "fosters," a poetic form that is Greek in origin as a means of exploring this discrepancy, an equally significant reference to Greece occurs in this poem's allusion to sacrifice in the fourth stanza. Through this allusion, tragedy—the exemplary form of sacrifice that dominated early-fifth-century Athens—is evoked. But Keats does so in a way that questions the history tragedy establishes by sacrificing an individual. By this questioning, Keats resists understanding the moment of sacrifice as a denouement loaded with the promise of a freedom that may be experienced vicariously by its spectators. This resistance, as a reading of Schelling's last letter from his *Letters on Dogmatism and Criticism* amply demonstrates, resists a history in which a literary genre is made to define the political history of a nation in an aesthetic experience of freedom. For Schelling, the individual's act of sacrifice is the highest example of freedom, and the form in which this act is best expressed is Greek tragedy. Yet, for Schelling the experience of freedom must remain a negative one. It is realized in the failure of the individual to surpass the limit of their individuality. Fate enforces this limit, but it is experienced (as a limit) in the formal requirements of a work of art. While this implies that every work of art is such because it offers an experience of limits, tragedy is a special case because its form exemplifies what its hero struggles against. By interpreting Greek tragedy as the form of this struggle, Schelling provides an account of why Greek tragedy is so exemplary in literary history. His account, like Winckelmann's account of Greek art and sculpture, defines the significance of art in terms of a freedom whose realization remains bound equally to its aesthetic representation and to the negation of that representation.

The question of tragedy and its relation to Greece's freedom arises nowhere more emphatically than in two lyrical dramas of Shelley, *Hellas* and *Prometheus Unbound*. In *Hellas*, this question is historically topical. The play, as Shelley indicates in his Preface, is written with reference to the Greek war of independence. Yet, the political and historical dimension introduced by this reference can hardly exhaust its story. Like *Prometheus Unbound*, *Hellas* poses a question about its Greek literary precedent. By referring to the two plays of Aeschylus—*The Persians* and the lost *Prometheus Unbound*—these two works by Shelley point to how Keats's reflection on the relation of poetic language to the concept of culture represented by Greece becomes the question of how a literary model can address Greece as a paradigm within our literary and political histories. By relating the literary to the political and historical, Shelley not only takes up the concept of culture bequeathed to modernity by Winckelmann but also does so in a context that presents freedom as a question posed by the nature of poetic language.

In *Hellas*, this question emerges from a crucial difference between the historical relation of Aeschylus and Shelley to the subject matter of their dramas. Aeschylus writes of an event whose outcome is already known to its audience; and Shelley writes of an event that has not yet attained historical existence—the independence of modern Greece from Turkey. Freedom in this context is articulated with reference to an earlier literary model that would appear to guarantee the modern occurrence of freedom in Greece and so affirm a modern history for freedom. But in this history, as the classical model also points out, the story of freedom is told through the medium of another; that is, the story of Greece's freedom is told by the Persians. In both Shelley and Aeschylus, the freedom of Greece is thought by means of what is different from itself. As a result, rather than persist as a historical model of freedom, Greece becomes the model of a freedom that cannot tell its own history. This account stands in stark contrast to Winckelmann's *History of Ancient Art* as well as the tradition it inaugurates through Goethe, Schiller, Hegel, and Wagner.

While *Hellas* poses the question of freedom as a question about what modernity seeks to free itself from, *Prometheus Unbound* defines modernity as what Greece must be freed from. Here, the emphasis falls upon an act of freeing or, in the language of this poem's title, an act of unbinding. Exploring an act no longer bound to that from which it seeks to free itself, this poem shows how any treatment of the question of freedom is involved with that of judgment. To be recognized, freedom requires judgment. But, as this play points out, Prometheus seeks to be free from judgment. This situation is complicated further, because judgment cannot be separated from memory. Judgment can only take place if it is preceded by what it is meant to judge. In this respect, judgment always takes place with respect to the past (and this is so, as Shelley's *Hellas* points out, even when the future is being judged). Since the past exists only in the form of memory (mere objects or artifacts are not enough; they have to be the memory of something), the exercise of judgment is an exercise in representing memory as an event: judgment is always a decision about reference. For such judgment to be effective, it must not only occur at a time different from what it judges but also it must occur as an event, as a moment, in a time that is the time of judgment. Here, judgment reveals the temporal problem central to the question of freedom as it is articulated within romanticism. The medium in which judgment occurs—namely, time—is also the medium that calls upon judgment to decide its significance. Judgment is afflicted by the very problem that causes it to exist, just as freedom, once attained, is constrained by the referential restraint that demanded its existence. A fundamental noncoincidence appears inherent to any attempt to define either of these terms. Such a noncoincidence defines the beginning of *Prometheus Unbound*, when Prometheus seeks to recall the curse through which he had judged Jupiter's judgment upon him. As the complexity of the word "recall" indicates, Prometheus seeks through memory to revoke the judgment of time. Yet, when the curse is spoken to Prometheus, he cannot recall his words. When the judgment of time returns to its source, no sense of the word "recall" (remember, revoke, repeat) operates: judgment cannot remember what it once judged. From this Shelley's reflection on freedom arises, a reflection that poses the question of how freedom is to be conceived if judgment cannot recognize its occurrence.

The Hölderlin texts discussed, "Andenken" and "Mnemosyne," also address the question of freedom in relation to memory. However, in Hölderlin this folds into a reflection on the individuality of the modern. Here, Hölderlin's thought engages directly with the tragic, at least in the sense Schelling gives to this form when he analyzes it as resolving the question of freedom with respect to the individual subject. In Hölderlin, however, Greek tragedy is not easily sustained as an example to which modernity should subordinate itself. Already in his translations of Sophocles, another kind of relation can be discerned. In his letters, Hölderlin is explicit on this point, particularly when he says, "We must not share anything identical with [the Greeks]."[4] For modernity to share the identity of the Greeks would require modernity to surrender its freedom to the Greeks. Yet, as Hölderlin also knew, modernity's freedom is not gained by the rejection of Greece, since in this rejection Greece attains the identity of a tradition only modernity could give it. For Hölderlin, the task of modernity as it is expressed in the formation of the "national spirit" of Germany is to face what is "most difficult," namely, "the free use of one's own."[5] Modernity defines itself by rejecting Greece: its freedom is conditioned by affirming what it rejects. At the same time, this rejection refuses to raise the possibility that Greece too sought the free use of its own before it too fell victim to a history that sought to ensure its future by denying the individuality of its freedom. Hölderlin turns to such an individuality as both the source of his relation to Greece and, at the same time, the source of his poetic language. Here, the question of Greece (not to mention the question of romanticism) becomes the question of individuality.

Several issues arise when one focuses romantic Hellenism on the question of individuality. Though these issues are initially literary, they are not unrelated to the cultural and political concerns informing the practice of modern criticism. The criticism of a work of literature always occurs as a judgment of its relation to something other than the work being judged —not even New Criticism could stop this referential movement. How to define the individuality of the work in question consequently becomes insurmountably difficult. Is this why our literary history can be no more than the record of repeated attempts to circumvent this difficulty, of repeated attempts to achieve a modernity that would always be modern? From within our critical traditions, literature appears never to be free from criticism's tendency to deny individuality to what it reads, and to do so in the name of asserting its own individuality. That literature should be the arena in which this tendency is played out suggests that what remains most resistant is the very medium of literature. Ultimately, criticism cannot avoid this. In literature criticism must face the medium of its own insight, a medium that is at once familiar and yet no longer quite its own. The evasion of this medium may be called the *culture of modernity*, because we owe our modern sense of criticism to the generalization of the literary as culture. Such a sense first takes form within Winckelmann's *History of Ancient Art* and then becomes known as Hellenism once the identity of culture and history has exerted its conceptual power over the medium of its expression. From Winckelmann we receive the understanding of culture that informs not just our modernity but also the critical vocation through which modernity repeatedly defines itself.

As recalled by this preface, this book is more than an examination of how the discourse that founds art history migrates to other disciplines. Rather, it examines how the relation of history and culture has defined the nature of criticism within our modernity. The significance of the reflection undertaken by the romantic poets discussed here is derived directly from their treatment of this relation. By questioning the critical power invested in the relation between history and culture, the poets open the question of freedom for modernity at the very moment when modernity asserts itself as a critical force arising from Winckelmann's founding relation between history and culture. That this question is so quickly foreclosed testifies not only to the force of our desire to be modern but also to our commitment to a concept of criticism in the service of such modernity. The question of freedom is still one that modernity has to pose, and it is the question of a freedom no longer established through the limits set by criticism. This book is directed toward the opening of such a question within our modern understanding of criticism.

We believe to be saying all kinds of new things and, still, all this is reaction, as it were, a mild revenge against the slavery with which we have behaved toward antiquity.

—FRIEDRICH HÖLDERLIN

Introduction

In recent years, critical thought has devoted itself to reevaluating the cultural influence history has accorded Greek literature and art. This reevaluation has occurred within an intellectual context marked by a willingness to question the persistence of traditions, which are now regarded as out of step with the premises of our critical modernity. A drive to place the study of art and literature within a broader historical and political frame, one no longer circumscribed by the narrow confines of a Western and specifically Greek tradition, fuels this willingness to question such traditions. This expansion has been accompanied by an increased attention to culture as the broadest possible umbrella under which the modern task of criticism may plot its course. In this role, culture has become the medium through which we are able to analyze a totality of influences affecting not only artistic expression (as it has been traditionally recognized in "high art") but also those other forms now competing within academia for the attention historically restricted to canonical texts. While this shift to "cultural" analysis has had the local effect of causing the value, or significance, of a particular text or group of texts to be reappraised, its real significance may be found in the way that such a shift takes up, once again, the possibility of defining our modernity in a representative manner.

An immediate effect of this shift is that the name of Greece can no longer stand for the cultural and political values it has traditionally been accorded. Indeed, if we are to remain true to our modernity, we must now refuse precisely the tradition fostering such values. But, in pursuing such a refusal, care needs to be taken to distinguish between historical Greece and the later cultivation of Greece as a reference point for all subsequent art and literature—a role it did not assume until the advent of Hellenism in the eighteenth century.

A number of factors explain how the influence of Greece develops at this particular historical moment. The publication of the archaeological discoveries at Pompeii and Herculaneum is certainly crucial, but more decisive is the reconfiguring of the aesthetic as a source of historical knowledge. The Greece that appears in the eighteenth century, as the writings of Johann Winckelmann most clearly reveal, embodies this reconfiguring. Indeed, it is only after Winckelmann that the aesthetic aspect of art and the political existence of a nation become bound indissolubly to one another.[1]

For modernity to reject the tradition that originates with this joining of the artistic to the political, it must also dismiss the first example of the source from which it draws its own critical power—its ability to reveal the political significance of aesthetic works. Whenever modernity performs such a dismissal it does so as a means to establish itself as the historical moment best able to reveal the hidden or even unconscious political agenda of a past consumed by the ideology of its aesthetic practice.[2] With such a performance, there is, however, always the suspicion of a misreading, of a desire to totalize the past and then dismiss it because of its totality. The presence of such a desire indicates that what is at stake is the need to establish our own historical significance, against which the meaning and influence of Greece is revealed as an aesthetically constructed ideology. The recognition that such a necessity is at work in this gesture should cause us to hesitate, because its logic presents a troubling question: Will the historical significance we ascribe to the present become as ideologically suspect as the one we now reject? If the present is to suffer the fate of the past it has just rejected, then our willingness to represent Greece as the source of an ideologically suspect tradition suggests the desire to sustain the modern role of criticism as the unmasker of ideology, as the guardian of an ideology free modernity, is the real issue.[3] Yet, by no means is modernity on sound historical ground when it pursues the purgation of ideology. Indeed, the confusion of Greece with what became known belatedly as a "Western tradition" indicates how much more is at stake in the modern refusal of antiquity than Greece.[4]

Beyond the assertion of our historical significance, beyond the desire to unmask ideology, there lies the task of identifying the confusion of myth and history that characterizes the ideological. Such identification presupposes the ability to tell the difference between myth and history as a prelude to extricating oneself from a mythical past. In the eyes of modernity, the past and its traditions always labors under the illusion of this confusion. Modernity's insistence that the past always fall victim to a confusion of myth and history requires a consideration of the extent to which modernity draws its critical power from the production of such a confusion. Here, the difference between modernity and tradition is confined to their relation to such a confusion. In both cases, this confusion is productive of history: tradition realizes history *through* this confusion, whereas modernity realizes history as a consequence of this confusion. Either way, confusion, whether unconscious in the case of tradition or conscious in the case of modernity, provides the basis for the critical and historical origin of both tradition and modernity. The rejection of tradition by modernity makes no meaningful difference to this basis. This is nowhere more evident than in the example of Greece since the cultural influence, and thus the significance of Greece, is affirmed at the very moment it is unmasked as myth or ideology.[5] In this case, criticism practiced in the name of modernity will always be in flight from the ideological confusion that justifies its existence.

The distinction between history and myth or ideology is always a critical distinction. As such, it is a distinction in which criticism discovers and then justifies itself by the fact of having made such a distinction. In this respect, what is called criticism here may also be known by what appears to name an historical epoch: modernity. But this modernity, as Nietzsche recognized, is less a historical period than a critical relation to history or what, if we had not decided to become modern, would still be recognized as the present.[6] What occurs through such a relation does not belong to history, but rather to a change in the subject of history. Despite this recognition and the lack of historical specificity modernity suffers from, the moment through which it comes into existence always occurs as the discovery of a new historical significance—much like the one presented by Keats in the sestet to his sonnet on Chapman's Homer when he describes the discovery of a new planet. This moment is crucial if criticism is to avoid divorcing itself from what it perceives as the source of its power: history. But should this divorce occur, the need for history increases to the point where it will be bought even at the price of critical self-contradiction, that is, when it is grounded in and makes use of the methodology it rejects.

While the present conflict between traditional and modern interpretations of Greece may appear to arise within the development of critical history in the nineteenth and twentieth centuries, this conflict is, in fact, nothing more than the modern world's evasion of a difficulty posed by the ancient world. Like modernity, Greece also had to forge a history freed from the myths of its predecessors. That this freedom is obtained by the appropriation of preceding myths or by the invention of its own myths does not, in the end, matter.[7] A critical gesture grounded in the ability to represent history as myth matters far more. Through such a gesture the historicality of the present stands in stark contrast. But, if we accept that Greece would also have had to make this gesture, then, and despite the claims of modernity, Greece will have arisen from what, for once, Greece did not achieve.[8] Only the critical relation to the past expressed by modernity could give the myth of Greece the history that was beyond its grasp. This does not mean that Greece did not desire to realize its own in the legacy called the "Western tradition."[9] Rather, as is now apparent, Greece's desire to know its own myth as history has become the desire of modernity to know Greece as the repetition of this same desire.

Although antiquity exerts considerable influence on the Renaissance, Greece does not become more than a textual heritage until the eighteenth century.[10] Only at this historical point does Greece emerge as the cultural icon of Western art and literature. While this emergence coincides with the beginning of modern archaeological research into antiquity at Herculaneum and Pompeii, such research was not enough by itself to determine the influential role Greek culture assumed during this period.[11] Despite the appearance of this material, the archaeological discoveries at Herculaneum and Pompeii could neither provide an interpretation of their own significance nor could they produce the kind of systematic account of Greek politics, culture, and history that allows Greece to develop the par-

adigmatic significance it attains in Winckelmann's *History of Ancient Art*
(1764)—a significance already present in his *Reflections on the Imitation of
Greek Works in Painting and Sculpture* (1755).[12] One cannot overlook the
fact that this significance developed as an effect of Winckelmann's writing.
Nor can one overlook how Winckelmann's writings generated such significance despite the paucity of authentic examples of Greek art extant during Winckelmann's lifetime as well his own failure to travel beyond Rome
and the Vatican.[13] Since Winckelmann's work treats a Greek art that does
not yet exist in material form, his writings provide an unparalleled example for studying the formation of a culture in the absence of direct experience of that culture's own artistic productions. At the same time, by reference to the limited examples of Greek art available at the time, these
writings indicate the power of synecdoche as a means of presenting a conceptual understanding of culture as if it also possessed a material form.

To establish the cultural significance of Greece, Winckelmann adopts
a procedure that begins with extant textual descriptions of art from antiquity and then builds a history of actual art objects on the basis of these
descriptions. Obviously, for this procedure to work, Winckelmann's history must assume that language possesses an unquestionable ability to
serve as a substitute for the visual property of sculpture and painting. This
assumption implies nothing less than the ability of language to create an
object, which may then become the subject of his writing. This assumption subsequently gives rise to not just a model of history but also, more
importantly, a means to define culture as an object that may be embodied
through description. This movement from language as a translation of the
visual (whose objects, by definition, have material existence) to a model
of history and culture is a defining step for both the understanding of history and culture in the modern period and for the critical power now invested in history and the material expressions of a culture. In effect
Winckelmann achieves through his treatment of Greece an ability to define the critical development of modernity as a historical consciousness of
culture. After Winckelmann, the presence of this definition can be discerned in the way that all assertions of modernity express a change in
what culture represents, yet nowhere do they change the model of understanding linking history and culture in Winckelmann's writings.[14] As a result, the legacy of Winckelmann should be sought less in the discipline of

art history than in this understanding of modernity through which history and culture are linked during those moments of crisis repeatedly punctuating the modern experience of the humanities. In the end, such crises indicate our perpetual quest for a modernity in which we will recognize ourselves without the rage of Oscar Wilde's Caliban.[15]

Given the historical conditions under which Winckelmann wrote, difficulties and inaccuracies can be anticipated in his writings on Greek art and culture. Lessing was among the first to point to these in his *Laocoön* when he documented errors in Winckelmann's attribution of certain Greek art works to one or another of the periods of historical development described in the *History of Ancient Art*.[16] Nevertheless, these inaccuracies have had little effect on Winckelmann's influence, largely because they are insignificant when compared to the dominance enjoyed by his account of the interrelation of history, politics, and culture. This influence can be seen most clearly in the pervasive presence of Winckelmann's understanding of culture as the representation of the political existence of a nation (thereby confirming the political as one of the primary subjects of historical inquiry). This conjunction of the aesthetic and the political in culture now governs the critical practice of modernity even though the terms in which we discuss this conjunction are no longer those of Winckelmann. Yet, despite these changes, one element remains constant throughout this transformation, and it appears as an essential goal toward which our politics, our culture, and, above all, our modernity, is directed: freedom.

While freedom persisted as a subject of philosophical reflection long before the eighteenth century, not until the work of Winckelmann did it migrate from its place within philosophical and political discourse to become the animating principle of aesthetic inquiry. Winckelmann, by giving freedom such a determining role, has already established the parameters within which the modern vocation of criticism would develop. But modernity, by rejecting the history of Greece and its influence, would seek to separate itself from the Hellenism that Winckelmann defines as the essential characteristic of the culture it celebrates. In this instance modernity seeks to distance itself from the historical form in which Winckelmann embodies freedom, but it does not separate itself from a relation of politics, culture, and history grounded in freedom.

Our critical modernity has willingly accepted the conceptual link between the aesthetic and the political and historical significance of freedom (even though it may reject the historical form—Greece—in which this link is first expressed). Yet, this has not always been the case. More than at any moment since the eighteenth century (including the contemporary critique of the culture and history of the West) the place and meaning of freedom within this relation of culture and history was taken up within the romantic period and, in particular, within that expression of its poetry and aesthetics that we now refer to as romantic Hellenism.

Since the publication in 1931 of Harry Levin's *The Broken Column: A Study in Romantic Hellenism,* the subject of romantic Hellenism has enjoyed a recurring, yet limited, existence as a topos within literary romanticism.[17] But, more often than not, romantic Hellenism has been reduced to one more example of an uncritical acceptance of an ideologically suspect cultural patrimony. This uncritical reception practiced by such a Hellenism fosters the idea of Greece as a model that criticizes the present while at the same time providing the example of what the present should strive to invent for itself. As Winckelmann would have it, then, Dresden may become another Athens. According to this Hellenism, Greece plays a double historical role; it is both a model and a curse (as *the* model of cultural achievement Greece is ceded an unattainability that curses every attempt to recreate its achievement). But, this treatment of Greece conceals within its hellenophilia the role that such an example played (and continues to play albeit under other identities) in establishing a point of reference for critical judgment: Greece becomes the name that grounds judgment. Viewed from this perspective, the treatment of Greece within romanticism records a history that has less to do with either Greece or romanticism than with the persistent difficulty criticism has experienced in its pursuit of a ground for its judgments.[18]

The significance of Greece within the study of romanticism may indeed reflect a difficulty inherent to the project of critical reflection on literature and art. However, the rejection of Greece as a point of reference has given voice to a modernity that pursues not just historical freedom but also freedom from such critical problems. Modernity is, after all, the moment in which we judge history and literature in reference to ourselves—otherwise what point would there be in being modern? For modernity to establish itself as a point of historical reference, it must not just reject Greece but also the past in general. But, by so doing, it affirms the curse from which it seeks to free itself. This step is necessary because it allows modernity to reject a particular example of the past while at the same time affirming the possibility of itself as an undisputed source of historical reference. As before, what point would there be in rejecting Greece as a historical point of reference if it had not been regarded, however fallaciously, as such a point? Here, both Hellenism and modernity uncritically accept Greece as the locus of a cultural achievement. In the case of the former, this judgment of Greece establishes a critical relation between the past and the present; in the case of the latter, modernity uses such an affirmation to establish a critical relation between itself and the past. Despite this critical relation, modernity reserves the possibility of such cultural achievement for itself as it embarks on a historical course defined by the continual displacement of a past it can no longer recognize as its own. In the failure of such recognition one can locate the sense of crisis so frequently associated with the advent of modernity. Indeed, modernity may be nothing other than the repetition of this sense of crisis, this sense of separation.[19] A criticism guaranteed by a sense of history seems to be at stake in this separation. But where does this sense of history come from?

As stated above, Winckelmann's history is written in the absence of what historians would regard as the facts of their trade. Faced with such a situation, Winckelmann has no option but to invent a body of artwork to which history can refer. Lacking direct visual experience of ancient art, Winckelmann is in the position of writing an account of ancient art whose historical claims are aesthetic in the sense that they only exist as the representation of an art that survives in the scattered documents of antiquity. Since Winckelmann's historical undertaking is, in effect, derived from an aesthetic account of an aesthetic object, his *History of Ancient Art* should be considered as more a model for an aesthetic form of history than a history of aesthetic form.[20] Here, a crucial break occurs within eighteenth-century aesthetics. The aesthetic moves from a science of sensation (how it is presented by Baumgarten for instance) and becomes a mode of historical understanding (precisely the shift that finds its most extensive and magisterial expression in Hegel's three series of

Berlin lectures on the aesthetic delivered in the 1820s). Because this shift in aesthetic understanding gives rise to the sense of history underlying Greece's role as a cultural model to be either emulated or rejected, the critical positions taken by Hellenism and modernism can be traced to an aestheticization of history shared by both. Only through this aestheticization does Greece become the Greece that, to recall the title of Edith Butler's study, tyrannizes the literary, cultural, and political traditions of the West.

Much is at stake in this shift since it calls into existence dominating tendencies in our literary and critical histories, tendencies whose source can be traced to an understanding of visual art.[21] Because the origin of history can be traced to the visual, the aesthetic emerges not as a mere sign of beauty; rather, it takes on a central role in our interpretations of literature as well as the sense of culture from which the historical context of literature is derived. The aesthetic operates in this guise (as it has done since the eighteenth century) as a form of mediation that plays a perceptual role: it presents what is to be understood and it is also the mode in which this understanding takes place. This doubling of the aesthetic as representation and perception explains the powerful hold the aesthetic has had on critical interpretation—a role by now so ingrained that its operation is effectively transparent. The fundamental guiding principle of the modern study of culture makes this point clearly: since culture is an invention that has no claim to natural existence it may always represent whatever is invested in it. In effect, it can have no natural content or source. As a result, cultural criticism always runs the risk of being consumed by what it casts its gaze upon. Here, the question of *how* one sees is taken over by *what* one sees.[22]

This question of how one sees is taken up by romanticism when it incorporates and reflects upon the Hellenism it receives from the eighteenth century. Within romanticism, Hellenism is far from being a mere repetition of Winckelmann's veneration of Greece. Romantic Hellenism views Greece not just as a means of reflecting upon its modernity but also as a means to pose questions concerning the conflicting roles played by judgment and freedom in the realization of modernity. These are precisely the questions that modernity would evade by presenting itself as the consciousness of a crisis from which it gives birth to itself. Where these questions occur romanticism can be said to undertake an inquiry into the aestheticization of history that has dominated literary and cultural interpretation, including that of romanticism. The existence of such an inquiry will require us to rethink both the relation of romanticism to modernity and also the aesthetic account of freedom that this relation contains. As such, this moment within romanticism cannot be separated from an inquiry into the critical project that now defines our relation to all cultural production, a project whose claim to significance takes place in the name of freedom and whose history can be traced to Winckelmann, who was the first to articulate this claim in relation to aesthetic works. Such an inquiry should not be avoided at a time when the criticism of art and literature has become the privileged means of articulating not just resistance to ideological oppression (to the extent that criticism—especially literary criticism—fashions itself as the preeminent medium for the unmasking of ideology) but also a vocation for academic study in its own right.[23]

Within this context Greece is not simply a synonym for cultural and intellectual achievement; rather, it is the name through which the theoretical and critical possibility of modernity is decided in the eighteenth century. This is the possibility that modernity's rejection of Greece has been unable to see, because its desire for self-identity requires it to be the historical source for such a possibility. But, in this desire, modernity repeats the gesture already contained within Hellenism. In the form of modernity, Hellenism persists beyond its actual occasion; its significance is not derived from antiquity, but rather from its ability to establish the critical relation through which modernity relates to the past. Modernity's rejection of Greece as the paradigm of a Western tradition confirms this significance in an act indicative of what is at stake: the construction of an ideology for the sake of criticism, a criticism validated by the ideology it would unmask. But, what if this Greece could only have come into existence as a result of the conjunction of history and the aesthetic developed by Winckelmann? What if Greece only became Greece in the eighteenth century?[24] If this is indeed the case, then what is being rejected is only the particular form that was given to a critical paradigm in the eighteenth century. Here, it is the failure of a paradigm that is being rejected. But this takes place within a history owing its systematicity to the predictability of such a failure. Ironically, the critical need for paradigms is never more evident than when paradigms are questioned and rejected in the name of a history conceived on the back of their repeated failure.

While the treatment of Hellenism within romanticism indicates a questioning of how history and the aesthetic come together in the eighteenth century, this does not mean that romanticism can simply evade what it questions. Here, it is important to remember that it is one thing to reject a given paradigm for its ideology and quite another to view this rejection as part of a historical pattern that sustains itself by repeatedly recognizing false history. The former distinguishes between history and ideology in the interest of the critical position it desires to maintain; the latter would question this distinction and the critical judgment that arises from it. Through this questioning, the unmasking of ideology is shown to turn on itself in the same way that modernity turns critically upon itself in the interest of becoming ever more modern (in the sense that modernity seeks an ever more adequate representation of itself). Since such unmasking is invariably oriented toward achieving freedom from false history, the questioning undertaken by romanticism becomes an inquiry directed at, first, the conceptual role played by freedom within the formulation of a critical position and, second, the role of criticism in discovering a form in which such freedom may be recognized. Since it is within this questioning that the significance of Hellenism to romanticism occurs, such Hellenism is less a geographical, historical, or literary reference than the means through which romanticism focuses on an issue that cuts to the core of our modern critical vocation.

The present taste for an ideologically oriented study of culture remains ill equipped to question this vocation. Unable to relinquish this vocation, the questioning practiced by this criticism has merely transformed the experience of freedom attributed to an object such as the art of Greece with a freedom invested in a subject who now experiences freedom through the rejection of a past, for example, the art of Greece. In this transformation, one of the paradigmatic shifts of which our literary histories are so fond can be perceived. Like romanticism before it, at least the romanticism of our traditional histories, such a shift is explained as the expression of a profound shift in perception. One must not overlook that romanticism is known as the moment ushering in the sense of such a shift for our historical sensibility. What in effect is ushered in and first receives the name of romanticism—namely, a shift from a mimetic model to a model of individual perception—is a foundation for the practice of criticism. Our modern form of this shift has been expressed in the movement that seeks to embed the literary and artistic object in the widest cultural, sociological, and historical context conceivable. This is indeed a move which effectively decides that the limited view of the past is to be refused. While the articulation of such shifts clearly demonstrates how we perceive our intellectual progress, a question remains: To what extent have we merely bought time for the critical project of our modernity before history will exact its revenge in the form of our rejection by an as-yet-unborn but inevitably newer modernity? Clearly, the significance of these shifts would be enhanced greatly if they did not carry with them the critical dilemma they desire to leave behind in the prison of a false history.

This dilemma is most easily discerned when modernity is regarded as less an historical movement than the attempt to articulate freedom within the passage of history. Because this articulation relies upon the formulation and refusal of paradigms, it is caught within an understanding that does not function apart from these paradigms (and the hope that there will always be a new paradigm unaffected by the problems of past paradigms[25]). Caught by what it wishes to escape, modernity will lack historical specificity and will instead be confined to the kind of thematic history that literary history and the history of criticism have not ceased to practice. The impermanence of such a history is to be welcomed more than the assertion of a rigid tradition whose only reason for existence is the claim that it has "always" been so. And yet there still remains the issue of whether this impermanence is nothing more than our response to a dilemma from which other generations had sought refuge in tradition. This dilemma (and it is a dilemma in the strict sense of the word since it produces two diverging responses) arises from the attempt to find an answer to a question that is first articulated in and by the movement now known as romanticism. The question, as the debate from Lovejoy on indicates, is the question of romanticism,[26] a question about both the nature of the object regarded as the focus of our critical understanding and the possibility of its historicization.

The persistent difficulty of this question remains unaffected by the thematic diversity the field of romanticism now experiences. Indeed, this difficulty is expressed by the growth of such diversity as ever more voices add an answer to the nagging question: What is romanticism? Yet, every answer is also a missed opportunity to engage the question posed by romanticism itself. By asking "What is romanticism?" we have directed our questioning toward a movement that, since it now has all the characteristics of a cultural object, can be addressed as such. This assumption leads directly to the inconclusive nature of the critical discourse that has tried to define the name and nature of romanticism. That this discourse is fated to rehearse its inconclusiveness over and over again indicates the parallel existing between it and what has already been discussed as modernity. Rather than pose this question yet again, this book aims at an understanding of precisely *why* such a question must be repeated, the question of why we will be trapped by our modernity.

The question of romanticism can be construed as a question about this literary period and its movement. However it is more helpful to understand this question not so much as our response to what has passed, but rather as a question belonging to the past and yet remaining in force despite our best efforts to evade it. "What is romanticism?" is a critical question directed against a literary movement, while the question posed by romanticism is directed against the conceptual machinery that has already decided on the answer to such a question in advance. In this case, the question of romanticism—that is, the question posed by romanticism—has everything to do with the difficulty of formulating a question that does not already demand an answer varying only in the object or concept it emphasizes. As such, the question of romanticism addresses freedom as a question, rather than as a concept that fosters critical and historical illusion in either its individual or general form.

Within romanticism, this question is taken up most directly by those texts in which antiquity figures most prominently, those grouped under the name of romantic Hellenism. Far from being a refusal to recognize modernity, these texts pose the question that is central to any attempt to assert modernity: the question of freedom.

While Shelley's *Prometheus Unbound* offers one of the primary reflections on this question within romanticism, his treatment of freedom is far removed from any reenactment of a battle of the books (as a merely thematic reading of the content of romantic Hellenism might suggest). Nor can Keats or Hölderlin be accused of repeating a battle that had already had its day earlier in the eighteenth century. What distinguishes the presence of Greece in their poetry is that, through Hellenism, antiquity had changed. This change, as outlined above, bequeathed to them a legacy determining the essential configuration of how modernity came to conceive of culture. The work of these romantic poets contends with this legacy, namely, the production of a concept of culture out of the aestheticization of history. And they do so at the very moment when such a legacy has put into place everything necessary to invent a tradition. From this moment, the question posed by romanticism wanes as the modern understanding of culture waxes without restraint—an understanding that persists despite the critical and theoretical reflection undertaken in recent years. In this relation to culture—articulated through the espousal of and reflection on Hellenism—romanticism poses the question of a freedom which would not be the product of a critical project (by this is meant the kind of project that, since Kant, turns to critique as the means to ground knowledge). Whether this critique is directed at separating illusion from knowledge, or myth from history, it requires, first, that such a separation occur in the interest of attaining freedom and, second, that judgment and criticism have the power to determine what gives their activity significance—freedom. In this context, the question posed by romanticism faces an insurmountable difficulty addressed as much to itself as to any other period.[27] Is freedom subject to critique? Is it subject to a critique performed by a history mediated by art? The difficulty of such questions resides in their demand that there is a necessary relation between critique and freedom.

The difficulty of the question posed by romanticism accounts for why our literary history should have preferred a dialectical model originating in the symbolic. After all, isn't restricted freedom symbolic of an unrestricted freedom? This configuration of the past as symbolic of a present freedom, or even of the present as symbolic of a freedom yet to come, evades the real presence of the question of freedom within romanticism. Such configurations have little to do with freedom. Instead, they are symptomatic of the critical need for a subject since it is through this sense of having not been free that a subject tells the story of becoming conscious of itself as a subject. Within critical history, this narrative may be perceived in the frequency with which we are reminded that the romantic subject overcomes the failed objectivity of the past. This model instills a sense of history as a consciousness of individuality. That such consciousness is derived from its opposite is transcended by the fact that it has been derived at all (just as, to recall Johnson's remark on the *chien savant*, we are less astonished by what the dog performs than by the fact that the dog can perform at all). Astonished at the derivation, the question of the means by which this consciousness came into existence can be forgotten. Indeed, the story of consciousness may be no more than this forgetting. Our history would have to be seen then as the active forgetting of the question posed preeminently by the poetry of romanticism.

Greece and the Invention of Culture: Winckelmann

A cursory reading of history would show that the culture of Greece has not always enjoyed the kind of significance it came to possess in the eighteenth century. While Greek authors appear as examples of classical learning during both the medieval period and the Renaissance, these references appeal to a general sense of antiquity as an unquestioned source of learning in philosophy, moral example, and science.[1] In the eighteenth century, antiquity and, in particular, Greece superseded its status as an example of learning and became a measure of the highest cultural achievement. This emergence can be attributed to the work of a single figure, Johann Winckelmann, who, in his *History of Ancient Art*, goes beyond the Renaissance emphasis on the written documents of Greece in order to develop the total account of a nation's aesthetic and intellectual production. In this work, Winckelmann systematizes the influence of Greece according to an aesthetic through which every aspect of a nation can be conceived as part of a total cultural representation. Greece assumes such a representation whenever it is evoked as the highest example of Western culture, and, above all, when it is evoked by the Hellenism that Winckelmann's work fostered in the late eighteenth and throughout much of the nineteenth centuries. Such a Hellenism, as should already be apparent from the foregoing remarks, is more than the sociological phenomenon suggested by recent studies of the Victorian period.[2] Indeed, the signifi-

cance of Hellenism does not lie in its occurrence as a historical phenomenon, but rather in its establishment of a concept of culture that went by
the name of Greece. This same concept reappears insistently within the
modern history of the aesthetic as it develops from Hegel's Berlin lectures
on the aesthetic through Wagner's *Gesamtkunstwerk* and into the *Gesamt-
gesellschaftwerk* of modern cultural study.

Although Winckelmann provided the foundation for the emergence
of Hellenism in the eighteenth century, the significance of his work lies
less in its interpretation of Greek art than in the historical model it established.[3] This point is emphasized by the fact that the two aspects of
Winckelmann's work that remain in force have little to do with what he
says about individual works of Greek art and everything to do with how
those works are organized and given significance: first, his principle of periodization, and, second, the concept of culture articulated along with this
principle. This continuing influence, even in domains where Winckelmann has no acknowledged influence, indicates that the Hellenism his
work gave rise to should not be viewed as an historically limited aspect of
romanticism or any other modern historical period. What the rise of Hellenism gave a specific expression to is an understanding of history mediated through a concept of culture. For such an understanding, culture acts
as a common denominator allowing access to other fields and other expressive forms that would otherwise remain isolated by the particularity
of the critical discourses to which they had hitherto owed their significance. This is why, under the name of culture, political life, artistic and
nonartistic productions, intellectual achievements, history, popular expressions, and even the body can all be treated as expressive forms representing a common significance: culture becomes the medium through
which every form of human activity may be examined.[4] In this respect,
culture still affirms the role first given to it by Winckelmann in the late
eighteenth century; it expresses a totality.[5]

In both Winckelmann and the modern period, the abstractness of
this totalizing inclination is disguised by a tendency to define and discuss
culture only in terms of the material forms in which it appears. The recurrence of such a tendency indicates the extent to which cultural study is
deeply rooted in the traditions of historical materialism. The exclusive
pursuit of such a tendency is also the sign of a turn away from any theo-

retical reflection on the critical position such a pursuit also implies. Admittedly, the failure to reflect on this critical position is both the appeal and the strength of this kind of study. Still, this should not prevent a critical accounting of such a mode of interpretation.[6] Admittedly too, there is good reason to avoid such a reflection since it must raise questions about not only the relation of materiality to history but also the concept of culture through which this relation is so frequently expressed. Both find themselves in the greatest difficulty when such a reflection is undertaken. Indeed, if cultural study is to undertake such a reflection it must undertake the task of theorizing what it does. In this case, it must account for a critical approach whose central insights and methodology are deduced from the axiom that all reality, or what is called reality, is a social construct. At this point, the cultural status of the concept of culture becomes an issue as one is forced to consider whether the belief in the social construction of reality is itself real or whether it is also a social construction.

Ironically, we must turn to the eighteenth century for an awareness of the difficulties posed by such a reflection, in particular to the work of Winckelmann, whose elaboration of a concept of culture as the general medium in which the historical significance of humanity is at stake is directly related to an awareness of these difficulties as well as the promise of their being overcome. By regarding this promise as if it were now materialized as history, our critical modernity has in effect forgotten the very difficulties to which its own origin may be traced. For this reason, a return to the moment at which history, culture, modernity, and the political life of a nation are first articulated in relation to each other becomes imperative. Such a moment is nothing less than the origin of Hellenism.

The role of Winckelmann's writings on Greek art and sculpture in fostering the Hellenism that arises in the late eighteenth century has long been recognized. While this is not the first moment when the significance of antiquity is recognized in the West, this later occurrence is to be distinguished from the Renaissance and its turn toward the classical. Unlike the strictly textual basis through which the influence of antiquity is felt during the Renaissance, the eighteenth century developed an understanding of antiquity that was based on a negotiation between the visual and the linguistic. This understanding, typified by Winckelmann's *History of Ancient Art*, generated a view of antiquity as the model of a general cultural context in which the aesthetic served as a mode of historical knowledge. In this way, Winckelmann's work, by producing a history for the nonliterary art of antiquity, not only gave visual art a discourse in which its significance may be expressed but also, at the same time, transformed the aesthetic into a medium for expressing the social and political significance of all art. In this respect, Winckelmann already negotiates the relation between heterogeneous mediums—the visual and the linguistic—so necessary to the development of modern cultural study and the critical tradition within which it operates.[7] Yet, this development still poses a series of questions that have important consequences beyond their historical context. First, we may ask, what allows the nonverbal arts to establish the context in which literature and its study subsequently take on central importance within what we now call the humanities? Second, what is established within this context that leads to the eventual loss of this importance for literature?

A preliminary answer to the first question directs attention to the way in which Winckelmann's history undertakes the construction of a cultural context out of the reconciliation of two heterogeneous mediums —and the means of achieving this reconciliation is nothing less than an aesthetic form of history.[8]

Winckelmann's construction of an aesthetic history begins with a discussion of Egyptian and Etruscan art. Despite this recognition of art prior to Greece, Winckelmann does not attempt a history of the aesthetic in which the art of earlier periods contributes to the development of art at a later date. Unlike Hegel's history of the aesthetic in which symbolic art already contains the seed of the classical and cannot help but develop into it, Winckelmann's history does not consider Egyptian or Etruscan art as a necessary precursor to classical art. Because of this distinction, Winckelmann's understanding of art is not, as Hegel indicated, properly philosophical since it is not a history that narrates the unfolding of an internal logic across its different national manifestations.[9] In Winckelmann's account, the development of art cannot be separated from the development of a nation because its whole history takes place within the rise and fall of a single nation. This does not mean that every nation provides a full account of the development of art. Winckelmann also argues that since a nation develops in relation to external factors, the absence of one or more of these will dictate the stage to which art develops in that nation. Of these factors only political freedom, as Winckelmann repeats in his account of Greek art, assures that a nation will attain the highest development of art. A consequence of this argument, as Alex Potts has indicated, is that Winckelmann's *History of Ancient Art* should be read for the way in which it expresses the freedom of the individual through a relation of the aesthetic to the political.[10] When viewed from this perspective, Winckelmann's account of classical art becomes a history in which a perfected relation of national identity and individual freedom is to be celebrated. But, here lingers the danger that what Winckelmann (and Potts) may offer is nothing less and nothing more than a classical account of the legacy of Greece, a portrait of Greece copied from the image through which Greece sought to present and define itself.[11] To regard Winckelmann as merely repeating this self-representation is to ignore his role in inventing an essentially modern image of Greece and then transforming this image into a principle of history. As such, Winckelmann's *History of Ancient Art* opens the question of how an image becomes historical, or to put this another way, it opens the question of how his image of Greece became the historical reference for a past it helped create.

From the very outset, the historical is a problem in Winckelmann's account of antiquity particularly if the historical is understood to require at some level an empirical source. At the time when Winckelmann writes his *History of Ancient Art*, the only examples of Greek art and sculpture available to him are in the form of largely unauthenticated Roman copies. Of these copies, only one could be identified in Pliny as an authentic and important example of Greek sculpture, namely, the Laocoön. Despite a lack of comparable textual evidence, other sculptures such as the Niobe, the Apollo Belvedere, and the Belvedere Antinous were also famous as examples of surviving Greek art.[12] The difficulty facing Winckelmann is therefore one of constructing a history when there is little to refer to in the way of material evidence. Given such a difficulty, it is to be expected that this lack of actual historical evidence should be compensated for by another means. What now becomes significant about Winckelmann's achievement is not that he produced an historical understanding of Greek art under such unfavorable circumstances, but rather the significance of his achievement lies in the means by which he developed such an understanding.

Faced with a lack of authentic evidence, any history would have to recognize the presence of a considerable, if not insurmountable, difficulty. For Winckelmann such a difficulty cannot be admitted and, accordingly, his *History of Ancient Art* proceeds as if the extant examples of classical art were in fact authentic visual evidence. This is why Winckelmann, in his opening remarks, can declare that he does not use the word *history* in its modern sense, but rather according to "the extended significance it has in the Greek language."[13] What Winckelmann has in mind is the use of ἱστορία to indicate a knowledge obtained by observation. Evoking the extended significance of ἱστορία becomes in this case a means to provide a sense of historical facticity. Such a sense is important, not just because of the lack of actual examples, but because Winckelmann's stated intention in the *History of Ancient Art* is to "attempt to produce a system" derived from visual observation ("meine Absicht ist, einen Versuch eines Lehrgebäudes zu liefern") (*Geschichte*, 9; *History*, 1.3).[14] Winckelmann defines this intention by emphasizing that his history will no longer take the form of linking art to the histories of individual artists; rather, it will take as its "principal object the essential of art" ("Das Wesen der Kunst ist in diesem sowohl, als in jenem Teile, der vornehmste Endzweck") (*Geschichte*, 9; *History*, 1.3). Here, in the desire to uncover the essence of visual art, a fundamental heterogeneity arises between the medium of this art and the medium in which its significance is given. As such, Winckelmann's *History of Ancient Art* can be read as the attempt to resolve from a systematic and historical point of view the difficulty posed by an essential heterogeneity between visual art and the linguistic medium in which reflection on that art takes place—in effect a systematic and historical account of how to read visual art. In this case, the significance of Winckelmann's *History of Ancient Art* is to be found less in what it says about Greek art and more in its ability to justify what it says in the general name of art.

This is the point where another sense of the word Winckelmann uses in the title to his major work must be insisted on: *Geschichte* in its extended signification in German means what has been structured in layers, a meaning to which Winckelmann's understanding of systematicity tends.

Winckelmann describes the stratification his history seeks to demonstrate as being discernible in four stages: "the origin, development, change, and downfall of art" ("Die Geschichte de Kunst soll den Ursprung, das

Wachstum, die Veränderung, und den Fall derselben . . . beweisen") (*Geschichte*, 9; *History*, 1.3). That the essence of art may be found in a paradigm that insists on origin followed by development, change, and downfall will not strike the late-twentieth-century reader as a groundbreaking insight. It was hardly such an insight in the late eighteenth century either. Indeed some of the last Etruscans may at least have been aware of this pattern. Yet, the fact that Greece is associated with this historical cliché is of significance to the extent that it sets up the confusion of the actual historical existence of Greece with an aesthetic account of this existence (in so doing, it may also be developing within the historical frame of origin, development, change, and downfall, the representation that late Greece sought to give itself). In this respect, the cliché has a significance that far exceeds the recognition of its presence, because it allows art to be separated from the actual history of the age in which it is produced.

While this separation has the effect of affirming art as an aesthetic production, it does so in order to make the aesthetic an index to history. According to this figure then, and the cliché is a figure, the aesthetic is at the same time historical and independent of history.[15] The paradoxical relation demanded by such an understanding of the aesthetic also reappears within the larger scheme of Winckelmann's presentation of Greece to the extent that Greece serves as a model that modernity can neither escape nor supplant. For Winckelmann, we are tied historically to Greece, but we remain independent of it in the sense that we cannot attain its history. Rather than become a sign of mere failure, however, the recognition of such a paradox succeeds by instituting failure as the moment when modernity attains consciousness of itself by becoming conscious of the history of Greece. Since this paradoxical history is based on the recognition of failure, it opens the door to a systematic account of history that no longer requires a definitive end: the very element that would threaten systematicity, its failure, is established as the systematic essence of a history that may repeat itself infinitely.[16]

Why Winckelmann should be forced to pursue such a systematic development results from the aesthetic understanding his study cannot help but embrace. According to this understanding, art is known as representation yet to be so it must always be understood by its difference from what it represents. This difference, the aesthetic aspect of art, is what Winckelmann systematizes in the name of history. In other words, Winckelmann systematizes as history precisely what must distinguish itself from history in order to be related to it: the aesthetic. Yet, what persists, even in this distinction, is an account of the aesthetic that parallels how Winckelmann articulates a consciousness of modernity and history. Just as the history of Greece is known by its failure so does the aesthetic become known by its failure. Here, Winckelmann establishes the modern historical significance of the aesthetic in terms of the exhaustion or dissolution of the representative function of the aesthetic.[17] Through this exhaustion the aesthetic, like Greece, attains a history. But, this parallelism begs another question: To what extent does this parallelism result from a need to provide a systematic account? To what extent is it a product of systematic thought?

To address these questions, it is more profitable to read Winckelmann's *History of Ancient Art* as the production of a sense of history for modernity, a sense articulated through a system that takes the name of Greece. Since such an articulation establishes our ability to define how art exists for our modernity, what is then at stake in Winckelmann's systematicity is the ability to establish, through art, a consciousness of our historical significance. Because this consciousness is so dependent on a moment of failure, classical art offers Winckelmann distinct advantages since it already provides a model for the historical failure of art to sustain itself. As such, the classical offers Winckelmann a model through which the end of art may be thought as the governing idea in modern histories of the aesthetic. To think the essence of Greek art, which Winckelmann declares to be his aim, is therefore to think the possibility of the end of art. To think this essence (and therefore to think a history for art within modernity) is to demand that the aesthetic becomes the source of our ability to recognize when a history has come to an end, in short, its downfall. But, precisely how is the historical significance of such a downfall to be thought when it is already an aesthetic category, when such a downfall only has significance within an aesthetic history?

Here emerges the crucial issue linking Winckelmann's history to a critical practice that, from romanticism onward, came to define itself in terms of its modernity. As evidenced by Wordsworth's Prefaces to the *Lyrical Ballads*, a new standard of critical judgment arises by denouncing the aesthetic understanding of the past. Yet, what is never denied at such moments is the aesthetic mode that poetic language is subject to whether it belongs to the past, present, or future. The specific meaning the aesthetic had been granted in the past is now denied. As a result, modernity leaves untouched its consciousness of the aesthetic as a representation of meaning. Indeed, what is so essential to an expression of modernity, the possibility of a critical relation to the past, rests on an affirmation of this aesthetic understanding.

Judged only by its thematic content, Winckelmann's emphasis on the art of antiquity would indicate an unlikely place to be able to trace the critical relation that modernity holds with the past. If anything, it would seem to be the other way around, since the aesthetic significance of Greece sets an example that continually criticizes modernity as being inadequate. Although the idealization of Greece that feeds the development of Hellenism is most prominent here, it is only part of the story. Such idealization occurs after the fact; it marks how a later era attempts to define its own significance. In the case of Winckelmann, this significance is decided through an aesthetic construction of Greece that is at the same time a systematic account of the aesthetic as a mode of historical understanding.

At its most essential, Winckelmann's *History of Ancient Art* represents an attempt to totalize in a systematic manner our ability to decide on the significance of art. However, this intention cannot be sustained unless the visual is translated into the necessarily linguistic mode of any systematic presentation. This systematic presentation is necessary because in the *History of Ancient Art* Winckelmann possesses so little in the way of actual material visual reference. To be successful, Winckelmann's account of Greek art must refer to itself in the place of the visual material it wishes to interpret.[18] This account demands a systematic presentation since it is only by such means that Winckelmann can give coherence to a history so limited in external material evidence. This systematic tendency also affirms that Winckelmann writes an account of art in general under the name of Greece, which is why Winckelmann dismisses other art histories because it is only in a systematic account that "the essential, the interior of art" can be expressed. With this intention to express the essence of art, Winckelmann's systematic understanding is nothing less than the attempt to determine the meaning of art from the perspective of its totalization. Winckelmann's division of the classical into distinct periods clearly exhibits this.

   More than any other epoch in the development of art, the classical defines for Winckelmann a movement of origination, followed by a period of development, then a period of change before it arrives at its downfall. While this movement can be examined historically according to these four stratifications, Winckelmann describes only three stages when he accounts for art and the general productive activity to which it belongs. Downfall is omitted, since it is not, properly speaking, a moment belonging to the history in which such a development takes place. Winckelmann describes these three stages as follows: "The arts which are dependent on drawing have, like all inventions, commenced with the necessary; next, beauty was sought; and, finally, the superfluous followed: these are the three principal stages in art" (*Geschichte*, 25; *History*, 1.29). Of these proposed three stages in the development of art, the first two differ from the last to the extent that they also provide causation. The third stage lapses into the descriptive language reserved for the effect of a historical movement, rather than what governs it. This distinction can also be perceived in the phrasing of this statement: Winckelmann only refers to the superfluous as something that "followed" ("zuletzt folgte das Überflüssige") as if its appearance was unrelated to the seeking of beauty, as if its appearance had no causation; it merely showed up. The omission of a link between beauty and the superfluous marks the central issue that Winckelmann's understanding of art must contend with if it is to be both systematic (expressing the essence, the interior of art) and, at the same time, account for its historical appearance. If the superfluous is to avoid becoming superfluous itself, then it must be given historical significance, it must be shown to be historically necessary. Winckelmann's *History of Ancient Art* will only articulate this necessity in the form of modernity. Only through the advent of modernity can the downfall of the past (and hence the superfluousness of what immediately precedes this downfall) be recognized. Here, it becomes readily apparent that the very possibility of idealizing Greece as a cultural model is unthinkable without a consciousness of modernity. By the same token, it would also appear that modernity itself cannot be thought without such a model. Here again, modernity and antiquity are revealed in their dependence on a model that is hardly historical, but rather aesthetic in origin. For Winckelmann to sustain this model, his *History of Ancient Art* must establish the aesthetic as the historical medium par excellence.

As Winckelmann's argument is only too aware, the possibility of systematizing the stages in the development of art requires an account of the medium in which this development can take place. History could clearly provide one such medium. However before this can be asserted, the relation of the aesthetic and the historical needs to be established. For the *History of Ancient Art* to account for art as an activity possessing both historical principle and significance, Winckelmann will have to account for a relation of art to the historical in which the former is recognized as the aesthetic representation of the latter. Through such an accounting art will acquire a subject in the form of history. According to the stages characterized by Winckelmann as necessary to the history he develops (the stages marked by beauty and superfluousness), it is to beauty that one must turn for the subject expressed by classical art. However, since beauty provides the source for such a subject, it will be necessary, as a first step, to distinguish carefully Winckelmann's treatment of beauty from a merely aesthetic interest (as if such an interest were ever merely aesthetic —an understanding that the aesthetic as a mode of representation gives the lie to in any case).

Beauty—defined by Winckelmann as that which art seeks as its highest achievement—arises in the *History of Ancient Art* from what may be understood as culture in its root sense, namely, something to grow, a medium for growth, and a climate that conduces growth. Because these are the conditions under which art originates, no single nation, as Winckelmann observes, can claim the privilege of originating art. According to this understanding, art is not the specific possession of one nation even though a nation will be an essential requirement in its development and in the possibility of its future occurrence. Winckelmann writes, "Art appears to have originated in a similar way amongst all nations that have practiced it and there is no sufficient reason for assigning any particular country as the land of its birth, for every nation has found within itself ['bei sich'] the first seed to what is necessary ['den ersten Samen zum Notwendigen']" (*Geschichte*, 26; *History*, 1.30). While this sentence does raise the question of a nation that does not pursue the practice of art, no such eventuality is entertained by Winckelmann. Indeed, the phrase "amongst all nations that have practiced it" implies that the possibility of art is always present within a nation whether or not it is practiced. This implication points to the presence of a fundamental aesthetic relation between art and nation in which a nation's possession of the aesthetic grants it access to the historical.

As Winckelmann states, it takes a nation for art to originate. But, since art is a seed that every nation finds within itself, the nation stands as the medium in which the seed of the aesthetic will be both discovered and cultivated as a sign of that nation's historical development. Because art, according to this understanding, is always the art of a nation, the interpretation of art becomes the interpretation of the social and political history identified with a nation. Such a relation of art to nation contains no necessity except for the fact that a nation exists and an art has occurred within it. Winckelmann only says that a nation finds within itself the first seed to what is necessary. Clearly necessity is only realized as a result of this first seed, the nation lacking necessity prior to this discovery. To regard this necessity as belonging to the historical existence of a nation and its people is to say more than Winckelmann says at this point in the *History of Ancient Art* even though such a belonging will clearly be assumed in later sections of this work. For this belonging to be accounted for, a nation's discovery of art must be shown to be a necessity that arises from within the nation at its origin. Winckelmann does not hold to such an account when he says that from art first arises an understanding of the necessary. The account implies that art alone is the source of the necessity a nation may subsequently call upon to explain the relation between itself and the aesthetic. In this case, the aesthetic will, in effect, provide an account of how the relation between a nation and the aesthetic is conceived. To account for art as such a medium while maintaining the separate existence of the nation (so that the aesthetic can be read as the record, rather than the invention of, its history) is the essential difficulty Winckelmann faces.

In his description of the earliest records of art, Winckelmann indicates the development that his account of art as an aesthetic medium will turn to in order to confront this difficulty. He writes, "The most ancient records teach us that the first figures represented ['vorgestellt'] what a man is and not how he appears to us, his outline ['Umkreis'], not our opinion ['Ansicht'] of him" (*Geschichte*, 25; *History*, 1.30). While outline and opinion are both representations, the distinction intended here marks the passage from outline to opinion as the passage leading from the presentation of what is to the *aesthetic* representation of what is. The aesthetic emerges as both a mode of appearance and a perception of something that exists. The difference at stake here is comparable to the difference between the fact of an event (the outline of history) and its interpretation. As is frequently the case, and Winckelmann is no exception, when such a pairing is introduced, one begins to take precedence over the other. This move is apparent in the sentence that follows the previous quotation: "From the simplicity of this shape ['Gestalt'], an inquiry into proportions began from which correctness was learnt; this correctness gave confidence to risk the magnitude whereby art attained grandeur and, finally, amongst the Greeks, acquired by degrees the highest beauty" (*Geschichte*, 25; *History*, 1.30). The shape that merely shows the human form becomes the source for the portrayal of the human form as appearance. For art to take part in this development, it must be understood as presenting whatever exists in a mode different from the way in which it actually exists: art must be seen as appearance. As the passage from *Umkreis* to *Gestalt* already indicates, it is only after art is recognized as appearance that it is able to develop; only as appearance can art have a history.[19] This conception of art as appearance is essential to Winckelmann's history for two reasons. First, only in its appearance does art change (and such change is necessary if a history is to be perceived). Second, as appearance, art will already indicate an essence unfolded over time. Yet, as Winckelmann adds, this essence of art also includes its end. Winckelmann writes, "After each part of art was united and their embellishment sought, the artist fell into the production of superfluousness in which the grandeur of art was lost and finally there followed its complete ruin ['Untergang']" (*Geschichte*, 25; *History*, 1.30). Within this history, art unfolds its essence by transforming its appearance or shape to the point where its purpose is to become a medium of embellishment. In the pattern of development Winckelmann describes here, this is the point at which art comes to an end for a nation. At the same time art preserves itself as a possibility for the future.

The development undertaken by art as it moves from outline to medium of embellishment presents an evolution guided by an internal necessity that is nothing less than its "complete ruin." Through this necessity, art achieves a history of its own. Since this history is what Winckelmann finds most fully expressed in Greek art, the historical paradigm (rather than the ideological paradigm which remains subject to the historical) offered by Greek culture is one of failure: Greece is the ruin to which all ideological yearning must yield whether in the form of emulation or rejection. The ability of art to possess such a pattern of development poses the question whether the pattern present in art is determined by the history of a nation, or whether this pattern is what first allows a nation to perceive the historical model through which it arrives at an understanding of its own existence. It is this question that Winckelmann takes up in his discussion of the ideal of art. This ideal is presented as central to the historical consciousness governing the *History of Ancient Art*.

Within the *History of Ancient Art* the ideal represents a point of reference for history that announces the highest expression of its cause (the separation of the aesthetic and the actual). Crucial to this understanding of Greek art is an account of how the medium in which art is presented can be both the representation of a history (its outline) and an interpretation of this outline as something that expresses more than the mere fact of its existence. To realize such an account, the role performed by the aesthetic will itself have to be accounted for; the aesthetic's ability to represent something other than the aesthetic must be determined. This demand places the aesthetic in the impossible position of having to adopt its representative and perceptual roles before it has accounted for such roles for itself. While this situation produces a logical double bind, it would be shortsighted to see this bind as a threat to the history that arose in the wake of Winckelmann's work. Rather, recognition of this bind expresses precisely how this history is articulated. It is one moment in a history punctuated by a recurrent consciousness of the inadequacy of the aesthetic upon which it depends. At such moments of recognition the aesthetic becomes insignificant, or in Winckelmann's words, the aesthetic becomes defined by superfluousness, the unnecessary ("das Überflüssig") as art declines into the mechanical repetition of its formal properties.[20]

Like so much of the aesthetic tradition that followed Winckelmann, his understanding of the development contains a movement toward insignificance, to what the modern age would recognize as merely aesthetic. Why the end of art must be thought of with such predictability has everything to do with the nature of the aesthetic through which the meaning of art is perceived. This aesthetic character, as Winckelmann's account of the origin of art within a nation already indicates, is necessary ("for every nation has found within itself the first seed to what is necessary"). The account of the origin of art as an activity explains that art is initiated through the representation of an individual as something other than what that individual is. If the nation is considered in conjunction with this activity on the part of the individual, then Winckelmann's text points to the nation as the source of the consciousness of this necessary characteristic of art: to portray the outline of the individual. By this means, the nation is already complicit in defining art as the medium (the individuals that comprise the nation) in which its own existence is affirmed. What constitutes a nation is therefore a medium in which its existence can be seen and nothing answers this need more than an art based on the individual. The movement from outline to form or figure is, in this context, the first seed of what is necessary to a nation: an individual that belongs to it.

Winckelmann accounts for the development of this seed—its culture—by the experience of freedom. Since freedom, according to Winckelmann, produces the conditions under which art flourishes, a history of the development of art is a history of freedom; as a history of freedom, it is a history of the relation between individual and nation. In the *History of Ancient Art*, the political freedom associated with Athenian politics is expressed in the necessary development of art toward the beautiful. Here, the cultural achievement of Greece, its aesthetic achievement, is explicitly linked to political freedom. By defining art in this way, Winckelmann can equate the end of art with the loss of freedom—a move that still insists on accounting for the aesthetic in terms of a political context that is itself defined according to freedom, albeit negatively. In such terms, Winckelmann's understanding of the beautiful expresses a determined trust in the political significance of the aesthetic and in the role the aesthetic plays as the medium for realizing the significance of the political.

If Winckelmann had merely depicted the development of Greek art as the expression of its political environment, then his *History of Ancient*

Art would stand as simply one more monument to Greece. Further, the phenomenon of Hellenism would be difficult to account for except by the Hellenism it professes. As the context in which Winckelmann worked (not to mention his own text) confirms, it is not the art of antiquity that fueled Hellenism, but rather the thought of what that art was and could be, that is, its essence. The possibility of such an essence is not only central to the development of Hellenism but also remains in force wherever such a Hellenistic account of art is refused. The historically unspecific name of modernity now expresses our desire to know this essence in an always different form. But, like Winckelmann, modernity offers a judgment that is simultaneously an account of what art was (what it refuses) and an assertion of what art could or should be. Here, Winckelmann can be seen as having already taken the decisive step that initiates a modernity in which the critical judgment of art becomes indistinguishable from historical knowledge.[21]

For Winckelmann, historical knowledge is embodied in the nation and the nation as an expression of political life (the freedom of the individual) is embodied in its art. This narrow relation of history, nation, and art is what has assured the survival of Hellenism as it has undergone a transformation into the superfluousness of our modernities. What Hellenism expressed in this relation was nothing less than the aesthetic future of art in which it is affirmed that without a nation (the setting of a politics) there will be no art worth possessing. Art will no longer be worth possessing because it is no longer a medium of political and historical knowledge. In this case, the political meaning of the nation defines the possibility of a future for art, and art is the chosen medium of this meaning. The survival of this possibility explains why art must rise and fall with Greece: if Greek art were to survive Greece, the political and historical judgment of modernity could no longer claim the aesthetic for itself: it would still be Greek. Art, in this instance, could not have a future understandable in terms of a history, because it would have no freedom of development. This is why Winckelmann's *History of Ancient Art*, as much as the Hellenism it fostered, is already part of a history that cannot be confined to Greece. It articulates the paradox that the end of art guarantees a history for art, the same paradox that defines the historical existence of modernity. Since Winckelmann frames this end in relation to the decline of freedom within the Greek state, freedom is the stake around which a history of nation and art gather. The individual as the first seed of what is necessary becomes in this context the first example of freedom. So conceived, both art and nation in Winckelmann are meaningful only as an account of the experience of freedom: the extent to which art develops being the sign of the freedom experienced within a particular nation.

Although the articulation of art and nation occurs in the name of freedom, and although this freedom is persistently present as what is necessary within both art and a nation if it is to develop and have a history, all this still hinges on that other necessity, whose significance belongs less to history than to the discursive realm of conceptual thought. This other necessity is nothing less than the complete ruin in which the end of art or a nation as well as the paradigm of art and nation is conceived as the possibility of all future art.

In a work published prior to the *History of Ancient Art* Winckelmann articulates the necessity that art come to an end by defining the future of art as a future still determined by mimesis.[22] In his 1755 text, *Reflections on the Imitation of Greek Works in Painting and Sculpture*, Winckelmann relates the achievement of Greece to modernity in the following terms: "The only way for us to become great or, if this be possible, inimitable, is to imitate the Greeks."[23] Winckelmann, in stating what modernity must imitate if is to become great, establishes Greece as the future possibility of history. But, what this modernity strives for in the name of Greece is less a return to antiquity than the inimitability through which the relation of antiquity to the modern is defined as a gap that may never be bridged. Modernity, in effect, seeks to affirm the necessity of its existence, and this necessity is discovered in the impossible example of Greece. This impossibility is expressed by both the inimitability of Greece and the paradoxical demand that this inimitability be imitated. Faced with such a demand, modernity has no choice but to produce its own history. The necessity of this path is clearly dictated by the inimitability of a Greece whose achievement is so complete nothing can be added to it. Since nothing is to be added, Greece can be said to have attained the most perfect representation of itself: Greece is now completely embodied by its representation. (In this context, completeness and closure have traditionally marked the point at which further reliance on mimesis becomes superfluous.) In its quest for the new, modernity is led to reject mimesis; but this rejection, as Winckelmann's remarks on the relation of nation and the aesthetic to the individual already indicate, does not allow modernity to distinguish itself so easily from the legacy that was invented for Greece in the eighteenth century.

Much depends on how one understands the inimitability of Greece. One can mechanically repeat over and over again one's belief in the transcendent achievement of Greek culture, politics, and so on. Repeating this belief does no service to Greek culture or politics, but rather entraps it within the kind of formulaic tradition that makes it so easy a target for the critical character of our modernity. Instead of rushing once more to this formulaic answer and the sloganeering it engenders, it will be more instructive to follow the argument of a text that reflects the kind of inconsistencies abounding at a moment when no such tradition as yet exists to support this argument. What then constitutes the inimitability of Greece in Winckelmann?

Winckelmann defines the task of modernity as the task of freeing itself from the legacy or, to use E. M. Butler's phrase, the tyranny of Greece.[24] This tyranny, so easily associated with historical Greece, is, in effect, the result of our desire to be modern. Without an inimitable Greece modernity has no reason to rebel. In this case, Winckelmann is not only the architect of Greece as an unattainable ideal but also the theorist of a modernity that sought to preserve its revolt in the form of a history. For modernity to attain this history, the inimitability of Greece is essential. However, when we consider how Winckelmann defines such inimitability, it emerges that the failure of Greek art is already an effect of modernity. Such a downfall, or what Winckelmann refers to as its *"complete ruin,"* is the source of its inimitability. If Greek art had not been brought to this decisive point by Winckelmann, then the historical separation that prevents us from repeating it could not be asserted so forcefully. Inimitability is, in fact, another name for history. If modernity is to imitate Greece, then it must imitate the history that makes Greece inimitable, and this history is nothing less than its failure, its complete ruin. Modernity, in this context, becomes the repeated downfall of Greek art as it imitates the inimitable moment of Greek history and culture. As a result, the onset of such a thing as modernity will always announce the failure of the past to sustain itself. Yet, such an announcement does not preclude the possibility that modernity still promises to itself the achievement, if not the form of the past it separates itself from. The historical separation Winckelmann draws upon to confirm the inimitability of Greece is essential to this possibility. In the case of both Greece and modernity, such separation serves to protect the concept that must fail in order for it to have a history—the history of its repeated failure. But what is preserved through these repeated failures is not the inimitability of an historical Greece, but rather the inimitability of a relation between history, nation (or identity), and the aesthetic. This relation persists as the promise of modernity even when the name of Greece is rejected by that same modernity.

What now becomes evident from Winckelmann's *History of Ancient Art* is that modernity, whether or not it turns toward or away from Greece, is animated by the pursuit of a greatness that would belong to it. Since modernity must always fail in such a quest (and rejection of the past is a sign of this failure whether modernity likes it or not), then the pattern of history it identifies and rejects in Greece is the same pattern that defines its course. What this indicates is that Winckelmann's account of Greece is in fact an account of the relation of modernity to Greece. In other words, Greece is the historicization of modernity's relation to the past. This is why Nietszche can speak of the thoroughly historical nature of our rejection of the past. What we would reject is the failure of the past so that what failed may succeed for us. In this context, Winckelmann's Greece is less the representation of a past that tyrannizes the future. Rather, the *History of Ancient Art* is an account of how the failure of a concept of the aesthetic becomes the sign of what the concept failed to account for.

The periodic awareness of this failure gives rise to those moments that claim attention as examples of a crisis in understanding. Such moments prepare for the assertion of one critical paradigm in the place of another. This crisis, as our literary histories teach it, is already legible in the eighteenth century as we pass from the Enlightenment into the period that marks the beginning of our modernity: romanticism. Romanticism, however, does not govern our modernity; rather, from this moment, our modernity, as Kleist is the first to witness, is defined by an unfailing willingness to recognize and respond to crisis.[25] This response is so unfailing that we can suspect the assertion of modernity to be the origin of this sense of crisis. While the adoption of crisis as the source of aesthetic development occurs explicitly within romanticism (and one thinks of texts such as the Preface to the *Lyrical Ballads* as well as the more obvious sources within German romanticism[26]), this articulation of modernity-as-crisis remains the legacy, whether intended or not, of Winckelmann's *History of Ancient Art.*

As Winckelmann's descriptions of the downfall of art all indicate, even at the moment of superfluousness—when art fails and turns to itself for its proper subject matter—the relation of art to the political history of the nation in which it develops never fails. This relation is maintained because art continues to be determined according to the specific character of a nation. As a result, if the art of Greece is to rise to the level of inimitability (a role to which it can only accede with the downfall of its art), then it must fail for reasons unrelated to the internal development of art. That is, the *history* of art must not be the history of *art.* This is why the art of Greece when it falls away from its highest achievement is still thought in reference to freedom even though at this moment freedom is recognized by its dying away. Even at the moment of its complete ruin, the aesthetic remains tied to the concept of freedom through which the significance of political and social history is always judged. In adopting this position, Winckelmann asserts the primacy of history and the political as the reference point for judging the significance of the aesthetic. In so doing, Winckelmann confirms that the aesthetic is to be understood aesthetically as the power of representing something as appearance: what it is, is not what it appears to be. Since this understanding even extends to that stage of development when the aesthetic can only reproduce the forms of its past achievements, there can be no moment when the aesthetic is only what it appears to be. To be merely aesthetic is always to be more than merely aesthetic. As such, the aesthetic is never really separated from the historical and political interpretation of culture, despite claims to the opposite by such politically and historically driven critics as Eagleton.[27] The aesthetic returns to haunt the source of its banishment in our modern republic of criticism because it remains the preeminent means of supplying a subject for art and culture. In the end, as Winckelmann's account of how freedom flourished in Greece indicates, this is what is still at stake in a modernity that would either imitate or reject Greece.

When Winckelmann first links art and nation, the link is located in a seed that the nation discovers and then allows to develop into art. For this development to occur, the seed must first be cultured, and it is this culturing that Winckelmann equates with the movement of a nation toward freedom. The nation thus serves as the medium in which art will grow; but freedom promotes the growth as well as the nation's development. While freedom becomes the index to the significance of an art and a nation, its occurrence and therefore the development of nation and art depend on another element that goes by the name of the climate.

In resorting to the climate, Winckelmann follows a tradition traceable to antiquity.[28] However, immediately prior to Winckelmann (and this is the important source), climate had been invoked in the eighteenth century by Montesquieu in his 1748 *Esprit des lois* as a means of accounting for the different laws of nations. While Winckelmann also turns to climate as a means of determining differences between the art of various nations, his account of how and what climate acts upon takes on greater significance since its effect goes beyond considerations of style or character. In the case of the classical, and the Greek in particular, climate produces the subject of art, and this subject allows a nation to be represented in art. The necessity of such a subject for an understanding of culture predicated on freedom can be easily perceived, since freedom is meaningless if there is not a subject or an individual capable of experiencing it.

Although Winckelmann evokes other elements such as the government and constitution of a nation as influences on the development of art and culture in ancient Greece, climate retains a centrality that none of the others can share. Indeed, without the climate and the subject it provides for aesthetic representation, the constitution and government of a nation would lack the means to interpret its significance, never mind its influence. In this case, the other elements evoked by Winckelmann owe their significance as influences to the medium in which this influence is expressed: the aesthetic. The influence of the constitution and government of a nation, which in Winckelmann's account of Greece means the influence of democratic freedom, is thus derived from the medium whose significance is traditionally attributed to the political and social reality it is said to reflect. The reflection becomes the source of the significance it is meant to reflect. The consequences of this situation go a long way toward explaining why Winckelmann gives no direct account of the constitution and government of a nation as external factors influencing the development of art. The only direct account of their influence is through the aesthetic productions of a people, as well as the political's aesthetic production of itself; therefore only in the aesthetic (and in the aesthetic treatment of nonartistic objects) can their significance and operation be realized. Because of these circumstances, it is difficult to pose the question about the existence of a politics not already implicated in the aesthetic ideology it would refuse. Since this is, in effect, a question about the political as a reality separate from the sphere of the aesthetic, what is actually being questioned is a meaning for the aesthetic.[29]

To evade such a question, Winckelmann separates his account of how the subject of art arises from any account of the freedom expressed by art at the highest stage of its development. As with the constitution and government of a state Winckelmann makes no attempt to account for the origin of freedom as an external factor; its provenance instead remains uncharted except through the cultural expressions in which it is represented. Since this condition would make freedom nothing more than an effect of the history that may be read in art, a separation of the aesthetic from what it represents becomes imperative. While this separation can be asserted by referring to the difference between a representation and what it represents (the most common of modern theoretical responses), such a separation quickly becomes the monotonous cry of a desperate plea for significance. Winckelmann's response is more resourceful and, instead of repeating a familiar rhetoric, permits the rise of an historical model from the very ruins it would find itself among if a direct account of freedom or the origin of constitution and government were attempted. Unable to achieve such an account, Winckelmann translates the problem of representing them into the effect of a temporal *décalage*. As a result of this temporal separation, art and the external factors governing its development rarely move in tandem with each other in Winckelmann.[30] If they did, then the aesthetic would be indistinguishable from what it is supposed to represent since, historically speaking, it would then be simultaneous with the events it reflects.[31] To maintain this separation is to maintain the aesthetic as the representation of history. Once this separation is accepted (and empirical experience is its most convincing witness), the aesthetic becomes a way of knowing the historical and external context of art. As a result, the aesthetic, in default of other external evidence, can be viewed as providing an account of those external factors it is said to represent.

Nowhere is such an account more needed than in the case of the freedom Winckelmann associates with the development of the highest art. But, as the *History of Ancient Art* makes clear, Winckelmann's account of freedom takes place wholly within his discussion of the aesthetic and its development in Greece. The description Winckelmann gives of the aesthetic development of Greece is, in fact, nothing less than an account of how the individual develops within a movement that begins with the domination of the external and ends with a self-determining autonomy within the state and its laws. In the following passage, this development is conceptualized in aesthetic terms as Winckelmann plots a movement from an imitative to an ideal mode of art: "The older style was constructed on a system composed of rules taken from nature. Afterwards art moved away from nature and became ideal. The artist worked more according to these rules than to nature, the object of imitation, for art had created ['gebilde'] for itself a nature of its own" (*Geschichte*, 216–17; *History*, 2.130). For this development to occur, art must separate itself from an origin known historically as an epoch of imitation, a step that will be repeated throughout the history of artistic and literary periods as well as within Winckelmann's own history.[32] Once in possession of a nature of its own, art is freed to express the highest beauty Winckelmann equates with the Greek experience of freedom. The distinction between an art with a nature of its own and an art of imitation does not account for the rise of an art of beauty. Such an account requires a further distinction if the relation between art and the state is to be mediated on the level of an individual. To perform this mediation, Winckelmann distinguishes two forms of beauty, individual and ideal. He writes, "The formation ['Bildung'] of beauty is either *individual,* that is, it concentrates on a single person or it is a selection of beautiful parts from many individuals that has been combined into a single form which we call *ideal*" (*Geschichte*, 151; *History*, 1.201). In these words Winckelmann describes a movement from a state of nature in which the individual acts as the point of reference and a state in which nature is transformed into a work that has no correspondence in nature. Politically, what is described here is the passage from a state in which the individual governs to a state in which the individual is recognized as part of a larger governing body. The model of freedom initially represented by the individual is repeated as an aesthetic state in which the most beautiful in each individual (what most expresses their freedom) is realized. In a rationalization of this development, Winckelmann articulates the kind of failing we have already seen to be built into the larger pattern of his history, a failing that makes the irruption of ideology inevitable while tracing its origin to the very thing it would now refuse. Winckelmann writes:

But nature and the structure of the most beautiful bodies are rarely without fault. They have forms which can either be found more perfect in other bodies, or which may be imagined more perfect. In conformity to this teaching of experience, those wise artists, the ancients, acted as a skillful gardener does, who grafts different shoots of excellent sorts upon the same stock; and, as a bee gathers from many flowers, so were their ideas of beauty not limited to the beautiful in a single individual . . . but they sought to unite the beautiful parts of many beautiful bodies. . . . This selection of the most beautiful parts and their harmonious union in one figure produced ideal beauty." (*Geschichte*, 155; *History*, 1.204–5)

In this passage, the example of the gardener's art acts as a correction to a nature that remains limited in its ability to express the highest beauty. The shift to the art of cultivation as a means of explaining this development is not an isolated example in Winckelmann's history. Rather, it marks the moment at which a systematic account of art and its representation of freedom (as the conceptualization of the individual) adopts the form of culture.

What constitutes this culture can be traced in some detail from the long fourth chapter on Greek art in the *History of Ancient Art*. At the beginning of this chapter, Winckelmann invokes the image of a seed in a description that once again connects the aesthetic and the nation while explicitly making the climate the source of their interrelation: "The influence of the climate ['Himmels'] must give life to the seed from which art is to be produced; and for this seed Greece was the chosen soil" (*Geschichte*, 129; *History*, 1.176). If every nation finds the seed of what is necessary—namely, art—within itself, then this discovery and the nation within which it occurs must happen as a result of climate. The primary role of climate may also be gauged by considering that without climate there would be no art for the constitution or government of a nation to act upon and influence its development. If climate fulfills a primary role as the agent that allows the seed to grow, then its necessity may be traced to what it allows to grow. Climate, however, is never presented outside of this metaphor of the seed as having a direct effect on art. Indeed, what could be more unnatural? Statues do not grow if we water them, and to say that watering a nation makes it grow is to invite the kind of catechresis lurking in every metaphor. Once the connection between seed and climate is made, Winckelmann will, however, tend to refer to climate as what acts directly on the physical formation, or *Bildung*, of an individual. Accordingly, the seed to be cultivated is not simply art since art is, from its inception, to be understood by what it is meant to represent: the human body. For Winckelmann, the cultivation of this body will be the origin of art. Winckelmann reiterates this to such an extent throughout the *History of Ancient Art* that art's role as an aesthetic or representative medium is viewed as having no other source than in the body of the subject it imitates.[33] For Winckelmann, as the following remark on the representation of the face indicates, this holds true for the classical as well as the modern age. He writes, "As man has been in all ages the principal subject of art, the artists of every land have given to their figures the facial formation peculiar to their nation; and the relation of art to its subject in modern times proves that the different shape in ancient art is to be attributed to the different formation of its subject" (*Geschichte*, 36; *History*, 1.54). Winckelmann observes in both the classical and modern ages that art finds its subject in the form of the individual as it exists in either age. Here, as with the metaphor of the seed, the model for understanding art appears to be an analogy between art and nature. But, just as the seed was not exactly art, but rather what art attempts to represent, the individual form from which art originates is not exactly natural either.

Throughout his discussion of climate Winckelmann makes clear that its influence on the development of art occurs because of its ability to cultivate the beautiful. Winckelmann refers to a "noble ['hohe'] beauty" whose "formation and shape ['Bildung und Form'] is found more frequently in countries which enjoy a uniform mildness of climate" (*Geschichte*, 40; *History*, 1.56). The reason for Greece's preeminence in the development of art is thus due to a climate that produces the individual body as a beautiful formation ("the nearer we draw to the climate of Greece, the more beautiful, lofty, and vigorous is the formation ['Bildung'] of human beings" [*Geschichte*, 39; *History*, 1.55]). This constant reference to the effects of climate as a means of accounting for the origin of art as an aesthetic medium will appear willfully mistaken to our late-twentieth-century sensibilities. The climate is not at stake here, but rather the generalization of a productive force. This force leads to art in whatever country it occurs—not to mention accounting for the country to which the development of art is preeminently tied. Such a generalization informs the modern study of culture except that we no longer evoke the climate to account for this interrelation of politics, history, and art. We now name Winckelmann's climate for what it does; we call it culture. Both are agents of formation that allow us to attach significance to artistic and nonartistic expressions alike. Winckelmann's explanation of climate as an agent of formation does however involve a step the modern study of culture no longer performs, largely because Winckelmann's success in translating the visual into an aesthetic history became a model that made it unnecessary to return to this step. (Such a return would, of course, be imperative if our modern understanding of culture had in fact broken with this history.)

While the beautiful formation and shape of the Greeks (what Winckelmann refers to as "the superiority of shape of the Greeks" [*Geschichte*, 41; *History*, 1.57]) gives to art its most essential and interior meaning, the formation of the beautiful by the climate will give beauty to the Greeks. In words appealing to the same aesthetic mode the highest aesthetic expression is meant to overcome, Winckelmann outlines how the shift from what the climate produces can occur: "The formation of beauty commenced with individual beauty, with an imitation of a beautiful male subject ['Vorwurfs'] even in the representation of the gods; and in the days when sculpture flourished goddesses were made after the likenesses of beautiful women" (*Geschichte*, 151; *History*, 1.202). The work of art imitates what the work of climate has wrought. As a result, by imitating what exists as beauty, the art described by Winckelmann imitates the aesthetic property defining it as art. The subject of such an art is the reproduction of the aesthetic that has been cultured by the climate. The climate performing such a task is not just an effect of the skies of Greece. Since it produces beauty, it produces the aesthetic model on which the possibility of Winckelmann's understanding of history is based. History in Winckelmann is then ultimately attributable to the climate, because it is the climate that provides the first step leading to the systematic and layered production of the visual Winckelmann refers to at the beginning of the *History of Ancient Art.*

While the climate accounts for the beginning of the history Winckelmann expresses as a systematic development, no such element is present to account for the end of this history. At this juncture one can more easily perceive the conceptual understanding to which the aesthetic has been subject. This understanding, if it is to maintain its significance, cannot simply come to an end but must in all instances survive its own end. If this survival is not built into the end that history records as the end of art, then there can only be one art. Accordingly, the interrelation of the aesthetic and the political on which the historical account of this art is based could no longer remain in force since it would be tied to one instance: the event of Greece. The negotiation Winckelmann must perform is between the national specificity of an art which assures the political significance of the aesthetic and the rejection of that specificity in the name of the concept it embodies. Winckelmann's *History of Ancient Art* is faced with the paradox it must incorporate within its understanding of history: what must survive the national specificity of art is its national specificity if it is to retain its political significance.

The way in which Winckelmann attempts to think of this end is through the inimitability associated with Greek art. At first sight, to think of the end of art according to this category asserts an understanding of art that is specific to one nation's achievement. At the same time, the simple acceptance of this assertion ignores the extent to which the topos of the end of art falls into the pattern of historical accounts that are repeatedly concerned with downfall and decline (and not just of art, culture, or politics but also of history itself).

Winckelmann's account of the decline of art is no exception to this pattern. His presentation of this downfall does make clear, however, that the problem his evocation of the climate helped to avoid can no longer be suppressed. Although this problem is expressed by the demand that art continues to represent the nation even as this same art marks its decline by beginning to imitate itself, the full significance of the problem is not articulated until the moment when the relation of the aesthetic and the historical can no longer be experienced. As Winckelmann indicates this end is a problem, but not a historical problem:

> Greek art has, like Greek poetry according to Scaliger, four periods yet, we could consider it to have five periods. For, as every action or event has five parts, and, as it were, five stages, namely, beginning, progress, position of height, decline, and end (in which lies the ground of the five scenes or acts of dramatic works)— so it is with the succession of time in art; but since the end is beyond the limits of art, so there are, strictly speaking, only four periods to be considered here. ["Denn so wie eine jede Handlung und Begebenheit fünf Teile und Gleichsam Stüfe hat, den Anfang, den Fortgang, den Stand, die Abnahme und das Ende, worin der Grund liegt von den fünf Auftritten oder Handlungen in theatralischen Stücken, ebenso verhält es sich mit der Zeitfolge derselben."] (*Geschichte*, 207; *History*, 2.116)

The systematic stratification of art requires five periods, yet one of these periods, in distinction from the real history associated with events and actions, has no history. The movement of Winckelmann's argument in this passage goes from an exact congruence between the historical and the aesthetic (as the basis of the formal organization of tragedy) to a marked distinction between the two. Why history and the aesthetic must be like one another in one instance but emphatically separated in another is the question posed by this passage.

The question arises because of a contradiction that lies at the heart of the historical project elaborated by Winckelmann. The contradiction can be expressed in the form of a question: Why, if the organization of an artwork is derived from history, is the last moment of this organization forbidden the ability to represent history? On the one hand, the aesthetic is related to history, but on the other, this relation is denied. One response to this question would assert that the end is beyond the limits of art because art cannot tell the story of its own downfall; only history can do this. Rather than answer the question, this response is a self-affirming example of the separation it wishes to explain. However, the repetition does point to the crucial importance of this assertion as a means of disentangling history from an analogy it needs: the analogy between the aesthetic (tragedy) and history (event, action) grants history a medium in which its meaning as a pattern of development may be recognized. But, when this pattern is read in a work of art, it is no longer a reliable reflection of the history that serves as its source. That is, the end belongs to history, not art, and the end in art is merely the simulacrum of an end. While this distinction is made in order to preserve history as the ultimate source of art's significance, this significance can only be articulated according to the pattern formed by the analogy between history and the aesthetic. Beyond the limits of art is the end of an event or action, or rather what is beyond is part of the pattern that art is already said to represent: the end of an action or event. To sustain the distinction, history has to refuse the pattern allowing it to be read as history (as a result it also refuses the pattern allowing history to become the source of art's significance). But what is asserted in the guise of this refusal is a history that still attributes significance to the repetition of a pattern. At the moment when history distinguishes itself emphatically from the aesthetic it does so by borrowing the kind of formal organization it sees exemplified in an aesthetic work: it models itself after an aesthetic it denies in order to be repeated *as* history.

While the necessity of a history that lies beyond art accounts for why art cannot come to an end in Winckelmann, there is more to this history than the experience of events and actions. Winckelmann's history of art is based on the development of the beauty of an individual; therefore the point at which art comes to an end would be the point at which art would no longer have a subject to express. As is self-evident, without a subject it can have no history, because history is the record of the existence of what art is modeled on either affirmatively or negatively: the human subject. To preserve the significance of this subject, art does not exactly end. Instead it fails in order to preserve a subject whose significance cannot be accounted for except in aesthetic productions. In this context, tragedy is an exemplary aesthetic form recounting the fate of an individual subject in relation to a destiny (the end belonging to history) that this subject cannot control[34]: tragedy fails before a destiny that belongs to history, but through this failure the recognition of the individual subject takes place.[35] Ultimately, it is such a failure that articulates the separation of history and the aesthetic, but, as indicated above, this separation remains the effect of an aesthetic work: tragedy. While the role of tragedy as an example of Hellenism will be the subject of subsequent chapters, its role at this point of Winckelmann's *History of Ancient Art* is to provide a means of thinking a history that cannot experience its end, or to put this less apocalyptically and thereby return it to its proper field, such an end is simply the moment or place where history's ability to confer significance is lodged.[36]

Maintaining that the significance of the historical lies outside the aesthetic denies the aesthetic its role as the origin of that significance. A study such as Winckelmann's thus occupies a difficult position, because it must assert such a denial and, at the same, present the kind of systematic, layered development (*Geschichte*) whose source, as the last cited passage indicates, resides in the formal organization of an aesthetic work, rather than in the singular occurrence of any event or action. Winckelmann's response to this situation is to separate the aesthetic from the historical. Yet, as Winckelmann's development of this separation makes clear, history would be brought to a standstill by such a separation since it will have no representative medium in which to view its movement.

According to the conditions and logic of Winckelmann's remarks, history is a Greek tragedy that cannot come to *its* end since to do so is to declare that the significance of history cannot be distinguished from an aesthetic performance. What Winckelmann's history must then become is an account of the failure of art to become history. As such, Winckelmann can do no more than elaborate a history condemned to repeat its disavowal of the analogy in which it first discovered its significance. The failure of the aesthetic to achieve historical completion becomes the subject of history, as Winckelmann gives voice to an essential trait of modernity and its repeated assertions of a history that will be our own. In this failure we can read how the consciousness of modernity arises as if it were the repeated incompletion of a Greek tragedy, always trying to rewrite the last act in its image but always telling the same story. Modernity offers the promise of a freedom from the tragedies of the past. But through such a promise it reenacts these same tragedies even when this promise takes the form of rejecting tragedy itself—as if such a gesture were not an act of katharsis, a purification of the aesthetic delusions that inform our ideologically tainted past. Not only is this why history is a Greek tragedy that cannot come to its end but also it is why Greek tragedy is no exception since its end—its catastrophe—is always an act that remains unseen, as if even its performance were an obscenity. Strictly speaking, such an end is not beyond the limits of art unless history is equated with the unspeakable, with what refuses language. Only through this equation can history preserve itself as something other than a deus ex machina, but then, as always, the unspeakable will have a voice so that its refusal may be attributed to a reality that language, and more generally the aesthetic, cannot experience. When all is said and done, the unspeakable will always have had a voice just as the facts of the past will always have a voice that pronounces their significance: the voice of history. This unavoidable necessity would be crippling if we were only concerned here with a simple notion of history. The history at stake in Winckelmann's *History of Ancient Art* is more complex; it experiences such an undermining as a failure that allows history to discover a subject in its own repeated failures. Such failures do not undermine history; rather, they provide it with a stage for its most resourceful performance.

As indicated by Winckelmann's remarks, art may be understood by analogy to a Greek tragedy that cannot come to *its* end. As tragedy, such an art is destined to repeat its fourth act while it bows to the history (and all this implies with respect to ideology and judgment) that reserves the final act for itself. The moment at which this repetition takes place is described as the moment of the downfall of art by Winckelmann, a moment marked by the failure of art to represent anything other than itself. In its downfall, art persists as a likeness of itself thereby preserving its mimetic character even as it no longer portrays a subject derived from the existence of something or someone. By characterizing the end of art in this way, Winckelmann defines the moment of Greece's downfall as the moment when Greece lives on by imitating the forms in which it had expressed its existence—precisely the kind of imitation that fuels the reproductive desire not to mention the politics of any privileged history or tradition. While such an end is necessary if Winckelmann is to preserve art as an imitative medium, this preservation also demands that Greece, at the moment of its downfall, must fail to bequeath what it is to be Greek. What survives Greece is the Grecian, like the Greek, and in this form the cultural achievement of Greece is defined by subsequent history. By cutting off the development of Greek culture at this point, Winckelmann is able to save art as a mode of imitation within which politics, history, and so on may be read. This legacy goes by the name of Greece. There is however another unavoidable consequence to this legacy: by failing to overcome the "limits of art" and establish the historical significance of its aesthetic productions, Greece bequeaths the problem of its own definition to subsequent history. Greece remains in order to be invented. Through his invention of Greece, Winckelmann achieves a model of history that preserves this problem as the problem of modernity whether it pursues or rejects Greece. Either way, this problem still defines the historical context of a modernity that can only assert its identity by recognizing the past in terms of a failure and downfall, in effect, a failure of the past to represent our understanding of the past. That Greece, in Winckelmann's account, is also a victim of this failure confirms the extent to which Greece is the form in which modernity first articulates itself as an event of historical significance. Modernity, in this instance, articulates the highest level that any art can attain by enforcing the separation of history and the aesthetic on which our ability to recognize and criticize ideology is founded. Modernity is, then, the moment that founds critical judgment through the assertion of a new history. Such a history, as Winckelmann indicates in the following passage, is conceivable only on the condition of failure:

As the proportions and forms of beauty had been studied by the artists of antiquity and the outlines ["Umrisse"] of figures had become so determinate that artists could neither work within them nor beyond them without failure ["Fehler"], the concept of beauty could not strive to go any higher. Since art cannot go any further, it must go backwards because in art as in all workings of nature, no stationary point can be conceived. (*Geschichte*, 225; *History*, 2.143)

As occurs so often in the history of the aesthetic inaugurated by Winckelmann, art fails where it begins. That is, as art fails it returns to the history that brings it to failure. This history, as Winckelmann's text clearly points out, is driven by an understanding of culture in which art becomes its most essential witness. By being brought to the point of downfall (when history and politics can only be known negatively, precisely the situation in which the modern critique of the aesthetic as ideology finds itself) art has already begun to repeat the history it would leave behind. For this reason, the moment of modernity, the downfall of the past's representation of itself, is the erasure of a history that takes place within a history that moves from one erasure to the next.

This movement occurs without regard for chronology since history is now a source of examples whether they be Grecian or otherwise. This can be seen in Winckelmann's description of the point when art begins to imitate itself. Faced with only being able to copy the outlines (*Umrisse*) of its own figures, such an art returns to its origin. According to Winckelmann's account of the historical development of art, this is the moment when it exemplifies the Egyptians[37]:

The decline of art must necessarily become perceptible through comparison with the works of highest and most brilliant period and it is to be believed that few artists sought to return to the grand style of their predecessors. In this way it may have happened, as things in the world frequently turn in a circle and return to the point from where they started, that artists concerned themselves with copying the ancient style which in the slight curvature of its outlines ["Umrisse"] comes nearer to the work of the Egyptians. (*Geschichte*, 227; *History*, 2.144–45)

The necessity ("Der Verfall der Kunst mußte notwendig") to which Winckelmann twice gives expression in the preceding passage emphasizes the decline is recognized by an analytic activity, rather than by an intrinsic quality of its art. By making recognition of decline dependent on comparison, Winckelmann establishes the "grand style" as an already known point of reference. But, since the highest and most brilliant art becomes perceptible only when it no longer exists (when few artists seek to return to it), this art becomes significant only when its decline has occurred. The circularity underlying this comparison becomes evident once one recognizes the decline through which this art is recognized will itself become perceptible only by comparison to such an art: the decline is known because of the grand style, and this style is recognized because of decline. The necessity Winckelmann turns to is not the necessity of a history, yet it is joined to an observation that would have historical weight. When Winckelmann says, "and it is to be believed that few artists sought to return to the grand style of their predecessors," he attempts to justify the decline by appealing to the intentions of its artists. The appeal to intention is an appeal to a decision that has historical existence; however, this appeal takes the form of belief. As if to give this belief historical support, Winckelmann resorts to

a generality as much rhetorical as historical: "As things in the world frequently turn in a circle and return to the point from where they started."

The return to the starting point marks the moment at which a systematic development would justify itself, since by returning to this point
it affirms the obvious: this point was the right place from which to begin.
But what sustains this return cannot be found in the art through which it
is said to occur. This is why Winckelmann's understanding of ancient art
(and therefore art in general) is only accounted for by external circumstances such as the climate and the government of a nation. Just as the climate produces the subject of art for Winckelmann, the nation will decide
on the freedom that allows such a subject to develop. But, the nation, as
Winckelmann's history makes clear, is the climate in another form, because it possesses a power to nurture the seed it finds within itself. What
assumes the role of climate within the nation is nothing less than freedom, and such a freedom is being thought by means of the aesthetic associated with art. As a result, the history of the aesthetic as Winckelmann
articulates it in the *History of Ancient Art* is a history of freedom. Winckelmann is emphatic on this point: "Art, which had as it were received its
life from freedom, must also necessarily sink and fall with the loss of freedom in the place where it had formerly flourished" (*Geschichte*, 332; *History*, 2.241).[38] As a history of freedom, Winckelmann's account of art is at
the same time an account of the rise and downfall of freedom. What art
then preserves in Winckelmann is an interrelation of politics, history, and
the aesthetic based on a concept of freedom. In this case, the necessity to
account for the failure of art has as much to do with the possibility of
thinking freedom in historical terms as it has with preserving the concept
of culture underlying the social, political, and cultural significance of the
aesthetic and the ideological critique made in its name. But, as Winckelmann's account of the development of art indicates, to think of the significance of the social, the political, and the aesthetic by means of culture
is to think of them according to a concept that can only fail to confirm
what it represents. However, to make this failure the determining principle of a history is to define such failure as an integral part of the very thing
it appears to disrupt. Far from bringing such a history to an end, this dis-
ruption is how a history of this kind preserves the conceptual understanding from which it emerges. This is as consistent in Winckelmann as

it is in Adorno who, almost two hundred years later, establishes the relation of art to history through the failure of the aesthetic made manifest by modernism.[39] Common to both Winckelmann and Adorno is the assertion that in the time of its downfall when art turns to imitate itself, it still represents the historical context it appears to refuse. To derive this moment from the experience of a loss of freedom is to insist on the representational ability of the aesthetic even in its failure.

With an aesthetic that can still represent when it fails, Winckelmann in effect develops a dialectically informed understanding of the aesthetic. Although such an understanding always contains its own negation, this negation in no way affects its continued operation. In fact, it assures its continuing operation. The decline Winckelmann describes as the final stage (but not the end) of art operates as such a negation. This decline is, as it were, the aesthetic end of art, and it occurs, as Winckelmann's emphasis on *Umriss* indicates, as a repetition of its starting point, that is, as a repetition of the history that leads, once again, to inimitability (the historical conclusion that the aesthetic can only write as an experience of its limits). But, this history, as Winckelmann's *History of Ancient Art* already points out, is less a history of cultural achievement than a history of how failure produces such an achievement along with an understanding of art as the representation of social, political, and cultural significance. Indeed, as the writing of Winckelmann's *History of Ancient Art* affirms, if there was no art for such a representation, then it would have to be invented.

Such an invention takes place in a history of the aesthetic that, like Winckelmann's, defines art as the representation of what allows art to be represented. In short, this is nothing less than an aesthetic history of the aesthetic, which can account for its failure and then treat its fall or decline as if it were a historical event. This failure, as Winckelmann's *Reflections* makes abundantly clear, is intimately related to a consciousness of modernity—a modernity born from the failure of its mimetic desire to produce an inimitable (that is, historically, politically, and culturally specific) art of its own. While this desire requires a rejection of the past, it also seeks to reproduce the relation of art and history being rejected in the name of a nation. By articulating this relation through its downfall, Winckelmann's legacy is not simply a Greece of the highest cultural achievement, but rather a history defined by the necessity of its own failure. Consciousness of this failure is the consciousness we call modernity. Thus Greece, as it emerges in the eighteenth century as a cultural phenomenon, may be better understood as the place through which our modernity is invented as a history that would celebrate the failure at the origin of its sense of history. At stake in this sense of history is not the work of Aeschylus, Pindar, or Praxiteles but a Greece that should be represented by their work. And this Greece is less a place than the interrelation of art, politics, and culture. Through the failure represented by its decline, this interrelation is defined by its negation so that this interrelation may still persist as the significance of the aesthetic. In this respect, our modernity persists as the possibility of what Greece represents. Whether we like it or not, so long as we subscribe to the aesthetic history of modernity, we are, as Shelley observed, all Greeks. Clearly, the climate is still a force with which to be reckoned, particularly when it forms the concepts that drive our aesthetic histories.

2

The Silence of Greece: Keats

In the wake of Winckelmann's *History of Ancient Art* arises the Hellenism from which Greece emerges as the ideal against which modernity has been fated to measure its aesthetic and cultural achievement. Nowadays Greece and the Hellenism through which its influence was established have become primary exhibits for a critical climate that has shifted the focus of its judgments from aesthetic to ideological concerns. Yet, even this shift and its accompanying recognition that the Greece of Hellenism may be nothing more than a "supreme fiction," as Martin Aske termed it in his book *Keats and Hellenism*, does not overcome the persistence of a critical and historical problem against which the idealization of Greece stands as one historically determined example. Indeed, what appears to be at stake both now and in the development of Hellenism has less to do with what Greece was than with the need to possess a point of reference for critical judgment—even if, as is the case in Winckelmann, the justification of that point should be ultimately attributed to the climate.[1] In this case, Greece, whether fictional or not, stands as the example of an authority to which modernity must either subjugate itself or else reject if it is to possess a history of its own.

As Winckelmann clearly articulates in the *History of Ancient Art*, the desire to emulate cannot be separated from a history whose development is defined by the failure of an art, such as that of Greece, to sustain itself historically.[2] Here, the significance of Winckelmann's thinking to literary history cannot be underestimated. Since Winckelmann thinks of this end as the moment when an art begins to imitate its own formal characteristics, such an end is conceived as the moment in which mimesis, representation, or whatever we use to access the meaning of art, becomes the subject of art.[3] While this failure of art to represent something other than itself (except through negation) establishes the historicality of modernity, this failure is also the means by which Greek art attains its aura of inimitability in Winckelmann's account. The moment of the downfall of Greek art, when art no longer finds its significance in its historical context, is the moment art becomes part of a history punctuated by our consciousness of being modern, of being unable or unwilling to imitate the Greeks. To the extent that Hellenism is fostered by this consciousness, it is a witness to our modernity despite its thematization of an idealized or fictionalized Greece. Like modernity, but perhaps less explicitly so, this Hellenism also pursues a refusal of a past, which takes the form of the inimitability of the past. For its influence to attain the highest level, Greece must be presented as what refuses imitation; only then can it retain its hold on modernity.

Through its recognition of a past so emphatically divorced from the present, Hellenism prepares the way for the emergence of a literary history whose points of reference are established in such divorces. That the emergence of this literary history occurs in the late eighteenth century should not be lost on students of romanticism, since nowhere has such a divorce of the present from the past been more emphatically asserted than with respect to romanticism and its break with the classicism of the eighteenth century.[4] The development of romantic Hellenism is already part of this break, because it already marks a divorce from a classicism that looked more to Rome than Greece even when it turned its attention to Homer.[5] The recognition of this separation falls clearly in line with a history that views romanticism's espousal of the Hellenic as the pursuit of a past more in line with its own imaginative yearnings. This yearning for an imaginative past also needs to be examined in the wake of Winckelmann's *History of Ancient Art.* Indeed, if it is considered within the terms of this work, the distinction between classicism and Hellenism is less the opposition of two historical modes of understanding than a distinction created by a model of history represented by Hellenism. This can be clearly seen when it is remembered that classicism is defined by its representation of a style, whereas the emergence of Hellenism as exemplified by Winckelmann owes its existence to an account of how style develops as an indicator of historical change. So viewed, Winckelmann's history of Greek art is, in effect, a history of style as a means of representation. Since classicism attempts to establish a particular style as the indicator of its historical meaning, the understanding of history that gives birth to Hellenism must already account for classicism as one moment within this history. In other words, classicism should be viewed as a moment within the development of Hellenism. In this context, Hellenism cannot be reduced to the mere representation of romanticism's imaginative yearnings. Rather, Hellenism represents the pattern of historical development from which romanticism emerges as the first example of our literary modernity.

This pattern is formed by an understanding of art as an aesthetic activity; therefore, the recognition of art that occurs within Hellenism is, as Winckelmann's *History of Ancient Art* reveals, a determination of the aesthetic from the perspective of history. The necessity of an aesthetic for the existence of this history exposes the historical to the dilemma that Winckelmann's *History of Ancient Art* would evade by making the aesthetic subject to a history defined by the downfall of art. Through this downfall, the historical existence of modernity is defined by the impossibility of a return to Greece—a classic formulation of romantic Hellenism. But, this return, as Winckelmann's text again shows, can only take place through a return of the downfall of Greece. In other words, modernity will always return to itself; it will always be modern. Such a Hellenism not only makes Greece the first example of an experience of modernity but also it defines subsequent aesthetic history in terms of the failure of modernity to overcome its own historical origin. As a result, any attempt to dismiss romantic Hellenism as an infatuation with a past that it cannot hope to attain misses the point. To see Hellenism as a fiction or ideology may well be accurate but to dismiss it because it is a fiction or ideology runs the risk of blindly repeating the *History of Ancient Art* as a *History of Modern Art*, a dismissal made in the hope that, by being modern, one is no longer Grecian.

The dismissal of romantic Hellenism as an ideologically informed adherence to a past that deforms history is symptomatic of a broader attack on romanticism as the repository of an aestheticism that, like the last stages of Greek art in Winckelmann, no longer feels the influence of an historical freedom and, instead, turns to itself as the source of its expression. This attack is most readily apparent at a time when the study of romanticism has turned away from the textual and linguistic emphasis of theory and instead pursued an increasing concern with literature as the reflection of pressing social, political, and historical issues. Through such a concern for history this attack defends itself under the aegis of a relentless searching out of ideology. Yet, even though this return adheres to history as a determining influence on the significance of literature (and in so doing subscribes to one of the two most important aspects of art for Winckelmann), it does so by denying the aesthetic history that is so much a part of such an understanding. That this history should remain at work even at a time when the aesthetic is dismissed in the name of modern critical insight betrays the extent to which the modern, like Hellenism, is tied to the fall of a past aesthetic.[6] The persistence of such a history not only indicates the persistence of a Hellenism but also the persistence of the aesthetic understanding that this relation to Greece embodied in the eighteenth century. This aesthetic continues as a mode of representation without which the historical inclination of current literary study is unable to determine the object of its inquiry. Yet, the tendencies within literary study that turn to the historical as the source of their critical insight have been reluctant to reflect upon the aesthetic despite the fact that it guides and enables their most alluring insights. It is as if any admission of an aesthetic presence would be in direct antipathy to tendencies that wish to distance themselves from the theoretical inquiries they have consigned to the judgment of history. Through the perception of the aesthetic as the sign of an art concerned only with its own formal properties (its own beauty) Hellenism would be dismissed as an ideological construct, or in less strident terms as a fiction—precisely the step so crucial to the possibility of Hellenism in the first place. Here, the ability to perceive ideology not only reflects the political tenor of our critical modernity but also does so in a way that would limit art to its historical understanding—precisely the driving force behind the Hellenism practiced by Winckelmann. However, in distinction to Winckelmann, the political attachment displayed by our critical modernity has also fostered a belittling of the aesthetic.

This belittling has appeared within literary study as if it were the direct result of a swing toward the historical and away from the philosophical character of our recent theoretical history. Although this swing has had the salutary effect of fostering an increased awareness of the political in both the literature we study and in the way we study it, the gains brought by this awareness should not blind us from seeing the extent to which this swing attempts to avoid the aesthetic moment that lies at the origin of all political and historical reading. A seductive absorption into the political is not what has made the aesthetic most difficult to discern; rather, it has been the way in which the political and the historical have made the aesthetic insignificant by rendering it utterly transparent. Indeed, what could be further from the political than the insignificance of the aesthetic qualities of art and literature? Or, to show how our current understanding of politics in literature operates, what could be more political than the insignificance of a poem's aesthetic qualities? The evasion of the political is, as we are always being reminded, a political act. Given this state of affairs, the aesthetic must always (and, as the saying goes) already possess a political dimension. By this reasoning the aesthetic becomes the representation of the political at the moment when it is said to represent only itself. But if the aesthetic is so defined no reflection on its own status as a mode of perception, still less its role in the creation of the political, can take place since the aesthetic will always be overshadowed by the political.

The means by which the aesthetic comes to represent the political even after it has been determined as insignificant arises from what Hegel recognizes as negative determination.[7] By negating one thing, another is determined. In the present example, the aesthetic, by negating the political, is said to point to it only more strongly. Within such an understanding, no such thing as the aesthetic can persist or have a history of its own, precisely because this understanding demands that the aesthetic undo itself or, to speak improperly, deconstruct itself. Through this undoing of itself the aesthetic declares itself to be insignificant and, in the same act, defines itself in opposition to the significance generated by political and historical forces. As a result of this self-negation, the aesthetic posits the political whenever it is criticized for its ideological, or as some might say its socially inadequate, character. Although the political has a vested interest in an aesthetic reduced to mere appearance, to mere beauty of form, this interest cannot be restricted to the political. What holds true for the political is, in this instance, also true for the historical, whose meaning continually demands the overcoming of the aesthetic. This overcoming, as already noted, finds its most effective expression through an aesthetic that negates itself as a source of meaningful insight into history or the political. This same self-negation defines the historical development of our most comprehensive account of the aesthetic, namely, Hegel's Berlin lectures. Despite the philosophical provenance of these lectures, their account of the aesthetic not only represents the fullest systematic working out of the historical understanding present in Winckelmann's *History of Ancient Art* but also establishes the fundamental basis governing subsequent critical treatments of the aesthetic: the aesthetic can only belong to history if it severs all meaningful ties between itself and history, that is, if it is relegated to the realm of appearance. Thus, what allows the aesthetic to belong to history, which in the case of Hegel is the history of philosophy,[8] is precisely what allows the aesthetic to be dismissed on account of its ideological (politically and historically deficient) character. Already an irrevocable contradiction can be seen in such a dismissal of the aesthetic: since the meaning the world of history and politics desires is affirmed by the negation of the aesthetic, neither history nor politics can become meaningful without such an aesthetic. The historical and political are dialectically tied to the mode of representation they must both refuse. Winckelmann's *History of Ancient Art* transformed this contradiction into a history of failure through which modernity may continually assert itself as the pattern of Hellenism repeats itself. Our modernity has merely reformulated this failure as ideology. In this reformulation three issues are at stake: the Hellenism mediated through Winckelmann's and Hegel's understanding of the aesthetic should remain unproblematic; the determination of its ideological character should be its definitive downfall; and this downfall should announce, but not for the last time, a political history of literature.

The most prominent and recent version of this attempt to overcome the aesthetic understanding that informs Hellenism has also adhered closely to the interpretation of romantic Hellenism figuring in traditional literary history. This attempt to overcome the aesthetic, as represented in Jerome McGann's discernment of a "romantic ideology," seeks to limit the aesthetic to a form of self-representation.[9] Here, literary history's view of romantic Hellenism as a projection of romanticism's own aesthetic concerns has been transformed into a general aesthetic tendency from which the study of romanticism is to be saved. In his presentation of a romantic ideology, McGann takes Hegel's treatment of the aesthetic as a primary example of the self-representation that informs such an ideology. The choice of Hegel as a primary protagonist in this ideological struggle indicates how high the critical stakes are for McGann. Given the importance Hegel attaches to the art of Greece in his lectures on the aesthetic, to identify Hegel in this manner is to take on an aesthetic history whose source may be traced to Winckelmann. For McGann to purge what he identifies as a romantic ideology is to purge a history that can more narrowly be referred to as romantic Hellenism. In the case of Mc-Gann, this purging will take place by limiting Hegel's lectures on art to a merely aesthetic significance. To put this in terms that are appropriate to both Winckelmann and Hegel, the aesthetic must be brought to a point of failure with respect to history, it must turn to itself and thereby name its downfall. In its wake, the historical is to assert itself.

McGann is, however, not content with limiting Hegel's lectures on the aesthetic to a form of self-representation, but, in a move that betrays his confidence in always knowing ideology when he sees it, McGann goes so far as to label Hegel's treatment of the aesthetic as "'pure' theory."[10] Predictably, this is not the only overstatement, or rather misstatement, of Hegel in a book that would sum up the "theory" of Hegel *and* Coleridge in four pages. Indeed, how can we accept an account of Hegel's treatment of the aesthetic that fails to distinguish between romanticism and what Hegel refers to as "The Romantic Arts"? As any reader of Hegel's *Aesthetics* must know, the two are not the same: the former is only a moment in a period whose beginning Hegel traces to the dissolution of classical art. This failure to recognize how Hegel understands the historical development of the aesthetic is a failure to recognize the dialectical dilemma haunting criticism particularly when it seeks to define ideology. Only such a failure can account for McGann's dismissal of what is in fact a sympathetic voice: when Hegel discusses writers now recognized as belonging to romanticism, his remarks are not just critical, rather they center on the self-representation that informs McGann's romantic ideology. For Hegel, what we now call *romanticism* is the moment in "The Romantic Arts" when art moves toward a purity, that is, it moves toward a total divorce from external representation, it becomes pure, it becomes insignificant, but it does so in order to represent something else. It becomes the prose of thought (*Prosa des Denkens*).[11] At this point one can see how Hegelian McGann's romantic ideology really is: at the moment he dismisses Hegel as pure theory, McGann has merely enacted what Hegel maps out as the historical passage of the aesthetic. To put this more succinctly, Hegel's account of the history of the aesthetic is the means by which McGann rejects Hegel in the name of history: the aesthetic (in the guise of history and politics) is criticizing the aesthetic in order to hide from itself. As McGann hopes, it does so in order to go where no aesthetic has ever gone: to a romanticism or even a Greece freed from the failure of ideology.[12]

If the aesthetic has a habit of reappearing just when it has been dutifully dismissed as the source of ideological fantasy, then the aesthetic cannot be restricted to the formulaic understanding that prevails in the literary histories of our time. As Hegel's *Aesthetics* emphasizes, the aesthetic is not simply an expression of the timeless beauty of, for example, a Greek sculpture, but rather it is always the expression of a difference between what is represented and the means of representation.[13] The aesthetic is always appearance; it is always the representation of something in a form different from itself[14] (and, as McGann should know, this is true for even self-representations of the self). Without this difference no such concept as the aesthetic could ever exist, nor could it ever exist as perception. But because this difference, essential to any theory of representation, does not itself belong to representation, it can always be appropriated as its negation (and thereby turned into a form of representation). Here, we can discern the strategy that always allows the aesthetic to return and represent the political and the historical: first, the aesthetic is said to represent only itself; second, this self-representation is said to indicate what it excludes. The whole argument turns upon the first statement, upon the demand that the aesthetic is essentially meaningless. Only then can it represent, by negation, the meaning it is said to exclude. This sharp distinction between the aesthetic, on the one hand, and the political and the historical, on the other, is how the latter denies any complicity with the object of its critique while using what it critiques as a means of representing itself. Such deniability is no stranger to politics and the dialectic explicitly present in this treatment of the aesthetic is no stranger to criticism, whether ideological or not.

Since the ideological dismissal of the aesthetic also requires it to be confused with history and politics, we may be forgiven the suspicion that we have returned, with a change of terms, to a critical commonplace of the late eighteenth century—the commonplace that offers such memorable critical advice at the end of Keats's "Ode on a Grecian Urn": "Beauty is truth, truth beauty." Tautologies die hard. We would now say: "Aesthetics is politics, politics aesthetics," or even "Aesthetics is history, history aesthetics." Yet, it would not be true to say that we have returned to the eighteenth century. It would be truer to say that we are still struggling, critically speaking, to get out of the eighteenth century. What has still to be digested is a romanticism that no amount of ideology finger-pointing will allow us to evade, a romanticism that undertakes a reflection on the relation of historical knowledge and aesthetic understanding that has defined the modern practice of criticism. To confuse this reflection on the aesthetic with an ideology of the aesthetic is to refuse romanticism in the name of an ideology that overdetermines the object of its critique in order to ensure its downfall. But in JM : to clear a space for romo.

As the motto on Keats's Grecian urn states, beauty and truth appear to be simply interchangeable with one another. For the distinction that ideological criticism aims at and in which its significance is embedded no such interchangeability can be envisioned: aesthetic and historical truth must be rigorously separated from one another whether or not the subject is romanticism. Clearly, such a separation should distinguish our age from the critical commonplace expressed in Keats's ode. Unfortunately, the logic that allows this distinction and, hence, ideology, to be recognized, is not such a one-way street. As a first step, this logic demands the interchangeability of its terms: a romantic ideology arises by arresting such interchangeability, and it is from this arrest that the history substituted in its place derives its critical force. As a result, the identification of ideology has a distinctly critical purpose: to preserve criticism from the confusion of history and the aesthetic that lies at the origin of its own judgments.[15]

If the recognition of ideology reveals a dependence on the confusion of the terms it wishes to keep separate, then ideological criticism feeds the context in which claims such as "every aesthetics is a politics" gain intellectual and critical currency despite the fact that they offer no more knowledge than the celebrated commonplace of Keats's urn. Claims of this nature avoid the question of what the political or the aesthetic is: since one is always enlisted as the representation of the other neither can be defined alone. This is particularly true in the case of the ideological dismissal of the aesthetic, because this dismissal can only define the political in terms of what the aesthetic excludes. Its subject defined in such a resolutely negative way, ideological criticism not only avoids distinguishing between the aesthetic and the political but also it refuses to raise the question of what a politics divorced from aesthetics would be either in the context of literary interpretation or historically (since the word does have a history that, as Hannah Arendt points out, begins for us with the Greek τὰ πολιτικά[16]). Indeed, how can we ever be taught anything about the relation of politics to aesthetics if the latter can only be seen through the other's eyes? In this case, the aesthetic could only be a transitory concept that will always be denied significance whenever literary interpretation lays claim to political and historical knowledge. But does this failure of the aesthetic before the judgment of history and politics sustain their claim to primary significance wherever art occurs, or does it belong to the history through which the aesthetic has been persistently mediated since Winckelmann?

Such a confusion can be traced in the historical pattern unfolded in Winckelmann's *History of Ancient Art*, when he states that the political decides the fate of the aesthetic ("art, whose fate had always been the same as that of Athens"[17]). As the downfall of art establishes its highest achievement so does the loss of freedom define Athens as the example of the political. This parallelism establishes the possibility of reading the political through the aesthetic; at the same time it establishes downfall or failure as a mode of perceiving something other than downfall or failure. In the recognition of ideology, the aesthetic is both the sign of such downfall or failure and the recognition of a history that survives this same downfall or failure. By asserting the political significance of this history, ideological criticism fails to distinguish itself from what it criticizes (thereby inducing a history in which critical judgment can only take place by celebrating the ideological nature of all critical judgments). This failing is also the strength of this history since it is based upon the susceptibility to ideology of its own understanding of art. The political and historical significance of art preserves itself, not by producing a critique of itself, but by producing a critique of itself in the safety of a historical Other whether this be Greece or romanticism. The question of how ideology is recognized is never raised since such a question would situate ideological criticism within the aesthetic history it both strives and fails to separate itself from. The history in which this critique takes place is precisely the legacy of Winckelmann's *History of Ancient Art.*

Thanks to this legacy, it cannot be forgotten that whenever the aesthetic is said to be the representation of the political, the aesthetic is always the means of representation. Whether one likes it or not, one still needs the aesthetic whenever the political or the historical is evoked. As Keats's ode states, that is "all ye need to know." In such circumstances, the political and the historical persist in a conceptual realm that cannot divorce itself from the mediating power of the aesthetic understanding. If so divorced, then the political and the historical would be meaningless, irrelevant, unknown. But, to be meaningful, the political allows itself to be represented by the aesthetic even to the extent of being indistinguishable from the aesthetic. Here, the central issue posed by the critical espousal of a romantic ideology is revealed: history and the politics it assumes are not the repressed content of the aesthetic, but rather one of *its* representations. The aesthetic is not one critical approach among others. Instead the aesthetic possesses a generality that is coextensive with the practice of criticism as well as the history in which this practice takes place. The discovery of ideology is the attempt to deny this state of affairs and then police the distinction between a "pure" aesthetic, on the one hand, and history and politics, on the other. As may be expected, the police in this case are aestheticians of such considerable dialectical dexterity that they can arrest themselves but put someone else in prison in their place. In effect, ideology is the police of a critical modernity that would no longer profess its Hellenism (the desire to define that past aesthetically) yet would see literature according to the representation of history and politics that fueled the significance of this same Hellenism.

The resourcefulness of this dialectical understanding is such that any critical interpretation, whether avowedly political or not, can always be analyzed as possessing some political intent. Allied to such a dialectic, the aesthetic can always access, like Winckelmann's account of Greek art, what is denied to sight. In this case, the aesthetic functions as both a source of mediation and as a mode of perception. This is why the aesthetic remains so necessary to any attempt to read literature in terms of history, politics, sociology, and so on. (Such attempts are unavoidable, otherwise everything we teach as literature would be merely ideological.) Thanks to this aesthetic and its ever attendant dialectic, literature is definitely not what Keats refers to as the "foster-child of silence and slow time," but rather appears as the authoritative child of a criticism seeking to sustain its perceptions as if they were as plain to sight and as legitimately real as objects belonging to nature. Here, mediation would be as real as what it mediates. The fundamental importance of this mediation can be gauged from its role in the formation of a history for both art and literature since this history is nothing less than the history of such mediation; it stands as the history of changes in what has been mediated in the name of literature. But nowhere within this history is there any questioning of the mediation that propels such a history. To do so is to stand outside this history and therefore relinquish the signifying power of an entrenched and institutionalized critical discourse.[18] So extensive is the reach of this mediation that any attempt to stand outside of it can always be recuperated as actually affirming it. Just as a refusal of politics can always be seen as a political act from within a context that regards every act or utterance to be political. What a critique of this mediation would entail then is a critique of the totalizing tendencies that have made the unreflecting pursuit of political and historical significance so alluring to the interpretation of art and literature. It is ironic but no accident that the place where such a reflection takes place is also the object pursued and so frequently turned away from by interpretation as it seeks a firmer footing for the significance it confers.

If literature, and more specifically poetry, can be construed as the place where such a reflection occurs, then it is not because it offers a more valid account of history or politics, but rather because it offers a meditation on the medium in which all such accounts take place. While narrative and prose will also engage in such a reflection and cannot help but do

what medium?

so, the tendency in criticism has been to co-opt their representative qualities as a positive example of the historical and political significance present in literature. When it comes to poetry, as indicated by McGann's reliance on the discernment of ideology as well as by related modes of reading romanticism such as Levinson's, the path leading to such significance is inherently negative.[19] In both cases, however, there is a preference for the taste of actual history, for its material evidence as the source of deciding the significance of literature. Yet, there is no place for literature to offer a reflection on the medium in which this kind of decision is made. This exclusion has made itself felt most forcefully in those attempts to define romanticism as a period, to totalize its significance as a historical moment. This is precisely what occurs in McGann but with the added twist that the definition of the dominant tendency of the period (its ideology) becomes the basis allowing another reading of that period to occur. This other reading, "the modern reading," as Winckelmann's *History of Ancient Art* indicates, derives its significance by repeating the history it would reject. Although this repetition can take the form of either imitation or rejection, neither of these options changes the fundamental underlying reliance on the aesthetic as the medium in which historical and political significance can be perceived. As pointed out in Chapter 1, this reliance is in both cases nothing less than Hellenism. To reject this reliance is to desire control over one's own ideological tendencies while defining the whole field of literary and artistic interpretation as a field of conflicting ideologies. The inclination toward such definitions can be read within romanticism and, particularly, within that area of romanticism covered by what we call romantic Hellenism. In other words, through Hellenism romanticism develops its reflection on the historical tendencies determining its significance as a literary period.

These tendencies are most obviously at work when we relate romanticism to the occurrence of an event such as, for example, the French Revolution. But such an event does not provide an account of what relation persists between romantic poetry and *its* past (as any historian—but not any literary historian—can testify, the events of the French Revolution were hardly poetic and are therefore unqualified to tell us about poetry and still less about a category that can hardly be compared to an event: a literary period[20]). What all this serves to indicate is the extent to which literary history has a fondness for adopting actual history whenever it turns away from "the silence and slow time" that, in Keats's most famous Hellenistic poem, characterizes the appearance of history in literature. By pursuing such a turn, criticism will refuse the Hellenism in which the necessity of this turn is first given expression as the basis of its own sense of historical development: the dismissal of Hellenism as ideology is also the dismissal of the source of criticism's own historical significance. But, as modernity is witness to, the marriage of history and aesthetics that produces Hellenism goes by more than one name.

To raise the question of romantic poetry and its configuration of the past is to reflect upon the historical and political implications of what we now study as romanticism. And to pursue this question is to reflect upon the persistence within romanticism of issues whose origin can be traced to classical rhetoric and a tradition that has as little in common with the classicism of the eighteenth century as it has with what now reigns as the political and aesthetic mores of our critical modernity. It is no accident that the aesthetic understanding through which literature is politicized and historicized (and on which our ability to speak of a political dimension in literary study is now based) is commonly interpreted in terms of an historical epoch whose emergence can be traced to the middle of the eighteenth century. With the rise of aesthetics, the rhetorical tradition loses its place as a point of reference for our understanding of literature and interpretation. But what is really lost with this tradition is a prolonged engagement with the medium in which literature is written.[21] Although such a focus on the medium of literature is ignored by an aesthetic understanding through which literature is always viewed as the mediation of something else, no such thing as the aesthetic could exist without first being a witness to the figurative nature of literature studied by this tradition. For our modernity to reject the aesthetic as the self-representation of an ideology (as McGann does when he impugns Hegel) does not herald a return to what constitutes the medium of literature. Rather, it repeats the founding gesture of the historical epoch (the epoch of the aesthetic) it wishes to bring to a close. Over and above its desire to separate itself from the era of the aesthetic, critical modernity exemplifies once again that a denial of the rhetorical dimension of literature and its understanding is part and parcel of the political and historical tendency that would now dominate the study of romanticism. Through this denial, the poetry of romanticism is being submitted to a political education, which is to say, it is being educated according to a political understanding that has already dismissed as aesthetic any understanding that does not accord with its determination of what can or should be mediated by literature. The etymology of education is given a perverse twist by this state of affairs since such a closed approach is in fact leading us away from romanticism and its place within our modernity while foreclosing any questioning of the historical and political dismissal of the aesthetic that has come to define contemporary critical practice. Given this situation, it should be clear that, at least in matters of education, we have not even progressed to Schiller's adoption of Kant, since Schiller, at least, recognized the political necessity of the aesthetic.

Rather than explore this issue by returning to Schiller and Kant, the following remarks will concentrate on Keats and, in particular, on the way in which a poetic reflection may use the aesthetic in order to develop its critique of judgment (for it is on judgment, as Kant implies by his discussion of taste as a *sensus communis*, that any account of the social and the political must be grounded).[22] Only by taking up the questions posed by the figurative nature of literary language can one begin to understand the role played by the aesthetic understanding within romantic poetry and poetic drama. To the extent that such questions are posed by romantic poetry and to the extent that such questions first arise within the classical study of literary language, the historical and critical tradition that has traditionally understood romanticism as breaking away from the traditions of a classical epoch will have to be rethought. Along with such a rethinking, it will be necessary to reconsider the place of the aesthetic within a poet such as Keats. Indeed, if we are ever to do better than Byron's intemperate remarks on Keats's poetry we will have to recognize that it is through the aesthetic that Keats undertakes a reflection on the relation of rhetoric to politics and history.[23] Two poems, one from October 1816, "On First Looking into Chapman's Homer," and the famous "Ode on a Grecian Urn" published in 1820 will serve as the texts in which this reflection on the aesthetic may be examined. In each of these poems, this reflection takes the form of an inquiry into the relation of modernity to Greece, and in both cases this reflection is involved with the question of judging history. In the former, this relation is explored through language and its translation and in the latter by the relation of language (the poem) to an aesthetic object that performs, like many of Winckelmann's examples, in the role of an historical artifact.

Keats's "Ode on a Grecian Urn" may seem at first an unpromising place to observe a critique of the aesthetic understanding that underlies the historical and political judgment of literature and art that arises from the Hellenism of Winckelmann. A critique of judgment seems far fetched in a poem whose aesthetic concerns seem to dominate beyond all else, concerns so frequently misread and dismissed as if they expressed the totality of Keats's poetry. In the "Ode on a Grecian Urn" these concerns may be easily summarized. The poem is presumably about a classical object, a Grecian urn. From this urn the poet seeks knowledge about what it represents, or rather to be more precise the poet seeks knowledge about what the representations on the urn represent. So understood we may conclude that what the poet seeks knowledge about is, in fact, the urn's aesthetic status; the poet inquires into the relation between aesthetics and knowledge, or to use the poem's own words for this relation, truth and beauty. Furthermore, the knowledge sought from this relation is historical in nature since what the urn is described as representing are scenes belonging to antiquity. In this case, the aesthetic understanding would demand that the urn only be understood according to the historical, political, and cultural events that define being Grecian. At this moment the aesthetic allows a historical knowledge to be recognized as the meaning of literature (this being the moment when literature fulfills the aesthetic requirement that it be understood as something other than literature). In this way, the aesthetic not only allows literature to be judged by history but also allows it to be overcome in the name of a culture and history whether that culture and history be Greek or otherwise.

To this point, Keats's "Ode on a Grecian Urn" reflects how the aesthetic seeks to appropriate a past that no longer has any historical significance of its own. The past in this case would be Greece as it is mediated by an urn that, we are told, is Grecian, or more precisely, is *like the Greek*. The urn that forms the subject of this ode cannot be historical in the strict sense of the word. Moreover, as various commentators have pointed out, there is no urn that represents all that Keats says this Grecian urn represents.[24] If the adjective "Grecian" in Keats's title as well as the later use of

"Attic" as an adjective in the phrase "O Attic shape" is taken into account, then there is a clear indication that Keats's ode reflects, but does not affirm, the substitution of aesthetics as a judgment from which we can derive knowledge. That the urn is Greek is an aesthetic judgment, but this is not a fact according to the language of the poem. To fail to read *this* fact is to permit a substitution through which the aesthetic judges historical as well as political knowledge.

Keats's relation to the Greek is complicated substantially by the persistence of antiquity as an adjectival, rather than a substantial, presence in the poem. This fact alone should caution us to tread carefully through the aesthetic history that views the rise of romanticism as the rejection of the classical. Most commonly, this rejection of the classical takes the form of a rejection of its presumed historical completion in eighteenth-century classicism. But, what if our understanding of classicism were no more related to the classical than the urn of Keats's poem? The question of classicism is not irrelevant to the issue under discussion here since, through it, the classical has been rejected by a model of education that has favored the political and historical definition of romanticism—all else being mere ideology. But does romanticism mark the date from which a classical education (traceable to the *trivium*'s insistence on grammar, rhetoric, and logic) loses its significance to a model of education based upon historical and political concerns? If romanticism does not mark such a date, then one must be careful to distinguish precisely what constitutes classicism, on the one hand, and the classical, on the other.

For romanticism to be proclaimed as heralding a model of education defined by an ideologically suspect aesthetic, it must first oppose itself to classicism and all that it represents in the name of antiquity. In other words, romanticism must first effect nothing less than the completion of the classical, because this opposition could not be thought unless such a completion is assumed. This completion, which we refer to as eighteenth-century classicism, marks the advent of the aesthetic understanding that history has associated with romanticism. In general terms, what is expressed through the relation of romanticism to classicism is less an historical development than the possibility of defining something such as the classical in terms of its historical completion. The need to possess such definitions is hardly new since one may already read it in Aristotle's

Poetics when Aristotle prefaces his analysis of tragedy with the comment, "for us, tragedy has now come to a standstill."[25] In other words, for Aristotle, tragedy has ceased to develop and is therefore susceptible to definition. Given this pattern, what takes place in the relation of romanticism to classicism is more than a mere skirmish in the unending disputes of literary history (of which, it might be added, contemporary criticism is always the best witness). Rather, the relation of romanticism to classicism reenacts an essential critical paradigm of which the historical epochs of classicism and romanticism are only particular examples.

What is at stake in this paradigm can be understood readily if one of the most frequently cited sentences from Hegel's *Aesthetics* is recalled, his announcement that "art is and remains for us a thing of the past."[26] The significance of this declaration is less well recognized than its currency would suggest. (If its significance were better understood, then such a statement would be less easy to use as a means of dismissing an aesthetics still practiced throughout literary criticism.) For Hegel, this statement heralds the moment at which art, or rather the aesthetic, is overcome— an overcoming that, in Hegel's case, occurs in the name of philosophy rather than a critical subject. The aesthetic in Hegel thus names a progressive understanding of the history of art, a history that is destined to produce the overcoming of art so that it will possess no significance of its own but will be defined by what it is replaced with. In such an understanding of the aesthetic nothing less than the overcoming of literature is promised, an overcoming that demands that art achieve its completion by becoming the representation of something other than art.

Significantly, the moment that signals this overcoming in Hegel occurs at the end of what he refers to as the romantic era—precisely what we know as romanticism. What occurs in the canonical version of how romanticism is related to classicism is therefore anticipated in the relation of philosophy to romanticism as it is thought by Hegel. As a result, in Hegel, the fullest philosophical and historical working out of the pattern to which the relation of romanticism to classicism belongs can be discerned. Hegel makes clear that the overcoming of literature takes place in order to turn its language into the medium for conceptual understanding.[27] (For Hegel, the aesthetic gives way to the philosophical; for our modernity, the aesthetic gives way to the political.) Arguably, literary history does not overtly proclaim such an Hegelian pattern for itself. Since we think of literary and critical history as progressing toward increased knowledge about the object of its attention, this pattern may be hard to discern. Yet, even a cursory view of the contemporary state of criticism should at least indicate to us that such is not the case. The question of what literature is has been subsumed by the self-determining nature of particular approaches that only see their own reflections (the rage of Caliban and the desire of Narcissus are equally present in this situation). Moreover, this has occurred under the aegis of an aesthetic understanding that persists in conceptualizing literature as if it were simply the aesthetic representation of history and politics (so that language emerges as the preeminent medium for such concepts just as it becomes the preeminent medium for philosophy in Hegel once art has come to an end). In both cases, literature will be overcome in the name of a subject that can only define itself through this overcoming. For this reason, we should be hesitant to speak about the overcoming of the classical in the name of romanticism since what classicism represents is less an epoch in literary history than the possibility of transforming literature into the aesthetic representation of a critical subject—a moment critical history has chosen to celebrate as romanticism although, once it has occurred, such a moment need not be restricted to just one literary period but can, by extension be claimed by all historical moments in the history of literature.

In the 1816 sonnet "On First Looking into Chapman's Homer," Keats takes up the question of this transformation in a poem specifically concerned with a subject that would define itself in relation to a classical past.[28] Curiously, this past does not appear to be susceptible to being read. The sonnet's title reminds us that the poem arises from the act of looking into Chapman's Homer. Even if this phrase is understood figuratively in the sense of inquiring into something, that does not change the fact that the poet's relation to the language of this text is announced in terms of simply seeing, rather than the understanding normally associated with an act of reading. This emphasis is reiterated in the opening lines:

> Much have I travelled in the realms of gold,
> And many goodly states and kingdoms seen;
> Round many western islands have I been
> Which bards in fealty to Apollo hold.[29]

As the locations described in these lines indicate, the poet is essentially a tourist who has traveled to both the political and poetic sources of antiquity. As a tourist the emphasis falls upon the visual; one does not, after all, become Oedipus to go sightseeing. Yet, the looking performed by the poet as tourist is an effect of reading and of reading in a certain way. The phrase, "realms of gold," if read as a figure for books, indicates that this poet is no ordinary traveler, but rather a tourist who regards books as a means of visualizing "states and kingdoms" and as a means of possessing such sights as if they were direct experience. This substitution of visual experience for a text is confirmed in lines 3 and 4, where poets are described not by their works but by the islands they hold "in fealty" to their patron, Apollo. Since it is to these islands that the speaker in this sonnet claims to have traveled by means of "realms of gold," antiquity results from not just a reading of books but an understanding of books as a figure for an experience that is essentially visual. In this movement from book to figure what has to be read is forgotten by the force of the visual experience that takes its place.

Keats's insistence on visual reference continues in the poem's only direct reference (unmediated by Chapman) to Homer. Like the bards of Apollo, Homer is defined by what has to be seen, a space, his "demesne." But here, a difference must be taken into account as Keats explicitly indicates the source of this visual understanding. Unlike the opening lines of the sonnet, what is known about Homer comes from the mouth of another, rather than the visual reference demanded by "realm" and "gold":

> Oft of one wide expanse had I been told
> That deep-browed Homer ruled as his wide demesne.

After its initial emphasis on the visual, the sonnet indicates the obvious fact about what takes place when we first look into its opening lines: the visual understanding offered by this sonnet does not arise from direct experience, but rather from the site it would always leave behind, the site we would always travel away from so that books may become realms of gold, states, kingdoms, and so on. By making Homer known through the voice of another, Keats explicitly defines the source that is always to be left behind. The visual, which here responds to the invitation offered by any recognition of metaphor, is sustained by what neither the medium of the poem nor the mouth of another can reveal to sight. The opening lines of this sonnet may now be put back into their context if we remind ourselves that they too are spoken, they are what we have been told by the mouth of another, the mouth of the poet.

By insisting that the visual is an effect of the words in which it originates, the sonnet merely prepares us for the terms in which Keats defines his relation to the classical. If, in distinction to the Renaissance, antiquity arises for the eighteenth century not through texts but through aesthetic objects, then Keats's insistence on antiquity as something that has to be told indicates his distance from the visual aesthetic that fuels eighteenth-century Hellenism and its concept of history. But, as Keats's sonnet continues, the terms in which this relation is presented also undergo a complication. No longer is this relation simply based on a distinction between a text and objects of visual experience. Now a text occupies the place of antiquity and it, too, becomes supplanted by a voice albeit a voice not its own. Keats continues the last lines cited with the following statement:

> Yet did I never breathe its pure serene
> Till I heard Chapman speak out loud and bold.

In place of the tendency to understand antiquity in terms of its aesthetic objects, Keats calls upon the Renaissance in the form of Chapman's translations of Homer. Antiquity now speaks but not through Winckelmann. Instead, it speaks through the text and voice of another. Only when Chapman speaks can Keats breathe the air of antiquity. That such emphasis is to be placed on breath as the means by which antiquity is received should not be overlooked. In its presentation of the poet's experience of antiquity, the poem indicates (and states first) that breath is essential. Only after this statement is given are we told that the poet heard Chapman. Through the ordering of these phrases, the poem gives the effect first then turns to grammar in order to invert the syntactic arrangement and produce historical causality ("Yet did I never . . . till . . . "). An even finer observation still needs to be made here. Although Keats says he hears Chapman speak, nowhere does he say that he hears the words of Chapman, never mind Homer. Keats only says that a loud and bold speaking out is heard. Is it to this loudness and boldness that we are to attribute the breath of antiquity? The emphasis falls on the fact of Chapman speaking, and, as such, the poet's experience of Homer falls on the breath of Chapman. But isn't Chapman as dead as the Homer he is supposed to give breath to? What, then, does Keats breathe in?

In the course of its development this poem enacts many substitutions: the Greek poets are spoken of in terms of the islands they hold; Homer is spoken of first by his demesne and then by Chapman's translation of his poetry; and now Chapman, the presumed source for the poem, is displaced by a subsequent reader. Chapman's translation, which gives breath to Homer, also requires breath. Through this chain we are led to believe, if the traditional view of Keats's relation to antiquity is accepted, that the essence of Homer's poetry is experienced. But, by detailing this chain so explicitly does Keats not draw attention to the substitutions, not to mention the interchangeability of Chapman and Homer, that this experience requires in order to be recognized?

Such substitutions are further emphasized as the sonnet moves to the two similes that form its sestet. The similes are as follows:

> Then felt I like some watcher of the skies
> When a new planet swims into his ken;
> Or like stout Cortez when with eagle eyes
> He stared at the Pacific—and all his men
> Looked at each other with wild surmise—
> Silent, upon a peak on Darien.

Both similes reassert the visual metaphors present in the opening lines of the sonnet. Rather than affirm the superiority of the visual over what is heard, these similes underline the role of the visual as a substitution for what the poet has understood as the poetry of Homer. As this is done, Keats also complicates the ability of the visual to fulfill such a role. By giving two similes for the experience that results from hearing "Chapman speak out loud and bold," Keats establishes a sequence in which the visual is subjected to the very substitution it ought to perform. Not only does this sequence question the role of the visual in the sonnet but also it does so by questioning the relation of the sestet to the effect of reading Chapman described in the preceding lines of the octet.[30] The visual emphasis of the two similes indicates a return to Chapman as the source of the text *looked* into in the poem, as the source who first brings antiquity to sight in the similes Keats now offers. As the first simile would have it, the poet passes from one who breathes the "pure serene" to one who looks at the pure serene ("some watcher of the skies"). But, rather than be inhaled, these skies become the backdrop for a new planet. This planet, in a metaphor incongruous to its immediate context, swims into the poet's ken or range of vision. By inserting the incongruity of a swimming that takes place in the sky, Keats makes known (the verbal sense of "ken") the extent to which the attempt to reach or even travel to antiquity can only access antiquity by means of what is out of place. If antiquity can be reached in neither its poetic, linguistic, geographical, nor historical context, then we will be forced to face the historical and cultural complications recorded by Keats's reflection on antiquity. To dismiss such complications as the aesthetic musings of an overwrought poet who knew no Greek is to invent a romantic ideology in order to refuse these complications. Here, Keats's sonnet indicates that what McGann and others propose as the antidote to romantic ideology is nothing other than the fantasy of a radical ideology waiting for its planet to arrive.

Despite the important reflection that Keats's relation to antiquity offers for the historical and cultural determination of literature, there is more to Keats's relation to antiquity. As the first simile in the sestet indicates, its central metaphor speaks of something new, a planet, appearing within what is already known, the skies. The effect of the translation appears to be exactly parallel to this since Chapman's translation provides the means of knowing a figure from antiquity (a figure previously known only by hearsay: "had I been told") as if it is being known for the first time. The relation of old to new presented in the first simile would appear then to clarify the effect of hearing Homer through Chapman. However, some caution is in order lest the parallelism obscure the means by which it is obtained. As we have already seen in the first simile, what belongs to the historical past (an as-yet-unknown planet must always exist prior to its discovery otherwise it could not be discovered) is now known in terms of what does not yet have a history: a new planet. The simile is explicit in this regard; it unequivocally compares antiquity to the arrival of a new planet about which there is no previous knowledge. Antiquity, rather than being the return of what is old, is presented by Keats as the arrival of the not yet known, the new, the modern. Antiquity, it would appear, has yet to happen, it too is waiting for the new, the modern. Keats, however, places clear conditions on its historical occurrence in this poem: it can only come into meaningful existence across a translation, that is to say, it can only become meaningful in a voice not its own. Prior to this it is like an undiscovered planet; it may exist, but for all intents and purposes, it is meaningless. If all this were not enough to pose the difficulty of understanding antiquity, then a historical incident recorded in Charles and Mary Cowden Clarke's *Recollections of Writers* makes clear that the translation cannot occur in its own voice either.

The incident recalled by Cowden Clarke tells of Keats's introduction to Chapman's translation of Homer. On this occasion, when Keats hears Chapman speak not only does he listen to another but also he is transported into a state of staring by a passage from *The Odyssey* that describes Odysseus arriving out of breath and voice on the island of the Phaiakians. Cowden Clarke tells the story as follows:

> One scene I could not fail to introduce to him—the shipwreck of Ulysses, in the fifth book of *Odysseis* [*sic*], and I had the reward of one of his delighted stares upon reading the following lines:
>
> > Then forth he came, his both knees falt'ring, both
> > His strong hands hanging down, and all with froth
> > His cheeks and nostrils flowing, voice and breath
> > Spent to all use, and down he sank to death
> > *The sea had soak'd his heart through.* . . . [31]

In its commentary on Keats's sonnet, this incident also records a movement from what is heard to the visual albeit a visuality in which nothing is seen. Keats stares. Language leads to sight but what is described remains unseen, or rather it remains untranslated as one sense fails to inform another. At the same time, this failure operates within each of the senses involved in this scene: hearing, as evidenced by the fact that each translation must find a voice different from its own if it is to give a meaning to a voice whose place it has already taken; and sight, as evidenced by the fact that the sestet offers two visual examples in order to recount what the poet has heard. As the latter case indicates, the appearance of antiquity has an unquestionable halting effect as the sonnet returns to the visual example of its origin: looking.

In the second simile, Keats compares the effect of hearing Chapman's translation of Homer to the arrival of Cortez on the isthmus of Panama. The incongruity of this geographical location in a poem about the text of a classical poet is not as easy to recuperate as the metaphor of swimming. Nor is it easy to ignore how this sonnet ends with an explicit act of looking that recalls the scene described in its title. On first looking into Chapman's Homer now becomes on first looking at the Pacific. The looking present in this ending also reenacts the scene described by Cowden Clarke. In that scene, Keats looks at what he cannot see (itself one definition of staring) and what has prompted this state are the words describing Odysseus emerging from the sea with no voice and breath left, emerging, it seems, from the passage cited by Cowden Clarke, in order to die. Faced with a figure of antiquity bereft of voice and breath, all that Keats can do is stare. This stare is carried over into the second simile, and an occurrence that, like the first simile, describes the effect of an antiquity that survives by traveling in a form not its own. As this second simile states, breathing the pure serene of Homer does not lead to the loud and bold voice of antiquity, but rather to a silence in which Cortez stands (*stare*) still staring. Brought to a halt in a gaze that does not see what it looks at, antiquity appears not as a history to return to but as the unseeing look through which antiquity is first seen (precisely the reputedly blind Homer?). Here, there will be no Odysseus rising from the Pacific: that alone would be the fantasy of a history which would meet itself at the end of its travels, the historical fantasy of the ideologically unbound. But at the end of these travels in the realms of gold promised by the Americas there is only the silence that invites our wildest surmises.[32]

A situation similar to the one Keats reflects upon in the sonnet on Chapman's Homer translation may be discerned in Keats's ode if it is only read as the representation of an urn—whether Grecian or not is irrelevant at this juncture. As the representation of an urn, the poem describes what it is judged by (and to sustain this reading we have to ignore the fact that Keats describes the poem as an ode, that is, it is an address, not a description). Yet, as always in these situations, we can neither see what does the judging nor can we hear its judgment. The judge is, in Keats's words, "the foster-child of silence and slow time." Only when the poem speaks on behalf of the urn is any judgment given. And what does the critical subject represented by the poem say at this moment? It judges beauty to be truth and truth to be beauty. It would be difficult to find a truer (*or* is it a more beautiful?) judgment. At the very point where the poem offers a judgment in the name of what the poem is about, this indecisiveness questions the very act of judgment that leads to a reading of this poem as representing either aesthetic indulgence or poetic truth. This is not, however, the first moment of questioning in this poem, but rather the culmination of a sequence that begins as early as the first stanza, a sequence that suggests our attention should be turned to the necessity of representing the ode as an aesthetic or true statement.

As many commentators have rightly noted, the "Ode on a Grecian Urn" develops out of the sequence of questions that dominates its first verse.[33] In Keats's poem, these questions express less a desire for answers than an exploration of the relation of language to an historical event which, in the terms of this poem, would also include the relation of the poem to the object it views. Keats's presentation of these questions proceeds in such a way that they express an inability to know precisely what is being looked at. Consider these lines from the first stanza:

> What leaf-fring'd legend haunts about thy shape
> Of deities or mortals, or of both,
> In Tempe or the dales of Arcady?

Presumably, if one knew what was being looked at on the urn, one could ask, What deities are these? or What mortals are these? To ask whether the shapes being looked at belong to deities *or* mortals is to state that one does not know how to decide between deities or mortals if one is to define the figures on the urn. This difficulty is compounded when the poet goes on to ask whether the urn depicts both deities and mortals instead of one or the other. At this point, one is justified in asking which question is in fact being asked by the poet. Or to put this another way, one can ask why is it that the poet asks a series of questions that confound, rather than lead to, understanding.[34] Part of the problem that Keats points to in these lines is that what is being looked at does not guide or define the poet's questioning. To know which god is represented on the urn presupposes that one knows that the figure is indeed the figure of a god. This is precisely what Keats does not know. As a result these questions are suspended because they cannot define what they ask after. They lack the normal structure of a question in which what is asked after is already represented by the question (e.g., What god is this? the figure is represented as a god by the question). As a result, Keats's questions indicate an insurmountable incompatibility between what can be said or heard (language) and what is seen.

To this point, Keats's "Ode on a Grecian Urn" is a relatively uncomplicated poem, at least if we reduce it to an opposition between language and the visual. However, as all readers of this poem must have noticed there is no visual reference other than what Keats tells us in the poem. The incompatibility just referred to is therefore an incompatibility between what can be said or heard and *what is said* to be seeable. The difference introduced by this complication is immense. No longer can we read the poem as being about an urn that the poem describes and comments upon; rather we are forced to realize that what we had taken to be a visual object arises from questions that do not know what they are asking after. In short, through these questions, the poem develops a reflexive relation to its language, but this is not a self-reflexive relation since, as we shall see, the only moment a self-reflexive relation occurs is by means of an assertion of voice when, at the end of the poem, the urn is said to perform what the poem cannot achieve. Only by reading such a performance in terms of what it represents can a romantic ideology be constructed, and such a construction, as Walter Benjamin has pointed out, is nothing less than the source of the political.[35]

By this reflection on the visual, the questions in the first stanza of Keats's ode would seem to lead us into an area that raises issues quite distinct from those raised with respect to ideological criticism at the beginning of this chapter. Yet, in both Keats's sonnet and ode, the overdetermination, that is, the classicism of an aesthetically programmed model of historical and political meaning, has never been far away since what would be represented by the visual is nothing less than the objective representation of the Greek world. That Keats's poem should resist the aesthetic understanding that permits language to become a means of accessing the visual is already an indication of the terms through which classicism may come into existence and in so doing supplant the classical. As an aesthetic category classicism demands the cultural and historical transparency of language. But, as stated earlier, such a classicism is a mode of relation to literature, rather than an historical epoch in the development of literature. This is why the overcoming of the classical is an overcoming performed by a classicism that desires to see literature stabilized as a mode of aesthetic representation—and this is the classicism now dominating the interpretation of romanticism despite the evidence of its poets. This evidence is nowhere more apparent than in the infamous closing lines of Keats's ode:

> When old age shall this generation waste,
> Thou shalt remain, in midst of other woe
> Than ours, a friend to man, to whom thou say'st,
> 'Beauty is truth, truth beauty,—that is all
> Ye know on earth, and all ye need to know.'[36]

After having been teased out of thought by the attempt to determine what the poem represents we are offered the consolation of a beauty that is also to be understood as truth. At the point where language fails to fulfill the demands of aesthetic representation, the urn is made to speak as if this device would overcome the aesthetic failing of the poet's language. For the urn to speak is to reassert the failing that the poem takes as the source of its language. What the poet cannot do has been displaced onto the urn so that it may be both the speaker and what is spoken about. This is the point where a self-reflexive understanding is performed but note that it only occurs as a means to preserve the aesthetic understanding that the poem cannot achieve. Not only is the urn represented as self-reflexive since it is both what speaks and what is spoken about but what it says would also take the form of the self-reflexive: "'Beauty is truth, truth beauty.'" If truth is beauty, then the phrase "Beauty is truth" means that beauty is beauty (just as aesthetics is politics means every politics is aesthetic).

At the heart of the aesthetic understanding through which literature would be overcome in the name of historical and political concerns is a tautology that not only sees knowledge and the aesthetic as being interchangeable but also views art as the medium of this exchange. If Keats's poem resists the view that literature can be such an exchange, then it is because language is not an adequate medium in which to decide what language represents, even if it is the only available medium. But, if language cannot be an adequate means of representing language, then this means the grounds of Keats's resistance can only foster what it wishes to resist. This is why the poem can say in closing, "that is all / Ye know on earth, and all ye need to know." The aesthetic understanding is all we know whenever the claim to knowledge can only be supported by the necessity of the aesthetic understanding. But if this is so, then it is already compromised by its necessity, the necessity of a classicism that the political and aesthetic education of romanticism would now foster as the condition of a knowledge of its romanticism. Perhaps, if we would be less willing to confuse knowledge with necessity, there would be no need to undertake the political and aesthetic education of a romanticism that our modernity has yet to catch up with. In such a case, the aesthetic would no longer need to be opposed to the political since it would then be clear that the aesthetic is, in fact, the rhetoric of the political, rather than an ideology to be opposed to history.

To recognize the aesthetic as the rhetoric of the political is to recognize how the critical function of political and historical knowledge is established through a rhetoric that, in the case of Keats's urn, may be termed a critical performance. As such a performance, the political can only adopt the aesthetic as its foster child. Accordingly, the promise of freedom that defines the political purpose of ideological criticism as well as its adoption of the aesthetic is difficult to sustain. Since it is in the interest of such a freedom that ideological criticism occurs, the question posed by Keats's reflection on the aesthetic concerns the possibility of thinking of not just freedom but also the judgment that would occur in its name—a question the systematic goal of Winckelmann's *History of Ancient Art* aims to deny by making freedom the historical self-judgment of a modernity that may perform as eloquently as Keats's ode albeit in the face of the urn's unforgiving silence.

Through this eloquent performance, Keats's urn signals the condition under which a synthesis of the political and the historical may be achieved in a cultural object. This performative aspect clearly distinguishes Keats's reference to antiquity in the "Ode on a Grecian Urn" from a Hellenism whose significance is tied to the promise of just such a synthesis. The fact that the thematic subject of this poem—the urn—has no material existence of its own is less an example of this resistance than an invitation to proceed as if it had such an existence. As Winckelmann's *History of Ancient Art* has already shown, a lack of authentic Greek art is hardly an impediment to writing a political history of art. The source of such an insight will tend to be forgotten once the force of the insight that the synthesis of culture, politics, and history offers to an aesthetic object is realized. Keats's ode explicitly emphasizes that this source does not lie in an external world, nor is it dependent upon an external world. Rather, it lies in the sole means by which such a world can be given significance and even a history. In the case of Keats's poem, this means has the status of an unavoidable necessity: the description of what could be seen on an urn relies solely on its language and, in particular, a language exemplified by two dominant modes of address—the question and the apostrophe. The meaning of such an urn, including its putative material existence, must then be derived from these acts of address, rather than from the precedent of a visual and material object.

An unforeseen consequence, at least for Keats, of this ode's emphasis on the linguistic origin of the urn's existence as a historical and cultural object, is the criticism that Keats now becomes another example of a linguistic prejudice associated with the theoretical inflection of modern criticism. Leaving aside the more practical question of why a poet should not be prejudiced toward language (for want of a better alternative), such a prejudice is more often repeated in the critique of postmodernism or deconstruction than in its defense. It is particularly prevalent in the kind of critique that relishes its perception of a metalinguistic bias if only because such a bias is so easy to refute. Indeed, the perception of this bias may be held up as proof of the critic's ability to judge language and therefore literature according to external objects.[37] While this misreading of postmodernism and deconstruction may or may not be deliberate (self-deception is indistinguishable from intentional self-deception since they are exemplified in the same way), its claims are not borne out by the literature it would save from the specter of a linguistic nihilism only it can see. The bad faith of such a critique is already perceived by Keats, when he makes the urn perform this critique by giving it the voice of judgment. But, when this voice takes on the authority to speak on behalf of what remains heterogeneous to it, *its* act of utterance becomes an appropriation of what Keats describes as the "silent form" of the urn, a language that neither possesses nor is possessed by the subject it addresses. Only by judging the silence of the urn in reference to itself—as if the urn were always speaking silently to itself—can such a judgment continue to assert an authority that has never ceased to reside in its power of address. The exercise of this power is also the assertion of its weakness, its groundlessness in such a thing as a ground. Since the meaning of the silence associated with the urn can only be recognized as a result of the judgments made in the name of silence, it cannot be the property of the urn. Urns are not silent, they are as Keats reminds us "silent forms." Silence is to be given a form in order to make it speak; silence is to become something other than silence. It must become an aesthetic object. Aestheticized as a silent form, the urn may be subjected to a dialectical reading in which it will be asserted that the urn, because it is silent, guards some secret by its refusal to speak. In this case, the silence of the urn is not only defined but also overcome by a judgment made on its behalf. At the same time, there is the necessity of teasing the urn into silence so that this silence can be subsequently broken by the dialectical power of criticism to confer speech where no speech is possible. As an object, the urn can refuse neither the silence nor the words through which such silence is judged. Through this inability to refuse, the urn, however, develops a critical relation to the judgment made on its behalf since it exposes that judgment not simply as the imposition of silence, but rather as the imposition of form on silence. As a result, the recognition of such an imposition points to the occurrence of judgment as the loss of the urn's freedom to exist apart from language. Such a recognition also points to the tautological and self-reflexive character of a judgment that would seek to invest its authority in an object: this judgment uses language to constitute the object as the authority of what is said by an object that exists separately from language. From this state of affairs, it can be seen from Keats's ode that the critique of a perceived prejudice toward language is far from extricating itself from the deconstruction it abhors. This critique exercises the prejudice of a judgment that adopts linguistic negation in order to establish a relation between politics and history, on the one hand, and language, on the other, a relation that can only occur as the effect of its most eloquent performance.

The tautological aspect of judgment already finds a precedent in Kant's declaration that he "can give nothing but tautological answers to all questions."[38] The inevitability of such a tautology should not be overlooked in a poem that is not only so full of questions but also moves toward a tautological judgment in its final lines. Yet, where Kant would establish the limit of human knowledge in the inevitability of its tautologies, Keats presents this attempt as already causing a violation of the medium in which this limit is established. For Keats, an urn in itself is unthinkable unless language is predetermined as an inadequate means of conveying the object or concept to which it is said to refer. In the phrase following the motto "spoken" by the urn, Keats places such an inadequacy in words asserting the possibility of human knowledge. The poem states "—that is all / Ye know on earth." But, does this phrase simply repeat the inadequacy of human knowledge expressed in a language that cannot transcend its origin? As ever, in Keats, the case is more complicated than it appears at first, particularly if the second part of the concluding statement is taken seriously: "and all ye need to know."

The last phrase of Keats's poem—"all ye need to know"—could easily be taken as merely repeating the sentiment expressed by the words it is immediately preceded by "—that is all / Ye know on earth." The relation of these two phrases rewards closer attention particularly if the repetition of "all" is considered according to its grammatical structure ("—that is *all* / Ye know on earth, and *all* ye need to know"). The first occurrence of "all" clearly refers back to the uttered motto, however, the second occurrence is more general, permitting the inclusion of the first within its reference. In this case, the necessity expressed in the phrase containing the second "all" should not be confused with the inadequacy of an earthly knowledge. Rather, the last phrase points to the need to know this inadequacy—a need that is not the same as simply recognizing such an inadequacy. To know this inadequacy in the context of Keats's poem is to know its performative role in establishing the knowledge of an object through the negativity (or inadequacy) of that same knowledge. Our ability to posit authority in an object is itself derived from an inadequacy of the means of knowing what is posited. Only then can we be sure that, despite this negativity, what we do not know has all the certainty of an object.

The exposition undertaken in Keats's "Ode on a Grecian Urn" is an exposition of how judgment is rescued in a poem that consistently fails to answer its own questions about the historical status of the urn. This historical failure sets the stage for the performance of judgment. While this judgment arises because history falters, this does not mean that history is over. On the contrary, history is now defined as the record of the necessity of judgment. In other words, through judgment, history is constructed out of its failure. This preservation of history follows the pattern of Winckelmann's *History of Ancient Art* in which the political, cultural, and historical significance of Greece is recognized through its downfall. From this downfall, a point of reference that may be pursued or rejected is established. In both cases, a Hellenism is at work, a Hellenism known by either the failure of modernity to measure up to the past, or the failure of the past to be a model for modernity. What Hellenism expresses is this failure as a principle of history. In this context, Hellenism is one expression of a paradigm that may change form according to the inclination of a critical will, but it remains essentially the same with respect to its operation. While this paradigm may be discerned in a historical pattern (since it is the means by which history judges itself as history), its purpose can only be described as historical if we mean by this word the attempt to preserve a concept (such as freedom) whose fate is never to realize the significance ascribed to it except by negation (as in modernity) or in a form different from itself (such as art). It is thus through the aesthetic that this concept survives its own downfall.[39] Keats's "Ode on a Grecian Urn" unmasks the source of such an aesthetic as the transference of a vocal ability to a silent object. Greece, like the aesthetic it embodies, now becomes the apostrophe of silence.

3

The Choice of Tragedy: From Keats to Schelling

Although Keats's "Ode on a Grecian Urn" and Winckelmann's *History of Ancient Art* both speak of antiquity by adopting objects and texts that stand in the place of Greece, the similarity between them ends there. Keats writes in full consciousness of such an adoption and, as a result, emphasizes the performance through which the past is given a voice. Winckelmann, however, offers only a text in which such a performance is muted in the interest of a systematic account of art that would also be historical. Indeed, only at the moment when Winckelmann speaks of the five periods of historical development as reflecting the organization of tragedy does something like the performative gesture of Keats appear (and only then because Greek drama is evoked). At this moment Winckelmann makes the inescapably aesthetic gesture of calling upon an essentially performative literary form as a model of historical development. But, by calling upon this form, Winckelmann adopts more than a literary genre but the Greek genre that Western literary history has regarded as one of its highest achievements, tragedy.[1] Here, tragedy enters as not just a central example of a form to be celebrated by Hellenism but also as the example in which an understanding of our historical development is at stake. In this respect, any reading of the Hellenism present in romanticism will afford the opportunity to ask why tragedy (in particular, its thematic concern with the sacrifice, the individual, and the state) should become such an example. Such a question arises not because poets such as Shelley and Hölderlin—as well as Keats—evoke Greece by means of a tragic form or by repeating a tragic mythical subject, but rather because these poets do not undertake such evocation in order to establish an historical point of reference. Accordingly, since none of these poets can be easily fitted within the Hellenism so frequently associated with Winckelmann, they are not the best examples for describing precisely what is at stake in this Hellenism's conflation of history and tragedy. To do this, we must first turn to the last of Schelling's *Letters on Dogmatism and Criticism.* A brief return to Winckelmann and Keats will serve as an introduction to the questions taken up by Schelling's text.

Although Winckelmann's reason for calling upon this genre at such a point in his *History of Ancient Art* is largely structural (it repeats the paradigm of historical development in which, for Winckelmann, Greek art and the classical Greek nation exist), he effectively puts in place an analogy between, on the one hand, an aesthetic form and, on the other, the political history of a nation whose development is measured by the rise and fall of individual freedom. The occurrence of this analogy marks the moment when Winckelmann's *History of Ancient Art* would regard Aristotle's classic description of the formal organization of tragedy as more than merely potential or possible.[2] What this analogy must then demand is that history follow the formal structure through which it is perceived (as such this history can only be the aesthetic reflection of an aesthetic perception). At this point the parallel between the pattern of development present in Winckelmann's history and the formal organization of tragedy raises the suspicion that Winckelmann's *History of Ancient Art* is itself an example of what became Greece's most exemplary of literary forms. Such a suspicion (as an example of our critical anagnorisis) is derived from the recognition of history's involvement with those aspects of formal organization that not only allow literature to be interpreted but also allow it to have a history. (What history of literature that focuses on the literary text is not a history of form, of the transformation of literature?) In each case, history as an account of the significance of past events, rather than the mere acknowledgment that an event did happen, reveals a reliance on formal structural elements if its account of the past is to possess significance and, like Keats at the end of the ode, be able to bestow significance through its rhetorical gestures. As Winckelmann recognized, this formal organization is nowhere more in evidence than in the genre that has exemplified so much of modernity's relation to Greece. In Winckelmann, however, the question of why tragedy should be so privileged remains undeveloped even though such a privilege may be traced to the concept of nation, the interrelation of art, politics, and history through which Winckelmann establishes Greece as the paradigm for interpreting the achievement and significance of subsequent cultures whether Hellenistic or not.

An opening of this question can already be discerned in Keats's "Ode on a Grecian Urn" even though the form it takes might qualify it as pretragic since it involves not the death of an individual, but rather the death of an animal. Still, it is clear that a reference to the central event of tragedy takes place when the poet, in the opening line of the fourth stanza, attempts to decipher an image with the question: "Who are these coming to the sacrifice?" The mention of a sacrifice that will take place before an audience points to an event that emulates the dramatic setting of tragedy (which allows the spectator to experience an event vicariously). The setting of such a tragedy is not so straightforward in Keats. The event—the sacrifice—has not occurred, yet it is this same event that stands as the historical reference for this episode. To this point, the significance of this scene within Keats's ode turns upon the promise of a sacrifice, of an event that will give rise to history since it will give shape and meaning to the scene being described by Keats. While such a significance indicates, once again, a difficulty in the movement from an aesthetic object to historical knowledge, this significance is relatively uncomplicated compared to what happens next.

Unable to know who is coming to the sacrifice, the poet asks, "What little town . . . Is emptied of this folk, this pious morn?" The question essentially repeats the opening question of the stanza from which these lines are cited, and again it presumes the existence of something (the little town replaces the sacrifice in this respect) in order to give meaning to the question. Here, what is depicted on the urn would be explained by an event that causes the town to act in one body. But in Keats's account of this moment the townspeople are no longer able to act; they can neither proceed nor return. While this inability can be all too easily traced to the existence of the townspeople as a frozen representation on the surface of an unchanging urn, such a reading would reduce the significance of Keats's ode to a formal generality whose insight is matched only by its banality. In the lines following the second question, the poet responds to his own questions with a statement presenting such a formal generality as a silence that cannot be broken. This silence also suggests that in the realm of the aesthetic representation we are witness to the sacrifice of more than a heifer:

> And, little town, thy streets for evermore
> Will silent be; and not a soul to tell
> Why thou art desolate, can e'er return.

The people of the town are described as on their way to an event from which they cannot return. If no one can return to tell why the town is desolate, then how can it be known that a sacrifice was the reason? The town, its people, and, presumably, the heifer are as silent as the urn. The only evidence indicating that a sacrifice is the reason remains the initial question of this stanza. Only by invoking Kant's tautology and turning the question into its own answer can such a sacrifice stand as the conclusive historical event through which the meaning of this scene can be spoken. At this point Keats speaks of an inability to return from such an event as the condition of the ensuing silence. Why then, if such a sacrifice takes place, can no one return from this event? Why is this inability to return from the sacrifice figured as a movement toward this event? Why does Keats invent a sacrifice and a town to act as its historical frame and render this frame uncertain by the way in which he presents it?

Preceded and followed by silence, the "sacrifice" is thinkable as an event precisely because in this setting nothing contradictory can be entertained. Here, all accounts of the past recognize the same enabling silence. What Keats offers in the place of this silence is a sacrifice and a town in which the former is the cause of the latter being able to act as a *polis*, as one body politic. The sacrifice in this context is the sacrifice of what is different from those who people the town; and this difference allows the town to be recognized as one body. This is clear from Keats's words since only the animal is differentiated (as a heifer) while the people of the town are referred to by collective terms: "Who are *these*," "folk." Indeed, the only point at which the townspeople could be said to possess an individuality is asserted when we are informed of their *inability* to relate what is happening ("*not* a soul to tell"). Here, individuality is only made known through a negation that demands the sacrifice of the speech in which this individuality would have been conveyed. But, more importantly, this negation denies the return of the body politic to the individual roles it practices within the town. Deprived of a means to tell (in two senses since they cannot return and cannot speak) the townspeople, in effect, share the fate of the sacrificial victim: they are sacrificed to an unwitnessed event so that their actions may be given historical significance. Here, Keats's ode engages with the tragic pattern requiring the individual to bow to the state in the pursuit of an event that this individual can neither control nor experience as an individual. To accede to this history is to accept a freedom determined by the political necessity of a state whose aesthetic powers mediate a sacrifice in the form of a history from which no individual can return (and to which no individual can proceed as witness).

In its account of sacrifice, the fourth stanza of Keats's ode remains consistent with the celebrated performance of the urn in the closing lines of this poem: just as the judgment that "'Beauty is truth, truth beauty'" speaks on behalf of an object that can never return the rhetorical gesture, the individual cannot speak against the history that demands its sacrifice as a matter of necessity. In both cases, freedom is subject to a history that demands the intervention of judgment in order to preserve freedom for history—the assertion of modernity being a primary, if not *the*, example of such an intervention. By preserving such a freedom for history what is in fact being preserved is the significance of history as the representation of a concept it must never realize. In Keats's ode such a concept is explicitly named "truth," rather than "freedom," as it was in the case of Winckelmann. But in either case the possibility of a concept for history, a possibility consistently thought by means of the aesthetic, remains crucial. By deriving this possibility from a performance for which the urn is a mask, Keats evokes a history in which judgment is exercised as a necessary consequence of history's failure to sustain the idea that set it into motion. This failure then becomes the ground of a judgment that constantly refers to such a failure as the source of its own significance. This pattern is precisely what may be found in the classic formulation of Greek tragedy as a struggle between an individual history and fate. In this pattern, freedom is thought in relation to a necessity or a fate demanding the fall of the individual. This formulation links Keats's address to a Grecian urn to a Hellenism that, in the case of Shelley and Hölderlin, is expressed most forcefully in their relation to Greek tragedy. Through this relation one can trace how a concern with the historical so central to the rise of Hellenism also became the means to question the relation of freedom to history. Such questioning focuses on both the conceptual necessity of history and, as Keats has taught us, on the aesthetic production of this necessity.

The role that Greek tragedy has played as the example of this necessity can be traced not only from the tendency to make Greek tragedy the primary example of literary achievement but also from a tradition in which the political significance and therefore the mimetic character of art is of paramount importance. This tradition, although present within the classical age of Greece, does not give rise to the systematic account of history and modernity developed by Winckelmann. For Plato, in the *Laws*, the best tragedy is a model for the state, and for Aristotle, tragedy is *the* example of mimesis. This emphasis reveals an added significance when it is recalled that, in both cases, the high point of Athenian drama had passed by the time it was granted such exemplary status (Plato was twenty-one years old when Sophocles and Euripides died in 406 BC; Aristotle would have to wait another twenty years to be born). As these dates indicate, Greece is already part of the history that would exemplify Greece in the form of its tragedy. In this respect, the treatment of tragedy as exemplary in Plato and Aristotle already shows a Greece performing a Hellenism upon itself, well before the rise of the Hellenism that flourished under the reign of Alexander the Great or in the wake of Winckelmann. In the case of Plato and Aristotle, what arises from their emphasis on tragedy is the marking of this genre as the chosen medium through which Greece will relate to itself—a choice that would later provide the model for an aesthetic understanding of history. The tendency to consider tragedy as a model for the political and literary aspiration of later history poses the question of why such aspirations are repeatedly thought according to a genre in which catastrophe befalls its individual protagonist—a question that points to the importance of the downfall of the individual to the historical continuation of a state or nation that served as a medium for the fostering of freedom.

Already the force the Greeks recognized as fate can be discerned in the downfall of an individual so central to tragedy. Although such a force may be placed in the hands of the gods, it operates as an indicator of human historicality to the extent that it guides a course of events to which an individual is subject. As such, fate would appear to exclude any possibility of freedom since the actions of an individual would always be directed by a necessity over which the individual has no control. In this context, it is easy to see how tragedy could be so attractive to the political since it describes the demands of the nation as fate while recording the individual's acceptance of those demands. Thematically, such a pattern can be deduced from Aeschylus's *Oresteia,* thereby affirming why Greek tragedy should be so compelling and recurrent an example whenever a politically oriented history is at work. If this is the sole reason why Greek tragedy should have such a hold on Western history and its political development, then the model of freedom we have been dealt is essentially dogmatic.

To regard Greek tragedy according to such a dogmatic model is to subscribe to two unavoidable consequences: first, freedom would be fate just as the urn's truth is said to be beauty and vice versa; second, history must deny the freedom that defines its existence. In neither case does one come close to the history articulated by Winckelmann—a history that also appealed to the form of Greek tragedy for an example of how art develops in relation to freedom. Central to Winckelmann's understanding of history is the possibility of art developing once again as it did in Greece (a possibility that literary history has adhered to repeatedly in its account of romanticism as the literary equivalent of revolutions in America and Europe before, during, and after the period). Yet, for this development to take place would again require a nation to find the first seed of art within itself and then to possess the political climate in which art may flourish. For this understanding of history to be sustained, the freedom that permitted the development of Greek art must remain a possibility—in other words the possibility of repeating the cultural achievement attributed to Greece is tied to a political history. Within this understanding of art, the downfall of Greece is not simply a reflection of the loss of freedom but also the means by which freedom is maintained as a possibility within history.

While a concept of culture is at stake for Winckelmann in pursuing such a possibility, the stake for Keats is considerably higher. Indeed, it is only by developing to its fullest extent Winckelmann's understanding of the relation of freedom to history that the issue taken up by Keats's reflection on the aesthetic can be perceived. Such a development not only occurs in Schelling's writings on art and freedom but also does so in a context that relies heavily on the paradigm of Greek tragedy. In the tenth letter of Schelling's *Letters on Dogmatism and Criticism* this development receives its most concise presentation, and despite the youthfulness of this text (it was written in 1795–1796 when Schelling was twenty-one years old), it provides the basic outline of his later remarks on freedom and art as discussed in his lectures from 1804–1805 (subsequently published in 1859 as *The Philosophy of Art*) and of the treatise on freedom published in 1809, *On the Essence of Human Freedom*.[3] In this letter, the philosophical question posed by Hellenism appears in its clearest form as a question central to the thought of the late eighteenth century, a question answered (despite what takes place in an ode such as Keats's "Ode on a Grecian Urn") by Athens's greatest performance: its tragedy.

Schelling's turn toward Greek tragedy as a model for his understanding of freedom repeats the frequent gesture of his work toward art as the place in which the historical development of philosophy can be fulfilled.[4] The tenth letter of the *Letters on Dogmatism and Criticism*, which contains Schelling's first account of the relation of freedom to art, begins with just such a gesture toward the aesthetic: "There is an objective force ['Macht'] that threatens to destroy freedom . . . to struggle *against* it and in this way to succumb to it is to call forth freedom in its entirety. . . . this possibility, which has been long invisible beneath the light of reason, must be preserved for art, for what is highest in art."[5] Obscured by the Enlightenment, freedom survives in art, and the art in which it is best exemplified is, according to Schelling, the art of Greek tragedy. The intellectual context in which this work appears may explain why Schelling turns to freedom and Greek tragedy at this point in a work that takes dogmatism and criticism as its subject. The context does much to define the philosophical issue that judgments made in the name of Hellenism would otherwise ascribe to history.

Letters on Dogmatism and Criticism marks Schelling's first important venture into the central question raised by Kant's *Critiques*. After Kant the question posed for philosophy is the question of its own possibility, that is, the question of the possibility of a ground for knowledge that would not rely on merely guiding principles or as the *Critique of Judgment* concludes when faced with a radical conflict within judgment: "We can do no better than eliminate this conflict."[6] The adoption of such guiding principles prevents a sliding back into a pre-Kantian attempt to discover the truth of reason, God, and so forth in an objective representation. Briefly, this attempt to understand the absolute in terms of an object is precisely the dogma from which philosophy is to be freed for both Kant and Schelling. But, as Kant observes and as Schelling will reiterate in the course of the tenth letter, dogma has a considerable attraction precisely because it is irrefutable: dogma requires an objective representation that cannot be determined by what it represents, hence, it can neither be proved nor disproved. (This is why the question of dogma and criticism, as Schelling engages with it, is relevant to a literary criticism, whose mediation of a literary work as the representation of an objective world is neither judged nor refuted by the work that, like Keats's urn, is said to provide such mediation.) Against such dogma and its attempt to locate the conceptual in something objective, Kant's critical method would stand as an antidote. This method, despite its name is not to be confused with criticism in the literary sense: the latter representing the extension of judgment whereas the former seeks to determine its limits.

Although the Kantian critique seeks to define the possibility of human knowledge in a way distinct from dogma, its overcoming of dogmatic prejudices does not protect it from an impasse arising from its own critical intentions. The difficulty producing this impasse is not that of locating something conceptual in an object. To see the impasse in this way is to place Kant's critique, as Heidegger observes, "negatively under the presupposition that beings as a whole must be knowable in the sense of experience or else not at all."[7] As Heidegger explains, what experience means in this instance is an understanding that views whatever exists in terms of an object.[8] Hence, whenever concepts such as God or freedom are subject to experience, they are to be knowable as objects or not at all. As Heidegger remarks, this represents not just a negative view of Kant's critical project but also is based on a presupposition Kant's work docs not support.

Heidegger continues, "Kant has only shown that what is meant by the Ideas is not knowable *if* it is an object and can only be made certain of as an object in the experience of things of nature. Kant has not shown that what is represented and meant in the Ideas, is an 'object.'"[9] The difficulty posed by Kant does not arise from limiting the dogmatic reign of objects in the realm of thought. Such a difficulty can only induce a crisis in the relation of thought to object. Nowhere does it raise the question of a thought no longer conceived within a positive or negative relation to the world of experience and its objects. Indeed, the refusal to judge thought in terms of an objective world puts thought into a crisis, from which it can easily recover by becoming the history of its own inadequacy. As Heidegger points out, the unknowability that informs this sense of inadequacy is only tenable if the existence of the Idea is not distinguished from one's experience of nature: to say the thing-in-itself is not knowable if it is an object, is not to say it is an object. Schelling's remarks on freedom are to be located in the opening created by this distinction. But, as Schelling and Kant are also aware, whenever experience is refused as an arbiter of thought, there arises a question about judgment, because judgment is now effectively cut off from the traditional source of its authority. That is, judgment must occur without reference to anything capable of confirming its judgments. And judgment can only appear to overcome this difficulty by emphasizing its inability to rely on an external source such as experience. It is this step that leads to the systematic development of thought that characterizes philosophy after Kant, a development in which thought is to experience itself as itself, and on the basis of this experience will arise a self-knowledge that obviates the need for judgment.[10]

As we saw in Chapter 1, this step toward a systematic understanding already appears in Winckelmann's *History of Ancient Art* as the result of Winckelmann's attempt to write the history of a concept ("the essential, the interior of art") that can only be known as an object to be experienced but which is not itself an object. The difficulty of this attempt is compounded further by the fact that even the material objects of classical art in which the essence of art is made manifest are few and far between at the time of Winckelmann's writing. Systematicity in this instance makes up for what is lacking from an objective perspective as internal coherence takes the place of external reference. As Winckelmann's work makes clear,

Hellenism is, in addition to the thematic infatuation with Greece that it became, also an historical expression of a systematic tendency that can only sustain itself by means of an unattainable past, in short, through the birth of a modernity to which Greece is no exception.[11]

From the Hellenism rising out of Winckelmann's work, the unattainability of what Greece represents fuels the desire for a return to the cultural achievement of Greece. This operates equally in Hellenism and in the modernity that would refuse antiquity, because to regard Greece as an unattainable object is to foster both a desire for Greece and a desire to reject it. In this aspect, Greece plays the role of an object whose existence (which is to say, whose significance) is protected by an unattainability that reflects the way in which the Kantian Idea, once regarded as an object, is deemed unknowable. But, as Heidegger's remarks on Kant indicate, the basis for asserting this unknowability fails to recognize that the condition governing this unknowability cannot be supported. Heidegger's remarks are also relevant to the systematic development of art and literature that we recognize as history (as will be seen, to be systematic does not necessarily mean completion or even the dominance of one account of the past). In the changes and developments plotted by such a history, a concept is to be made manifest; it is to be given as an object that can be experienced, even though this history cannot know the object that governs it (rather than knowing it *as* an object). As Winckelmann's *History of Ancient Art* realizes, such an unattainability may become the single most effective means of establishing a history or a system. That this gesture has all the marks of an assertion of modernity only confirms the extent to which self-relation has become the defining paradigm of critical modernity.

Although the generality and diverse forms in which such a paradigm is expressed would appear to resist any characterization of it as systematic, its insistent reliance upon the aesthetic establishes it within a systematically developed history that begins with Winckelmann. Only by recourse to the aesthetic can an unattainable goal be given a realizable potentiality that does not undermine its conceptual origin. The philosophical account of this recourse takes place in the tenth letter of Schelling's *Letters on Dogmatism and Criticism*, an account that faces the question posed by Winckelmann's work, namely the question of a knowledge that, to cite Heidegger on Kant again, "must know that it is not supposed to know objects, but rather to know what is non-objective, but still not nothing at all."[12] To know something that is also not objective is the legacy of a Hellenism that defines history as the attempt to resolve this problem by repeatedly turning away from it. The attempt to know its nonobjective source determines the project announced by Winckelmann's *History of Ancient Art* even if this project is not carried out in a philosophical manner (as Hegel notes in the Introduction to the *Lectures on the Aesthetic*, that was *his* task).[13] Still, to have given art an objectifiable history is to have given experience to a concept that has no objective existence of its own, but yet is not nothing—like the unheard melodies of Keats's "Ode." As in the example of Keats, although unheard, a melody is still a melody, just as to be "not nothing" does not exclude the nonobjective from a history. The question taken up in Schelling's treatment of Greek tragedy is then the question of the conceptual and its representation, how the conceptual may be experienced in language and thought. In short, it is a question of the aesthetic and a history that may be traced to the rise of Hellenism.

The terms in which Schelling treats such a question focus on the relation between an objective world, on the one hand, and freedom, on the other. The determination of freedom by an objective world would represent dogmatism; therefore, the possibility explored by Schelling is the possibility of a criticism that would not be merely negative. It would not merely state, for example, that our knowledge of literature reflects our inability to know it as an object. To subscribe to such an inability is, in any case, inverted dogmatism, because it requires that literature be understood as an object in order to assert that it sets a limit to our knowledge and accordingly determines our knowledge of literature. This is also why every negation of knowledge about literature becomes the ground for a phenomenology of literature.[14]

As Schelling is aware in the tenth letter, freedom poses a particular difficulty: as a concept, it possesses no objective existence. Unlike Winckelmann, however, Schelling will not turn to climate as a means of accounting for the historical existence of a concept (which is what Hellenism in the final analysis desires) but to a history founded upon a struggle that the individual must submit to, a history exemplified by Greek tragedy. Before adopting this example, Schelling situates freedom in relation to the historical facticity of the objective world. He speaks of this relation as one in which the objective world is understood as a threat to freedom. At the same time, freedom is penetrated with the conviction that it must struggle against the world that poses this threat or else relinquish the very idea of liberty and succumb to that world. The understanding of freedom represented here is agonistic: one fights to preserve freedom, that is, one is free to fight, and only fighting can affirm the existence of freedom. In this case, conflict constitutes the difference between the objective world and freedom, but it does so in such a way that the struggle is unending. In other words, Schelling posits as the origin of freedom an opposition that is preserved by the struggle that arises from this origin.

In remarks preceding his discussion of tragedy in *The Philosophy of Art*, the conflict that arises from the opposition of freedom and the objective world is presented as follows:

A genuine conflict is present only when the possibility exists that either side may win. Yet, this appears to be unthinkable on both sides of the case at hand, since neither of the two can really be overcome. Necessity cannot, for if it were, it would not be necessity. Freedom cannot, for it is freedom precisely because it cannot be overcome. Yet, even if it were conceptually possible for the one or the other to succumb, it would not be poetically possible since it would generate absolute disharmony.[15]

Ever mindful of the dogma that would make one subordinate to the other, Schelling attempts to think a freedom that remains free even as it recognizes the existence of necessity. In the terms already discussed, this attempt would preserve the nonobjective from being understood as an object without giving up its relation to such objects. At this point Schelling's relation to the legacy of Kant's critique can be seen most clearly; this understanding of freedom indicates how Schelling thinks the consequences of Kant's thought. If what Kant regarded as unknowable is no longer thought of as an object, then the ability to think something that is nonobjective, but not nothing, becomes the task of thinking of freedom itself. This is because any account of the nonobjective is an account of its freedom from the objective. To take up this task is to think of freedom as the ground of all knowledge, precisely what, in a less philosophical way, Winckelmann had developed as the ground of the highest aesthetic development. Yet, to take up this task is also to involve thought in a contradiction that will be regarded as being essentially systemic: freedom cannot be thought without the necessity of the objective but freedom cannot be thought in terms of the objective.

In his attempt to systematize such a contradiction Schelling resorts to the aesthetic as not just its manifestation but also as the form of its existence. Schelling would give this role to art in the opening paragraph of the *Letters on Dogmatism and Criticism* when he speaks of freedom as a possibility that "must be preserved for art, for the highest in art." The necessity that governs this preservation emerges almost immediately when Greek tragedy, as the example of a contradiction, first appears in Schelling's argument:

> One has often asked how the reason of the Greeks could have tolerated the contradictions of their tragedy. A mortal, by fate determined a criminal, yet himself struggling against fate is horribly punished for a crime that was the work of fate! The ground of this contradiction, what makes it tolerable, lies deeper than one suspects, it lies in the strife between human freedom and the might ["Macht"] of the objective world, a strife to which the mortal necessarily succumbs when the might of this objective world is overpowering. (106)

The contradiction Schelling presents as the distinguishing characteristic of tragedy takes place through an individual who admits to a crime that is the result of fate. The capacity to admit to and thereby become the agent responsible for crime defines the individuality of the tragic hero, but the consequences of this admission effectively negate this individuality. Here, the necessity that governs tragedy is the necessity of a transformation in which individuality is expressed when the tragic hero plays the role of a criminal. The expression of this individuality is, in Schelling's argument, the moment in which freedom occurs, because it is a moment in which innocent protagonists choose to accept responsibility for a crime of which they are innocent. In the same moment, freedom is both asserted and lost. But, since this moment depends on the protagonist's choice to accept a role, freedom and necessity occur as the result of the protagonist's acceptance of a performance demanded by fate or necessity. All the protagonist needs to know is that this is necessary.[16] In such knowing, as Schelling puts it, the choice becomes tolerable ("erträglich") because to recognize it as necessary is to recognize it as part of a larger strife: "The strife between human freedom and the might of the objective world." Here, the tolerability of admitting to a crime for which one is not responsible arises from the protagonist's understanding that freedom and individuality are both essentially aesthetic. For the protagonist's choice to become tolerable, it must be understood in terms of a general strife for which the individual is both victim and medium. Within this general strife (recorded of course by the history of the individual who is to succumb to history) the individual exists as an aesthetic object (not nothing but also not objective in its own right or freedom). As such, the individual becomes the aesthetic medium of a freedom that can only be realized by the denial of the individual.[17] For Schelling, the individual succumbs to a history they must choose if their freedom is to be known both to and for history. Knowledge of this freedom is what survives as art thereby making a history of the aesthetic, as Winckelmann's *History of Ancient Art* is already witness to, the history of a freedom that succumbs to and is thus preserved by the downfall demanded by its own presentation.

As Schelling's remarks make clear this is a demand made by the aesthetic form of a work of art. By being an aesthetic object, the work of art thus becomes the place in which the history of freedom is written as the limiting of freedom. This was already apparent in the sentences cited previously from Schelling's *The Philosophy of Art*: "Even if it were conceptually possible for the one or the other to succumb, it would not be poetically possible since it would generate absolute disharmony." The work of art, in order to persist as a work of art, must remain true to the formal conditions of its existence; while it can tolerate contradiction, it cannot tolerate absolute disharmony. In the tenth letter, Schelling makes these formal conditions play a defining role in the tragic hero's acceptance of fate: "By letting its heroes *struggle* against the superior might of fate, Greek tragedy recognizes human freedom; in order to avoid crossing the limits of art, it must *succumb* to fate ['Um nicht über die Schranken der Kunst zu springen, musste sie ihn *unterliegen*']."[18] To recognize human freedom is to recognize art as the aesthetic medium of not just freedom but also the individual for which freedom exists. Thus, the aesthetic tells the story of the necessity of succumbing to fate if the aesthetic is to exist as such a medium. Here, fate becomes the means by which the aesthetic is known to be aesthetic—a knowledge that may be traced back to the moment when the protagonist of tragedy performs the role of aesthetic object. What this knowledge gives rise to is, as always, of more importance, because it is there that what is at stake is invariably revealed.

When Schelling writes, "Even Greek tragedy could not maintain defeat and freedom side by side," he appeals to Greek tragedy as the highest example of an art in order to assert that even this highest example remains incapable of a synthesis in which defeat and freedom can coexist. Again, the reason for this inability is the aesthetic form of art since any such synthesis would erase the struggle in which the individual is brought to an experience of freedom.[19] Indeed, to ignore this inability is to cross the limit demanded by art as the limit of its form, of its difference to an objective world that would subject it to the banality of mere existence.

Why freedom must be experienced in an aesthetic form as the erroneous judgment of the individual becomes even clearer as Schelling recapitulates his remarks on Greek tragedy. At this point Schelling explicitly reveals the dialectical development of his argument as a characteristic of the aesthetic work. The loss of freedom signifies the occurrence of freedom in an act that defines the individual as the exercise of a will. Schelling writes, "This was a noble idea to admit that man consents to accept a punishment even for an inevitable crime and, in this way, displays his freedom by the loss of this same freedom and puts an end to the struggle by a declaration of his free will."[20] By means of its defeat, freedom comes to exist as what subjects itself to necessity and the force of the objective. But, rather than signify a return to the dogma in which a concept is defined by the objective, Schelling distinguishes this act of subjection from dogma by means of the act through which the protagonist of Greek tragedy accepts fate. As we have already seen, this act only has significance for Schelling to the extent that it is performed by a hero who cannot be held guilty of the crime for which this act takes responsibility. In this context, the act of taking responsibility and succumbing to fate points all the more strongly to the freedom that is lost and through which such an act can only take place. (For, as Schelling would argue, if one were not free, then how could one choose necessity?) Schelling refers to this articulation of freedom when he states, "Here, as in general, Greek tragedy is the rule/standard ['Wie überall, so ist auch hier die griechische

Kunst *Regel'*]" (107). And the rule of Greek art is nothing less than the rule of an art that must always reenact the sacrifice of freedom in order to preserve the aesthetic as the form of such reenactment (and therefore the form in which freedom occurs even if this occurrence can only happen as negation).

As the rule, Greek tragedy would express what Winckelmann refers to as "the essential, the interior of art." However, in the case of Schelling, this goes one step further since the essential of art is the essential of the individual's historical and political existence: it is the essential form of the individual's existence. The individual is, in this case, nothing other than the negative representation of a necessity whose rule is embodied by Greek tragedy, a rule that, at the same time, binds the Greeks. To use a form of argument common in Schelling, if it did not, then there could only be freedom for the Greeks. By extension, Winckelmann could not think the possibility of Dresden as another Athens since the necessity that commands the downfall of Greece as the tragedy of freedom could not take place. Schelling's example of Greek tragedy offers to modernity the possibility of such a freedom and, therefore, of such a Dresden. As such it is an offer that cannot be refused; to do so is to refuse the refusal in which freedom is thought according to a dialectic in which what is represented is not what is meant. Accordingly, this freedom is less what is represented by the aesthetic than an effect of how the aesthetic is understood as a means of representation.

How the aesthetic may become a model of freedom becomes clear when Schelling discusses the humanity of the Greeks and their relation to nature. This discussion of the human relation to nature is, at the same time, a continuing determination of the form of art. Not only is the vocabulary used the same vocabulary for discussing art and literature but also the problem broached is that of aesthetic representation. Schelling writes:

[Man] indicates the objective world by determining limits across which he must not step. In representing an object to himself, in giving a form and a continuing existence to it, he dominates it. . . . as soon as he crosses these limits, as soon as the object is no longer representable, that is, as soon as man ventures beyond the limits of representation, he feels lost and prey to the terrors of the objective world. To an object without limits he can no longer give a form. (107–8)

The necessity of form affects both the work of art and any attempt to understand the objective world. To be human, as Schelling explains it here, is to recognize this necessity. Since what makes Greek tragedy the highest art is also a recognition of this necessity, then it is through the recognition of its limit as art that Greek tragedy attains the highest level. To put this another way, only by recognizing that it cannot be confused with or determined by the objective world, literature can be an art, rather than, for example, sociology, history, and so on. Each of these would view literature as if its aesthetic representation of an objective world could be taken for granted. (Or even that beauty is the representation of truth either positively or as its ideologically determined opposite.)

Schelling's understanding of the form of art does not readily admit what criticism would now recognize as the political content of artistic productions. A politically oriented criticism cannot fail to demand that the objective world be the measure of art. Yet, to do so, it must pass beyond the limit that defines the literature it has taken as the subject of its inquiry. To sustain its understanding of art, political criticism must either revert to dogma or else use the limit that Schelling places between nature and the aesthetic as the means to maintain the study of the objective through its absence (ideological criticism). Given this insistence, one might say that politics in the academy is merely theoretical, its desire for a practical world being the impossible dream of an escape from the formal conceptualization that Schelling recognizes as central to any intellectual endeavor that remains human. But, such an escape is also dogmatism; as indicated above, it is theoretically irrefutable precisely because its practical claims (in Kant's sense of the practical as what ought to be) are regarded as theory (again in Kant's sense of the theoretical as being concerned with what is). If a political understanding of literature is to be possible, then it must recognize a question about the theoretical at the center of its critical endeavors. This question focuses on the formal limit that defines the aesthetic and provides it with its representative powers. As such, it also focuses on the extent to which this limit induces a failing from which the political and the historical arise as the record of a concept (freedom) fated to exist by means of a representation to which it must also succumb. Need one add that this is precisely the question that Keats's "Ode" poses for the sacrifice when the townspeople take on the silence of the urn? Here, the difference between silence and speech marks the limit between language and the world of objects such as the urn. As in Schelling, this limit passes no judgment on the event or understanding expressed in its name; yet no such event or understanding is conceivable without this limit, in which the representative power of the aesthetic discovers its promise. But, in order to sustain this power the aesthetic must not fulfill this promise: the limit that gives rise to this power is also what preserves it by establishing a constraint that constantly renews its promise. Like the protagonist of Greek tragedy, the aesthetic succumbs to a necessity of the limit that allows it to be known as the aesthetic (and therefore become the easy target of ideological criticism). In this way, the aesthetic submits to the condition of its own representative power in order to repossess that power just as the individual subjects freedom to necessity in order to experience freedom as the negation, but not the determination, of necessity.

The understanding of the aesthetic Schelling presents in the tenth letter of the *Letters on Dogmatism and Criticism* is indispensable to the concept of freedom elaborated there. So necessary is this aesthetic that Schelling's concept of freedom would be unthinkable without it. Without this aesthetic, it would require the impossibility of its own objective representation. The aesthetic gives freedom a means of representation that allows freedom to be recognized while avoiding the necessity of appearing for itself (if it could, as Schelling is aware, then there would be no such thing as fate and therefore no limit for freedom to struggle against). Here, freedom is thought not simply as an effect of the aesthetic but also as an effect of the self-limitation of the aesthetic, as an effect of why the aesthetic is so limited. In this instance, the aesthetic allows freedom to be thought and, through its formal limit, preserves freedom as the persistent but elusive subject of its own representation. That the aesthetic retains freedom as its subject can be deduced from this limit, because this limit provides the model to think of whatever exists as different from the objective world while at the same time recognizing that what is being thought is not nothing. Into such a category freedom falls. This means that the question of freedom may only be conceived according to the aesthetic. This is why Greek tragedy, as Schelling observes, gives a rule for the appearance of freedom that is also general. (Schelling writes, "Wie überall, so ist auch hier die griechische Kunst *Regel*.") Generalized according to the aesthetic, freedom continues to exist as a retreat from the limit that allows it to be thought and, at the same time, requires this retreat as a condition of such thought.

By conceiving freedom according to the self-limitation of the aesthetic, Schelling provides a philosophic account of a tendency already apparent in Winckelmann: the tendency to account for the significance of the aesthetic in terms of political freedom. This tendency establishes freedom as the essential theme of aesthetic representation precisely because our ability to understand the political and historical significance of aesthetic representation is tied to such representations. Since this effect is derived from the limit that allows the aesthetic to be thought, the political and aesthetic significance of art depends on the necessity that the aesthetic registers and submits to the boundary from which the political and the historical are defined. In this case, the political and the historical are preserved by an aesthetic separated from an objective world in order to become the representation of that world (whether directly or negatively by the exposure of an ideology is immaterial). This is how the aesthetic always retains its power to represent what does not have an objective existence of its own and, as a result of that representation, would not be nothing. In this form the aesthetic becomes both a subject for history and the means of telling that history. This means, in the terms of Schelling's letter, the form and subject of history is the tragic; that is, the story of an individual's sacrifice to fate and necessity, an act from which no one returns and to which one is always subject in the interest of a history or a crime not one's own, but which is recalled as if it was one's own. Like the urn, the individual must remain silent and not revoke the performance that takes place in its name. If it did, then, in the case of Schelling's discussion of Greek tragedy, there would be no recognition of freedom. Just as the urn's silence sustains the judgment made on its behalf as if it were a historical act, so does the individual's sacrifice sustain a freedom through a death that is equally silent.

As Schelling's reliance on the example of Greek tragedy in his account of freedom indicates, recognition of a performative aspect does not prevent the occurrence of judgment or sacrifice. In fact, the performative intervenes by necessity and, accordingly, is accounted for by the history that this aspect would appear to undermine, because this history is the record of what was and what will be necessary. In this context, the necessity expressed in Keats's words, "that is all / Ye know on earth, and all ye need to know" points to the necessity of this performance as history. Governed by the necessity of staging such performances as the source of its power of judgment, history becomes the record of its own objective failure as it strives to protect the concept to which it owes its significance. This protection is never more efficacious than at those moments when history is most threatened, that is, when it must succumb to necessity as it recognizes its representative power to be limited. Keats describes such a moment when, at the end of the "Ode on a Grecian Urn," history becomes a speaking object content to repeat that this is all we know and need to know.[21] But, as always such a moment reiterates the difference that allows history to transform itself from an account of what ought to be and become the means of representing what was. In this development the aesthetic history of modernity is played out but hardly brought to an end, for the principle that guides this history is the necessity of modernity as the moment in which freedom from the necessity of the past is asserted as the origin of history. Here, the insight of Hellenism is clearly stated: without modernity there could have been no history, since modernity is the moment at which history recognizes its failure and resets its course toward the freedom that the past failed to sustain. In such failure history persists as the record of a freedom it cannot do without and which, as Schelling's text states, it can only possess in a form that marks its retreat.[22]

To identify the form that marks this retreat as Greek tragedy would reflect a Hellenism that is nothing more than a single-sided turn toward the past. As Winckelmann's earlier *Reflections on the Imitation of Greek Works in Painting and Sculpture* indicates, Hellenism is not single-sided, but rather is an articulation of modernity constituted by a limit Winckelmann locates in Greece. Inasmuch as Hellenism defines this limit as Greece, it is also giving a particular historical form to a paradigm Schelling presents as a dialectically informed aesthetic. To think of Greece according to this paradigm (in the example of its tragedy) is to think of modernity according to a mode of history predicated upon the kind of failure that modernity always ascribes to the past. In this respect one can talk of the persistently Hellenic character of a modernity that would reject Greece. Schelling rationalizes this pattern as an account of freedom that is as historically predictable as the event of modernity itself. But, as Schelling's treatment of Greek tragedy indicates, this account of freedom, in which modernity's attempt to free itself from antiquity is inscribed, demands a concept of literature that is impossible to judge. The difficulty posed by this account is, as Heidegger remarks in his lectures on Schelling's 1809 text on human freedom, the problem of thinking something which is nonobjective but which is yet not nothing. To locate literature and indeed art within a history of the aesthetic that is nothing less than a history of freedom is to locate them within this question. Literature cannot be the objective form of freedom, because it is not itself objective (a confusion that is harder to resist in the case of nonlinguistic art but to which Diderot's later writings on the salons stand as a strong antidote). In this case, literature may be read as the nonobjective form of something that is not nothing. But, how can one judge when something is not nothing and has at the same time no objective existence of its own?

The freedom described by Schelling poses the question of what literature is when it can only exist in its difference to an objective world and when, because of this difference, its significance is restricted to the expression of a will. In the final analysis, a will to history is expressed here, for it is to such an outcome that Schelling's protagonist succumbs in a history demanding the failure of individual will. For Schelling, in this failure, the will and its freedom exists as its resists the objective world of which it cannot be a part. By making art the privileged example of this will to an individuality that can only take place by succumbing to what demands the end of individuality Schelling will, in effect, define the aesthetic as a mode of representing what is not itself an object but which is yet not nothing. This understanding of the aesthetic, as Schelling's example demonstrates, enables the concept of freedom he defines. Freedom becomes what must be recalled from the aesthetic. But when the aesthetic is also the means of recall, the only choice is to succumb to its limit, because it is only in such succumbing to necessity that freedom can be recalled. Although this is articulated by Schelling as a formal issue, it gives rise to no mere formal problem, at least if one considers how our inability to resolve it fosters the most rampant dogmatism. If one wants to be more literary, then it fosters the most practical (in the Kantian sense) readings, whose concern with what ought to be confuses freedom with a groundless moral imperative, which would view the objective world as the judge of the aesthetic and thereby become theoretically irrefutable and groundlessly correct. They are also evidence that we have not yet come to terms with a modernity whose desire to free itself from Hellenism is the ground of its critical judgment. For this to occur, Hellenism, like Keats's urn, must perform the tragedy of Greece in words that define our fate—"that is all / Ye know and all ye need to know." But, as Keats's staging of this tragedy already indicates, this is all we are free to know when the aesthetic is the medium and the subject of history. From such a staging the question of freedom and individuality returns as the most insistent question of the poetic thought of two of romantic Hellenism's central figures: Shelley and Hölderlin.

4

The History of Freedom: From Aeschylus to Shelley

Both Shelley's *Hellas* and Aeschylus's *Persians* would appear to be apt examples of the kind of struggle described by Schelling in the tenth of his *Letters on Dogmatism and Criticism*. Both are concerned thematically with the subject of freedom, and both use the generic form of tragedy to express this concern. Accordingly, one may expect that each play, by associating Greece with freedom, affirms the place accorded to Greece as a cultural and political reference point for history. On a merely formal level, this deference to a Greek past appears to be confirmed by Shelley's use of Aeschylus's *Persians* as a model. But, such a relation becomes more than merely formal to the extent that the recall of Aeschylus's *Persians* allows Shelley to argue that history, as Winckelmann understands it in his *History of Ancient Art*, is driven by and expresses freedom as its inmost experience. Given the repetitive nature of the relation between Shelley's *Hellas* and Aeschylus's *Persians*, the critical response to this lyrical drama, which has been somewhat muted in output, is not surprising.[1]

To have written a play that not only recalls the first of the Greek tragedians but also, by so doing, recalls the event that becomes the subject matter of the earliest extant Greek tragedy, Shelley would appear to accede to a Hellenism in which the whole history of Athens may be invoked by an aesthetic work.[2] Indeed, so strong is the sense that *Hellas* is a classic Hellenistic text that famous remarks from its Preface, such as, "We are all Greeks—our laws, our literature, our religion, our arts have their root in Greece," as well as the Winckelmann-like sentiment expressed at one point by the play's chorus ("Another Athens shall arise" [1084][3]) set Shelley up for the kind of ideological critique that Hellenism has brought upon itself. While Shelley's play is clearly written within the context of late-eighteenth- and early-nineteenth-century Hellenism, this does not mean that *Hellas* is simply an ideological document. As is the case in Keats's "Ode on a Grecian Urn," a reflection on the role of the aesthetic within the understanding of art should not be confused with a blind submission to the aesthetic. Here, a play that takes Greece as its subject should not be regarded as being determined by its subject matter, thereby leaving no room to read this text as an examination of how the historical significance of modernity is thought as an expression of freedom. Viewed from this angle, Shelley's *Hellas* can be read as a reflection upon its own intentions (the very intentions in which the ideology that fosters the politically and historically motivated critique of this play are embodied).[4]

In his Preface, Shelley emphasizes not just the subject matter of this play but also the manner in which it is to be treated. He writes, "The subject in its present state, is insusceptible of being treated otherwise than lyrically, and if I have called this poem a drama from the circumstance of its being composed in dialogue, the license is not greater than that which has been assumed by other poets who have called their productions epics, only because they have been divided into twelve or twenty-four books."[5] With the phrase "the subject in its present state" Shelley speaks of the modern state of what this play takes as its principal subject: freedom. When Shelley says that this subject can only be treated lyrically, such a treatment may be understood as resulting directly from the uncertainty of the historical events that form the subject of *Hellas*. In this case, Shelley's inability to know the historical resolution of the Greek war of independence invites the use of the lyrical as means of evoking this same resolution—as if to say that the lyrical always begins where history ends. This understanding of Shelley's purpose in resorting to the lyrical assumes, first of all, that the only reason for the existence of this play is the Greek war of independence. Secondly, this understanding assumes that the lyrical can only be understood with reference to history, whether or not this history has yet happened.[6] However convincing such an account of Shelley's use of the lyrical is, it still does not answer the question of the role played by Aeschylus's *Persians* as a source for *Hellas*. Indeed, there arises the question of whether the historical resolution so confidently recognized by Aeschylus and his audience is also being read lyrically. Furthermore, one may even ask if Shelley's lyricism is not already present in Aeschylus's account of Greece's freedom from the Persians—a presence obscured by our willingness to read this play as if it were only a celebration of the origin of Greek history in freedom. The pursuit of either of these questions first demands a fuller account of how Shelley positions both Aeschylus and the lyrical in his preface to *Hellas*.

Written eight years after the events it portrays, Aeschylus's play provides a model of historical certainty derived from the fact that the outcome of events it portrays are already known. Since *Hellas* is modeled on the *Persians*, Aeschylus's play could then be read as affirming the eventual occurrence of the freedom left suspended by *Hellas*. Here, Shelley's play would become the mere repetition of a ready-made history as Aeschylus provides the Salamis that Shelley lacks. But, such a repetition would be counter to what Shelley describes as a lyrical treatment of freedom "in its present state," that is, its modern state. If this predictable conclusion is to be avoided, then we would do well to remember that Shelley's lyrical treatment is directed at the subject of both his lyrical drama *and* the play of Aeschylus: Greek freedom. The following remark conveys that Shelley does more than write a play whose meaning is lodged in a historical precedent:

The *Persae* of Aeschylus afforded me the first model of my conception, although the decision of the glorious contest now waging in Greece being yet suspended forbids a catastrophe parallel to the return of Xerxes and the desolation of the Persians. I have, therefore, contented myself with exhibiting a series of lyrical pictures, and with having wrought upon the curtain of futurity which falls on the unfinished scene such figures of indistinct and visionary delineation as suggest the final triumph of the Greek cause as a portion of the cause of civilization and social improvement. (408)

As a mode of subjective writing, this recourse to the lyrical could be viewed as an attempt to evoke an event not subject to the demands of history. Such an evocation can be read in Shelley's description of "figures of indistinct and visionary delineation" that have been "wrought upon a curtain which falls on the unfinished scene." But, in these words, a convention of the theatre—the falling of the curtain—gives the lyrical this power of suggesting a historical and political resolution it cannot otherwise embody. The judgment of history can only assert itself as a result of the suspension occasioned by this curtain—as if history were always fated, like some nemesis, to put an end to the lyrical.[7]

However much the fall of the curtain on the last scene of *Hellas* suspends this play before the judgment of history and, in so doing, appears to draw a clear line between the lyrical and historical, the same cannot be said for the relation of this play to Aeschylus's *Persians*. Here, Shelley's "series of lyrical pictures" occurs within a form and structure that explicitly recalls Aeschylus's tragedy. This reference to a prior model would again suggest that a meaning for the lyricism of Shelley's *Hellas* is being sought, not just in an historical antecedent which happens to take the form of an aesthetic work but also in an antecedent which derives its meaning and its occasion from an historical event. Yet, to submit this play to the judgment of history (in the form of an antecedent) invites the kind of ideological criticism that has been directed at Hellenism and the traditions it has fostered (a criticism envisaging a history freed from the necessity of any aesthetic or even lyrical presentation). Further, it would separate the subject of this play from the only treatment Shelley will allow freedom: the lyrical. The lyrical treatment undertaken by *Hellas* is directed at both the Greek war of independence and also the play upon which it is modeled. By directing the lyricism of *Hellas* at Aeschylus's play, the relation of Shelley's lyrical drama to the *Persians* is not simply one of a model or paradigm to its expression. In this case, what Shelley is invoking in *Hellas* has less to do with history (and the subordination of the lyrical to the historical) than with the role of the lyrical in the formation of history.

By distinguishing Shelley's use of Aeschylus's *Persians* from the expression of freedom and political ascendancy Aeschylus's play is usually taken to exemplify, this reading already takes issue with the narrowly Hellenistic sentiment that has defined the meaning of Shelley's famous declaration in the Preface to *Hellas*: "We are all Greeks—our laws, our literature, our religion, our arts have their roots in Greece." In the sentence following this declaration, Shelley defines what he means by our Greekness when he describes Greece as an historical principle that has prevented "such stagnant and miserable state of social institution as China and Japan possess."[8] Greece in this case becomes a metaphor for historical development understood as a movement toward freedom. This movement, articulated negatively by reference to a political and social oppression Shelley associates with China and Japan, indicates that the model of thinking freedom (in which Greece is invoked as *the* model and *the* root) follows that of Schelling as a struggle against its opposite. Here, the Preface would define Greece as the source of a principle that has irrevocably changed Western history. In so doing, Shelley appears to give voice to the kind of blinding belief confusing tradition and history. But this is not the whole story. Having roots in Greece (or in a Greek play) does not mean that one is enslaved to these roots (as if such roots determined the shape and nature of the growth that appears above ground). Indeed, it is crucial to retain one detail to which Shelley draws our attention in the Preface, a detail that opens up the whole question of the relation of *Hellas* to its roots in Aeschylus's drama.

Despite the fact that both Aeschylus's *Persians* and Shelley's *Hellas* can be read as the embodiment of a freedom traceable to the classical age of Greece it is important to remember that Shelley, by refusing the catastrophe of Aeschylus, effectively rereads not just this political history of freedom but also the philosophical account given by Schelling. Shelley, in effect, suspends the struggle so central to Schelling's account of Greek tragedy and, in so doing, undoes the primacy Schelling accords Greek tragedy as an account of freedom. (This can be argued because in Schelling there can be no awareness of freedom without the hero's acceptance of the catastrophe—without a catastrophe no freedom is conceivable in Schelling.) What, then, is Shelley's purpose in distinguishing *Hellas* from the *Persians* on the basis of the catastrophe that, for Aeschylus, offers the historical affirmation of freedom?

To pose the question of why Shelley suspends the catastrophe of Aeschylus is also to raise the question of what Shelley really means when he says, "We are all Greeks." As the tense of this phrase indicates, Greece is not something from which we can easily free ourselves—as if Greece were merely limited to the significance of its historical moment. A clue to what the phrase "We are all Greeks" means can be deduced from its Hellenistic reading. According to this reading, the claim that our literature has its roots in Greece would suggest that *Hellas* is to be understood in terms of its model. Here, Aeschylus's *Persians* would promise a judgment that modernity cannot make. It is a judgment about modernity's historical existence as an expression of freedom—the need for such a model being itself witness to the difficulty modernity experiences whenever it would judge its own historical significance. But for modernity to rely upon the past as a source to judge its significance compromises not only the freedom to which it aspires but also its own existence. Unless, of course, modernity is to sacrifice such freedom for the knowledge of its historical existence, a gesture that expresses precisely the recognition of freedom in Schelling's discussion of Greek tragedy. Here, how we understand Shelley's use of the *Persians* as a model poses the question of the play's subject: the problem of possessing freedom as a subject; the problem of "the subject in its present state." Furthermore, through this problem the question of our ability to be Greek is posed—precisely the question that, as Shelley states, must be suspended as our history in *Hellas*.

Given the complexity these questions invite, it is easier to offer a philhellenistic answer to the question of what Shelley means when he says, "We are all Greeks." But, with such an answer, Shelley's reflection on freedom in *Hellas* as well as this play's reliance on the *Persians* will amount to no more than the sentiment that it happened in the past so it will happen again as freedom becomes the repetition of history. As a result, it is on the authority of a play about a decisive event in the history of Greece that we would all be Greeks. Such a conclusion is suspicious, particularly since the text that stands for such an authority—Aeschylus's *Persians*—is a text that will only relate the moment in which Greece becomes Greece from the perspective named in the play's title: the perspective of the Persians. Are we all Greeks because we may only know our social and political identity through the representation of another? In such a gesture, the past, represented by the Persians, appears as the authority for a modernity that discovers its significance through a past which tells the story of its own self-destruction, its sacrifice to a moment in which history is made, the moment of Salamis. Clearly, more is happening in both Aeschylus's *Persians* and Shelley's *Hellas* than would be admitted by the naive Hellenism from which the contemporary taste for ideological critique draws its strength.

Before discussing the lyrical intent that would separate Shelley's

Hellas from the *Persians*, attention needs to be paid to the relation of Aeschylus's play to the development of Greece as a historical, political, and aesthetic embodiment of freedom. As briefly alluded to already, Aeschylus's play takes as its subject matter the decisive sea battle of Salamis in 480 B.C. Historically, this battle marks the beginning of the ascendancy of Athens as it overcomes Persian domination and inaugurates the century that Hellenism will later take as its political, historical, and cultural reference.[9] At the same time, this battle is more than an historical event; it also became a sign of the cultural achievement of fifth-century Athens, because it is the one event through which each of its major tragedians are related to one another.[10] Whether apocryphal or not, the Athenian desire to accept this story as part of the mythology of Athenian history marks the extent to which the political, historical, and cultural ascendancy accorded to Greece by Winckelmann is already an issue in fifth-century Athens. Indeed, the acceptance of this story already indicates how much Athens had already invested in an interrelation of politics, history, and culture as the source of its significance.[11] In this respect, Salamis becomes the vehicle for cultural and political self-representation. In so doing, it reflects the transformation of history into mythology.[12] But, above all else, this transformation displays within fifth-century Greece a need for self-relation and self-representation that runs counter to the claims of a later Hellenism (for which Greece is inevitably so exemplary it would never have required such self-representation).

Within the extant corpus of Greek tragedy, the *Persians* is an unusual play. In its treatment of an historical event as its subject matter, Aeschylus's tragedy differs from the immortal or heroic figures that people the classical form of Greek tragedy. While this might suggest that the *Persians* should be viewed as belonging to the genre of historical tragedy, such a view would be historically imprecise. Only in the sense that it is a tragedy about history could it be considered a historical tragedy. As a tragedy about history, the *Persians* takes the relation of history to the form of tragedy as its subject matter—a relation that can be seen in the role Dareios plays as the figure who connects earthly events to divine knowledge albeit after the fact. But, a strong current runs against the connection forged by Dareios, a current exposing how Aeschylus already explores the way in which an event becomes the performance of history.

Already at the beginning of the *Persians*, the event defining this play is present as an uncertainty that demands, but does not yield, interpretation. In this respect, Aeschylus's *Persians* begins at precisely the point where Shelley's *Hellas* is suspended. The Chorus reflects this uncertainty in the following words:

> But come, Persians, let us sit down
> on this ancient building
> and engage in deep and careful
> thought; the need is urgent.
> How are matters proceeding for Xerxes the King,
> son of Dareios?[13]

Into this climate of uncertainty, Atossa, the mother of Xerxes, enters and first relates a dream in which her son falls after failing to yoke two women of the same parentage to his chariot. In this dream, one woman is understood to represent the Persian empire, while the other, who causes Dareois to fall, is Greek. Atossa then relates how, after waking, she sees an eagle being attacked and offering no resistance to a hawk. From the perspective of the Greek audience for this play, the words of the Chorus, Atossa's dream, and the attack on the eagle can all be understood as predicting an already known event. Since the Athenian audience of *Hellas* possesses such a knowledge, Aeschylus's play relies upon historical knowledge as a source of its meaning in the same way that Shelley's play can be said to refer back to Aeschylus as a source of its meaning. In each case, historical antecedent is already a factor in the performance and understanding of both plays, the only difference being that Aeschylus's play recalls a historical event, while Shelley's play recalls the aesthetic performance of that event. Although this comparison suggests that Aeschylus has taken the classic Hellenistic step of confusing the historical with the aesthetic (by concealing the aesthetic within the historical) the manner of the play's development suggests otherwise.

In the dialogue following Atossa's description of the dream and the hawk attacking the eagle, the Chorus offers an interpretation that runs counter to the historical facts known to the audience. The Chorus declares, "In our judgment these matters will work out well for you in every way" (225). The dramatic irony at work in this judgment is obvious, so obvious, in fact, that one can easily overlook the means by which the

Chorus arrives at this judgment. Although the Chorus ends its response to Atossa on a note of confidence, the remarks that lead up to this final pronouncement show the Chorus to be a passive interpreter of her dream. In the lines recording its response, the Chorus first reflects Atossa's sense of foreboding and then suggests that if she sees anything evil in her dream she should supplicate the gods and pour out libations to Earth and the dead so that "contrary fortune may be kept down by the earth in obscure darkness" (215–23). Through this passivity, the meaning of the dream not only remains undecided but whether the gods themselves have even given it any meaning remains suspended until the occurrence of an event that may correspond to what the dream describes. In effect, whether or not the dream has any meaning at all (divine or otherwise) is left to the unfolding of events.

In her reply to the Chorus, Atossa first offers her agreement with the Chorus's reading and then goes on to pose a question implied not just by this opening scenē but also by the whole setting and Persian *dramatis personae* of this play: "As first interpreters of these dreams you have pronounced them favorable to my son and my household. May everything work out for the best. We will do everything for the gods and our friends beneath the earth, as you instruct, when we return to the palace. But there is something I want to find out, my friends. In what part of the world do they say that Athens is situated?" (226–31). In these words, Atossa judges the reading of what she saw, but before acting upon this reading, she poses a question that expresses her ignorance of the very thing all these signs derive their meaning from: Athens. While Atossa's question can always be attributed to the hubris of the Persians and thereby repeat the Aristotelian model of Greek tragedy, doing so would miss an insistent aspect of this play: where Athens is, is also a question that can be posed to this text which is so resolutely Persian.[14]

To relate the outcome of the battle of Salamis from the perspective of the Persians provides no direct reference for Athens or the Greek world it represents. In this respect, Aeschylus has written a play in which a crucial historical event in the history of the Athenians is related as the downfall of the history governed by the Persians. Rather than distinguish the Greeks from the Persians, Aeschylus shows their fates to be tied to one another. In this context one of the details of Atossa's dream reveals its significance: the two women are "sisters of one race" (κασιγνήτα γένους ταύτοῦ).¹⁵ As such, what is told of the Persians is a family history within which the Greeks and their history are to be included.¹⁶ Moreover, as the first episode indicates, this history is an effect of interpreting events; whether they occur in the form of a dream, or the sight of two birds of prey fighting, or the sea battle of Salamis, the necessity of translating the visual into a language, which serves as the medium of their significance, is posed by these events. Here, the Hellenistic intention that can be emphasized in a reading of the *Persians* is shown to be a result of precisely the question Winckelmann had to face in elaborating the history that gave rise to modern Hellenism and the concept of culture it inaugurates: the translation of what can be seen into history. Since it is also such a translation that defines the relation of *Hellas* to the *Persians*, Aeschylus's play becomes the site in which its role as a model for subsequent history can already be read. This means the *Persians*, rather than unequivocally affirm the tradition within which this play has been read, already offers a reflection on the relation of history to freedom informing this Hellenic tradition. In this context the ability of Aeschylus's *Persians* to represent Greece to itself also becomes a reflection on this representation, precisely because the play is located in Persia.

The question that arises when Atossa asks to be told where Athens is situated, the question of what the unfolding history refers to, is, of course, meant to be swept away when the Messenger enters with the news of Persia's defeat. Indeed, the Messenger's news does little to answer the question of where Athens is, except to indicate that where Athens is, is where Persia was. Instead, the Messenger relates how a deception perpetrated by the Greeks was the decisive factor in the events leading to the defeat of the Persians at Salamis: "The whole disaster began, mistress, when some vengeful spirit or malignant deity appeared from somewhere. For a Greek man came from the Athenian force and told your son Xerxes this: when the darkness of black night fell, the Greeks would not stay there, but would leap up onto the benches and try to save their lives by making a furtive escape, each one of them going in a different direction."¹⁷ The Persian loss is presented as a failure to understand and recognize deception. The Messenger is explicit on this point, even as he invokes a role for the gods in the lines that follow the preceding quotation: "Because Xerxes did not understand that this Greek was tricking him, nor that the gods were against him, on hearing this he immediately gave a pre-battle speech to his admirals" (361–63). In this speech Xerxes commands his admirals to set a trap for the Greeks, but it is through the setting of this trap that Xerxes will himself be trapped and fall victim to what the Messenger goes on to describe as an example of "how badly he knew the future" (κακῶς τὸ μέλλον ἱστορῶν [454]). Xerxes's misreading of the future repeats the Chorus's interpretation of Atossa's dream and account of the birds. The difference is that his interpretation of the future treats what cannot be seen—deception—and therefore reads the words of the Greek as signs of what is visible. In effect, Xerxes's misreading inverts the Chorus's. In the former case, the historical meaning of an event is judged through language, and in the latter, the meaning of language as the description of what can be seen allows the flight of the Greeks to be judged as a historical event. In both cases, language fails as an index to history.

In the first two episodes of the *Persians*, this failure appears most clearly in the Persian inability to read a history in which something other than their own image is reflected. Although this inability provides an interpretation of their loss at Salamis, it also offers a warning that addresses this play's own relation to an event such as Salamis. In so doing, it also addresses what may be called the Greek reading of this play, that is, the Hellenistic reading in whose light Shelley's Preface to *Hellas* is so often read. Traces of this Greek reading already appear in the first two episodes, particularly in the Messenger's evocation of the jealousy of the gods. Through this evocation that aspect of the tragic genre Schelling describes as necessity would be introduced. But here it is important to remember the deception recounted by the Messenger. Necessity operates in this play by means of a control that relies on a deceptive relation between event and history (its significance). Actually, two levels of deception should be discerned, since Xerxes also perpetrates a deception in order to read the words of the Greek. In this case, the deception perpetrated by the Greeks requires Xerxes to deceive himself about the relation of language to history so that the history in which the Greeks wish to see themselves may occur. If such a history cannot occur except through both these instances of deception, then the interpretation of an event as the example of what can only be seen (or described as what can be seen) lies at the center of this play. As such, Aeschylus's play is about the way in which Salamis becomes a form of self-representation in which Greece attains a history through and from the Persians.

The central question of this play is posed most explicitly in its third episode when the Chorus calls upon the ghost of Dareios to explain the Persian failure to read what Shelley describes as "figures of indistinct and visionary delineation wrought upon the curtain of futurity." The interest of the Persians in raising the ghost of Dareios is again to control the future. The Chorus expresses this desire, "For if he knows any further cure for our problems he alone of men could tell how to bring it to pass" (631–32). In calling upon Dareios, the Chorus calls upon the leader who forged the Persian empire now tottering under the defeat of Xerxes by the Greeks. By calling upon this figure, the Chorus not only attempts to invoke the past of the Persians in order to safeguard their future but also it calls upon a figure who is referred to by the Chorus as a god. The Chorus's invocation reads, "Does my blessed king, equal to a god, hear me? . . . the Sousa-born god of the Persians. Send him up . . . send up the divine ruler Darian! . . . He was called godlike in counsel for the Persians, and godlike in counsel he was, since he steered the army well" (643–55). This invocation will also be repeated by Dareios's own words when he appears, "Leaving Hades is especially difficult, and the gods of the underworld are better at taking than releasing. Nevertheless, since I have authority amongst them, I have come" (687–91). In this way, the play calls upon a figure whose godly status promises a cure to the present state of the Persians. Yet, Dareios when informed by Atossa that Persia's power is "completely crushed" (714) only repeats his ignorance of what has just happened to the Persians: "How? Were they blasted by some plague, or was there civic strife?" (715). A mortal Atossa must inform him of what has happened on earth amongst the living. But, as if to make up for his ignorance, Dareios is quick to offer a divine account, one that, like the Chorus and Atossa before him, is based, yet again, on a reading of the future: "Alas! How swiftly the oracles have been accomplished! Zeus has hurled down on my son the consummation of prophecies" (739–40). With these words Dareios not only provides a controlling reason to the events that give history to mortals but also a reading that, through its reference to Zeus, is essentially Greek. Given the perspective adopted by Dareios, it is not surprising that, from this point on, Xerxes's defeat becomes the result of transgressing the gods, in particular, Poseidon, whose sea Xerxes bridged so that his troops might cross from Asia to Greece: "He transformed (μετερρύθμιζε) the very nature of the strait, and by casting around it hammered shackles furnished a great road for his great army; although only a mortal, he foolishly thought that he could overcome all the gods, including most of all Poseidon" (749–50). But when Dareios utters the question that follows these words, the origin of the transgression that fulfills the prophesy of the oracles is located in the mind of Xerxes: "Surely this must have been some disease affecting my son's mind?" (νόσος φρενῶν [750–51]). Here, the downfall of Persia and the prophesy of gods is accounted for as the result of a disease or sickness that afflicts the mind or wits of Xerxes. By locating this downfall in the mind, Aeschylus makes Dareios locate it in the place of transaction between perception and a world whose existence and events remain resolutely and merely visual until given significance. It is the significance Xerxes gives to what he sees that Dareios describes as a sickness of mind—a sickness that does not let Xerxes see the transgressive nature of turning a sea into a bridge. According to what Dareios says, the sickness that Xerxes cannot see is the power of his understanding to change, rather than reflect, the world in which he exists. Here, it is thought's inability to protect itself from deception—even at the moment of recognizing deception—that will account for Xerxes's downfall. But, does such an account justify the defeat of the Persians as a defeat at the hands of the gods of Greece?

As the Messenger informed us, the battle of Salamis is governed by a deception that cannot be judged as a deception, because the visual evidence that would provide such knowledge and therefore avoid the need for judgment is withheld on two levels. First, only the words of the Greek are offered for Xerxes's judgment; second, the visual evidence that would avoid the need for judgment can only occur at a time when such evidence cannot be known: at night. In this instance, judgment takes place because it has no guide to know whether or not what is being said has visual reference. Here, Aeschylus's *Persians* presents judgment as a problem onto which a divine account is superimposed by Dareios. But when Aeschylus accompanies this account with an insistence on a historical misreading caused by a sickness in Xerxes's mind, he emphasizes a current running through this play: the translation of the visual into language establishes the significance of an event, its becoming history, its becoming worthy of recall. In the case of this play (and for the Greeks), this translation occurs by producing history in the form of a prophesy of events that have already happened and which the Greek audience of this play know to have already happened. In this respect, Aeschylus's *Persians* prophesies a catastrophe whose outcome, unlike Shelley's *Hellas*, requires no suspension. This difference would suggest yet again why *Hellas* should be modeled on Aeschylus's *Persians*. The *Persians* presents the performance of prophesy as history, but this performance is enacted through a prophesy that only appears after the fact in a reading of events whose occurrence were unknown to its interpreter.[18] It is through a figure who only knows of the Persian's defeat by word of mouth—the same form in which Xerxes learns of the Greeks' intention to flee during the night—that the events recalled in this play are placed under the control of the Greek god, Zeus. Through Dareios, the Hellenistic reading of Aeschylus's play is shown to be already at work in the downfall of the Persians. This reading, however, depends upon knowledge of Zeus's prophesy as a completed act. Only through such a knowledge could Aeschylus's be said to attribute to the Greeks a history free from the misreadings of the Persians.

As Aeschylus's play points out, a history not subject to such misreadings (or deceptions) arises from the Persians' inability to distinguish fiction from history or what the Greeks are actually planning. But, if the Greeks' victory turns upon the failure of the Persians to perceive deception, then this does not mean that the Greeks are themselves free from the failure that led to the defeat of the Persians. Rather than possess an ability to distinguish between fiction and history, all the Greeks did was to exploit this inability in the Persians. Aeschylus, by emphasizing that the Persians' defeat resides in Xerxes inability to perceive deception, points to a failure of judgment as the crucial factor in the Greeks' victory. This failure is not something that Xerxes can avoid—as if he had the luxury of refusing the need to judge the veracity of events that cannot be observed. Above all else, it is the necessity of judging the truth of his words that the Greek who comes to the Persians imposes upon Xerxes. By locating the central act of this play's catastrophe in the necessity of judgment, Aeschylus cannot be said to be simply following the historical reading that only sees a celebration of Greece's freedom in the defeat of the Persians. In this reading, the necessity of judgment faced by Xerxes is avoided because the future is already known to have happened: the Greeks see a play about an event whose outcome is already known. Yet, by focusing on the moment before such an event occurs, Aeschylus indicates the extent to which this reading arises from a moment in which history must masquerade as fiction (when the Greek speaks to Xerxes) and still be regarded as history. In this moment, history risks itself precisely because it relies upon a deception that can only be judged as a deception by the outcome of Salamis. What is at stake here can be easily realized if the possibility that what the Greek says is read as history by Xerxes in order to trap the Greeks into believing that their deception controls what is to happen. Such a possibility must exist for the Greeks until the outcome of Salamis is decided. Only then can it be read as part of an historical development in which a prophesy is completed. Within the play, this prophesy is only presented after the event; therefore, it does not risk its relation to history, since at the moment the prophesy is given in the play it is already history. For an audience armed with such historical knowledge, the prophesy can never be the sickness of mind attributed to Xerxes when he listens to the description of an event that has no act to justify its meaning. By avoiding this sickness, Athens possesses a history for itself as Salamis becomes the myth sustaining its historical existence. As Aeschylus shows through the medium of the Persians, this is how Athens discovers in Salamis the formative power of the myth of its own history, the myth in which even deception (including myth) becomes the necessity of history.[19]

Through this treatment of the relation of Athens to its own history, Aeschylus's *Persians* discloses how Athens becomes a model for history. It becomes a model for history as a model of self-representation in which the risk of judgment is controlled by a deception that by itself cannot be judged historically. Rather, this deception must wait for the occurrence of an event it does not describe to take place. The *Persians* thus provides a model of self-representation that is at the same time a model of what this representation cannot control but without which it cannot be thought: the history in which Athens tells its freedom from the Persians finds its rationale in a failure of judgment that Athens stages in order to replace the necessity of that judgment with history. Since this failure provides for the catastrophe of Aeschylus's play, which Shelley correctly describes as "the return of Xerxes and the desolation of the Persians,"[20] then it is this failure that Shelley again correctly identifies as the source of history when he writes, "The decision of the glorious context now waging in Greece being yet suspended forbids a catastrophe parallel to that of Xerxes" (408). The nonoccurrence of such a failure suspends not only judgment but also its replacement by history. Through this suspension the lyrical character of Shelley's *Hellas* makes its entrance as the direct consequence of what Aeschylus has presented in the form of a historical tragedy: Athens's translation of its freedom into the principle of a history for which Athens serves as the example.

Taking his cue from Aeschylus, Shelley also makes an inability to know the difference between history and deceptive images central to the development of *Hellas*. In a recall of the opening episode of the *Persians*, these deceptive images take the form of a dream, a "gloomy vision," Mahmud is unable to interpret. The dream whose images portray events foretelling the fall of Turkish rule over Greece is described by Mahmud in the following way:

> Thrice has a gloomy vision hunted me
> As thus from sleep into troubled day;
> It shakes me as the tempest shakes the sea,
> Leaving no figure upon memory's glass. (128–31)

When the vision foretelling his fall jolts him awake into day, Mahmud complains that it leaves "no figure upon memory's glass." Mahmud's complaint is directed at precisely the one thing through which the meaning of the dream ought to appear: its figure. This figure, as Mahmud's words and actions subsequently make explicit, is how memory gives significance to a dream for which there is no corresponding historical event. In order to know the historical meaning of this dream (rather than the "truth of day" in which it is revealed as just a dream), Mahmud calls upon Ahasuerus. For Mahmud, Ahasuerus is not only a seer who belongs to a tribe known as "wise interpreters of dreams," but, more importantly, he is a "chronicle of / Strange and forgotten things" (133–36). So characterized, Ahasuerus promises an ability as well as a knowledge from which an historical figure for Mahmud's dream may appear. Yet, where Mahmud sees

in Ahasuerus a chronicle of the past, Hassan, his attendant, goes further
and describes the source of his interpretive powers:

> from his eye looks forth
> A life of unconsumed thought which pierces
> The present, and the past, and the to-come. (146–48)

In Hassan's words, Ahasuerus possesses an eye through which his relation
to the present, past, and future of the world is sustained by a "life of unconsumed thought." This last phrase is crucial for what is to come, because it locates Ahasuerus's relation to the world as not just produced by
thought but also by a relation in which this thought remains unconsumed. Already this emphasis shifts the Hellenistic reading of the play
(never mind the *Persians*) into a different context, since it is to the source
of history that Shelley's reflection on freedom is being directed from the
very outset.

Between the opening scene of *Hellas* when Mahmud reiterates his
summons to Ahasuerus and the arrival of the Jewish seer, accounts of revolts within the Muslim empire are relayed to Mahmud. In this context
Ahasuerus arrives and will be questioned by Mahmud in order to pierce
the "mist of fear" that the news of the revolts have brought. By way of
preface to this scene, Shelley makes the chorus of Greek women speak and
address the relation of Greece to thought, that is, the relation of Greece to
what Ahasuerus is said to exemplify:

> Temples and towers,
>   Citadels and marts and they
> Who live and die there, have been ours
>   And may be thine, and must decay,
> But Greece and her foundations are
> Built below the tide of war
> Based on the chrystalline sea
> Of thought and its eternity;
> Her citizens, imperial spirits,
>   Rule the present from the past,
> On all this world of men inherits
>   Their seal is set— (692–703)

While the sentiment expressed in these lines recalls the Hellenism so easily associated with Shelley's declaration, "We are all Greeks," it also offers

a clarification of where this Greekness is to be located. What the Chorus calls Greece is based on thought and its eternity, and from this basis, it controls all that may be known in terms of the present. The idealizing tendency present in these lines—especially in the way that Greece appears as something that transcends history—needs careful consideration if this play is to yield anything other than the easy discernment of an ideologically constructed Greece. These lines are explicit in pointing out that the foundation Greece represents is based on thought and its eternity, which is quite different from saying that Greece is the origin of an eternal thought to which all later ages are subject. As Shelley and subsequently Hölderlin make clear, the relation of Greece to history is being thought of in terms quite different from the aesthetic modernity ushered in by Hellenism and which has been resurrected as the object of the cultural and ideological criticism of our time. (This is also to say that the dialectical history in which this criticism, after Schelling, locates freedom is also being thought differently.) The above lines indicate that through thought itself and its eternity Greece not only exists but also the past rules the present. Thus we must turn to the role of thought in this play if the relation of *Hellas* to Hellenism is to be understood.

At the point where the play joins the dialogue of Mahmud and Ahasuerus, Ahasuerus's role as the embodiment of thought is repeated (when Mahmud describes Ahasuerus and himself as reflections of one another: what Mahmud is to power, Ahasuerus is to thought [739–40]). But, as this dialogue proceeds, the hope that Mahmud holds out for thought to fulfill is recognized as beyond the scope of thought. As expressed in Shelley's words from the Preface, this hope is to know what is written on the curtain of futurity or, in the words of Mahmud, to interpret his dream. But, Ahasuerus, as Mahmud comes to realize, is no Freud:

> I honour thee and would be what thou art
> Were I not what I am—but the unborn hour,
> Cradled in fear and hope, conflicting storms,
> Who shall unveil? Nor thou, nor I, nor any
> Mighty and wise. I apprehended not
> What thou has taught me, but I now perceive
> That thou art no interpreter of dreams;
> Thou dost not own that art, device, or God,
> Can make the future present—let it come! (751–61)

Faced with the impossibility of historical knowledge of the future, Mahmud expresses what is to come as an event about which one can only predict that it will occur. But, as Ahasuerus points out in his reply to Mahmud's pronouncement that he is no interpreter of dreams, such prophesy belongs to the realm of thought and its eternity:

> —Sultan! talk no more
> Of thee and me, the future and the past;
> But look on that which cannot change—the One,
> The unborn and the undying. Earth and ocean,
> Space and the isles of life or light that gem
> The sapphire floods of interstellar air
> The firmament pavilioned upon chaos,
> With all its cressets of immortal fire
> Whose outwall bastioned impregnably
> Against the escape of boldest thoughts, repels them
> As Calpe the Atlantic clouds—this Whole
> Of suns, and worlds, and men, and beasts, and flowers
> With all the silent or tempestuous workings
> By which they have been, are, or cease to be,
> Is but a vision—all that it inherits
> Are motes of a sick eye, bubbles and dreams;
> Thought is its cradle and its grave, nor less
> The future and the past are idle shadows
> Of thought's eternal flight—they have no being. (766–84)

As thought strives to understand what is heterogeneous to itself, it contends against the sameness of the one that is neither born nor given death. The world that thought would understand is presented in these lines as what repels thought even at its boldest, or, as would be said now, at its most radical. The "Whole of suns, and worlds, and men, and beasts, and flowers" becomes the same as the vision Mahmud sought to have translated into history by Ahasuerus. This is why the dream yields no interpretation, because the interpretation would, in Ahasuerus's terms, be itself a dream comparable to the "motes of a sick eye," or the sickness of mind of a Xerxes. Why the dream or vision can only inherit an obstruction to its sight is explained by Ahasuerus as an effect of thought's eternal attempt to overcome the condition of its own existence, to become in a misreading of Hölderlin's famous line from "Brot und Wein," a flower rather than like a flower ("nun müssen dafür Worte, wie Blumen, entstehn"). But, just as words are not flowers even though they may originate *like* flowers, so thought remains in eternal flight from itself and in so doing establishes itself as thought. In Ahasuerus's closing lines, our determination of history as future and past is defined by such a condition—as if to say the one thing that establishes history as a chronicle of human existence is its inability to be what it refers to. This is why thought is both a cradle and a grave: without it there could be no conception of past or future. At the same time, the price to be paid for such a conception is the eternal flight of thought away from what it represents to itself and in which it seeks to establish its meaningfulness.

As may be expected, what Ahasuerus says cannot be understood by a historian of Mahmud's inclination. He asks:

> What meanest thou? thy words stream like a tempest
> Of dazzling mist within my brain—they shake
> The earth on which I stand, and hang like night
> On Heaven above me. What can they avail?
> They cast on all things surest, brightest, best,
> Doubt, insecurity, astonishment. (786–91)

Where Mahmud had formerly experienced a "mist of fear" (641) after being told of the revolts within the Muslim empire, he now experiences a mist formed by the words of Ahasuerus. Mahmud's remarks are charged with the all-too-familiar accusation of linguistic nihilism that tends to appear whenever history, or whatever is asserted in its name, must defend itself against the condition of its discursive existence. This accusation and the condition by which it is governed are clearly present when Shelley makes Mahmud ask, "What can they avail?" The question can be read rhetorically implying that they avail nothing, or it can be read as a demand that they do avail something, that they have a purpose which can be revealed historically. In either case, for Mahmud to ask what the eternal flight of thought means is to miss the point since such a question seeks to arrest this flight, rather than to understand it. Ahasuerus is direct in his reply when he points to Mahmud's misunderstanding:

> Mistake me not! All is contained in each,
> Dodona's forest to an acorn's cup

Is that which has been, or will be, to that
Which is—the absent to the present. Thought
Alone, and its quick elements, Will, Passion,
Reason, Imagination, cannot die;
They are, what that they regard, appears,
The stuff whence mutability can weave
All that it hath dominion o'er, worlds, worms,
Empires and superstitions—what has thought
To do with time or place or circumstance?
Would'st thou behold the future?—ask and have!
Knock and it shall be opened—look and lo!
The coming age is shadowed on the past
As on a glass. (793–806)

The promise of prophesy (present in both the reference to the oracle of Zeus at Dodona and in Ahasuerus's closing words) offers a history that will occur by necessity. Armed with such a necessity, the future has no different relation to the present than the past does. Both are appealed to as a means of defining the significance of the present; both the past and the future tie the present to the kind of unfolding we recognize as history. However, in the lines just cited, thought is distinguished from this historical sequence, since, unlike prophesy and history, it does not die and precisely because it does not seek a significance derived from an objective world, the world of what the eye can see (rather than the unconsumed thought that issues from the eye of Ahasuerus). In this respect, the thought Ahasuerus explains differs markedly from the thought that Schelling makes subject to the objective world in order to recognize freedom. According to what Shelley's Ahasuerus says in the above passage, thought has dominion over such a world, since its mode of existence is not that of appearance (only in a world of appearance can there be mutability, empires, worms, and so forth). Thought alone is what it is, because it is not understandable in terms of time or place or circumstance: that is, it is not understandable in terms of change which, as Kant rightly points out, is only a category of experience.[21] To conceive of thought in terms of experience would be, as Ahasuerus points out in his last words, to see thought as the figure (shadow) of a past that can only be seen in a mirror. What Mahmud must see as history (his future) will therefore be his own image as another. Isn't this precisely the point of Aeschylus's drama, in which the Greeks are invited to read their history through another—the Persians—in a work that has no Greek characters? And, isn't this the moment in which thought is denied when it is usurped by history?

In what follows in the scene between Mahmud and Ahasuerus, the denial of thought is performed as Mahmud first experiences a vision and then, in a scene that repeats the appearance of the ghost of Dareios in Aeschylus's *Persians*, he is approached by the phantom of Mahomet the Second, the subject of his vision. The vision, rather than derive its meaning from history, must now find such a meaning in the mouth of a phantom. As before, Ahasuerus comments on Mahmud's attempt to join dream and history. First, with a direct reference to the subject of the vision as a source of history:

> Thou would'st ask that giant spirit
> The written fortunes of thy house and faith—
> Thou would'st cite one out of the grave to tell
> How what was born in blood must die—(808–11)

In the vision through which thought takes flight all that is to be learnt by Mahmud is the necessity of death as the future asserts an inevitability that Mahmud has no experience of except through another. Here, the flight of vision toward history experiences the condition of the thought in which it originates. In his last words, Ahasuerus comments on this flight in the following terms:

> What thou see'st
> Is but the ghost of thy forgotten dream.
> A dream itself, yet, less perhaps, than that
> Thou callest reality. Thou mayest behold
> How cities, on which empire sleeps enthroned,
> Bow their tower'd crests to Mutability.
> . . . —Inheritor of glory,
> Conceived in darkness, born in blood, and nourished
> With tears and toil, thou see'st the mortal throes
> Of that whose birth was but the same. The Past
> Now stands before thee like an Incarnation
> Of the To-come. (841–54)

The vision possesses less the promise of history than the ghost of the dream for which Mahmud sought historical interpretation through Ahasuerus. This ghost is itself referred to as a dream, even though what Mahmud considers as reality may be even more dreamlike. In this dream, as Ahasuerus points out, Mahmud can only see a mutability in which perception is figured as experience. Framing this perception is a history that experiences its birth as its death, as what it cannot experience for itself (this being its cradle and its grave). Within this frame, the past stands as the birth of what is to come. But, as Ahasuerus states, it stands before Mahmud "*like* an Incarnation of the To-come." Mortality may be the sign that guarantees the experience of mutability, but neither can predict history; they can only predict that change will occur.

In the place of prediction, Mahmud calls the ghost of Mahomet the Second, who in his first words says no more than Dareios does in his first speech and no more than what Ahasuerus said he would say:

> I come
> Thence whither thou must go! the grave is fitter
> To take the living than give up the dead (861–63)[22]

For the past to incarnate the future the grave would indeed have to give up the dead, a possibility that neither Mahomet nor Aeschylus's Dareios can perform. Mahomet's appearance here not only invokes the necessity of death but also, in an allegorical as well as lyrical picture, describes the historical change derived from this necessity:

> A later Empire nods in its decay:
> The autumn of a greener faith is come,
> And wolfish Change, like winter howls to strip
> The foliage in which Fame, the eagle, built
> Her aiëry, while Dominion whelped below.
> The storm is in its branches, and the frost
> Is on its leaves, and the blank deep expects
> Oblivion on oblivion, spoil on spoil,
> Ruin on ruin—thou art slow my son; (870–78)

The downfall of empire is predicted by a figure of the past. Although Mahomet predicts a "greener faith," the authority of this prediction can only be traced to the mutability that death exemplifies. The prediction is an effect of change that history records and then takes as its surest principle. Yet, such a prediction is not a guarantee of freedom as a principle of history or as the possession of an individual who submits to fate, to death. Rather, it is an understanding of the finitude of freedom, the finitude through which freedom persists as the vision or dream of a history that subjects even this dream to its principle of mutability and so preserves the promise of the dream's interpretation as event. In Mahmud's last words after the phantom of Mahomet vanishes, this promise is maintained by the inevitability ascribed to the mutability of the future even as the question of when and how an event takes place is abandoned. After hearing the cry of victory from without, Mahmud speaks:

> What sound of the importunate earth has broken
> My mighty trance?
> . . .
>
>   Do I wake and live?
> Were there such things or may the unquiet brain,
> Vexed by the wise mad talk of the old Jew,
> Have shaped itself these shadows of its fear?
> It matters not!—for nought we see or dream,
> Possess or lose or grasp at can be worth
> More than it gives or teaches. Come what may,
> The Future must become the Past, and I
> As they were to whom once this present hour,
> This gloomy crag of Time to which I cling
> Seemed an Elysian isle of peace and joy
> Never to be attained. (913–28)

Despite the cry of victory, what occurs outside reasserts the troubled day that marked Mahmud's awakening at the beginning of the play, but now Mahmud must ask if he is both awake and alive. The intrusion of the event offers no resolve to the failure to translate vision into history, to make the future become the past. There is no prophesy to recall after the fact. For Mahmud, it no longer matters if the events happening around him are actual or a dream. To distinguish one from the other—the essentially historical exercise practiced by ideological criticism—is to create, as the passage of this play makes clear, "a dazzling mist within the brain" in which history cannot be distinguished from the "ghost of a forgotten dream." All that remains for Mahmud is to assert that in either case, whatever we see or dream is worth less than it gives or teaches. But, for Mahmud, what is given and what is taught is a sense of the permanence of history derived from the necessity of change: "the Future must become the Past." History, as the record of change, would justify itself through the change it records, the change that makes history the record of what it can never be, unchanging.

It is at this point that the full significance of Shelley's reluctance, as stated in his Preface to *Hellas*, to produce a catastrophe parallel to that of Aeschylus's *Persians* can be realized. In the Preface, Shelley speaks of this reluctance as the result of a suspension derived from the fact that no point of historical decision had yet been reached in the Greek war of independence. His use of the word "decision" is important, because it invokes the judgment most under question in *Hellas*—the judgment of what will become history, the judgment of what history *will* teach us. Shelley sees this catastrophe as suspended in a text whose subject is the freedom of modernity. Through this suspension Shelley poses the question of freedom as a question about judgment. This judgment cannot be derived from a knowledge of history (the chronicle Mahmud seeks in Ahasuerus) or even a misreading of Aeschylus, because such judgment does not belong to the time recorded by history, but rather to the time that belongs to thought: the time of judgment. Here, the lyrical character of *Hellas* presents a refusal to turn from the question of judgment. In *Hellas*, such a turning away is exemplified by the desire for a history that can only justify itself as a record of change (and within such a record freedom can only be an agent of the change to which it will also be subject). This refusal, as the dialogue of Mahmud and Ahasuerus points out, is a refusal of thought, or to recall the words of the Chorus, it is a refusal to recognize the double crossing of the thought Shelley describes as the foundation of Greece, the thought that has no being, no objective form to call its own. In the realm of thought, the Greeks are like us, precisely because, like us moderns, the Greeks have no dominion over this realm. This sense that we are all Greeks (and not in the sense of the naive Hellenism) enables the ideological critique of the past. Hellenism, as Winckelmann makes only too plain cannot be divorced from modernity, but Hellenism in the hands of Shelley poses the question of judgment that modernity and modern criticism would refuse whenever it seeks to free us from the ideology of the past. Recognition that judgment is the central question suggests that, for Shelley at least, our relation to Greece may not be one of subordination to the model modernity has created for us. This question, as Shelley's earlier lyrical drama, *Prometheus Unbound*, indicates is bound up with thought as an act of recall. In Shelley's poetry, this question is addressed as much to the relation of language to thought as it is to the aesthetic understanding, in which the critical vocation of our modernity rejects the medium of its own history. When this rejection occurs, the freedom suspending judgment becomes a historical force as well as an event such as that celebrated at Salamis. Only then (and this does not indicate the time of history) can it be said to have a history.

5

The Time of Judgment: Shelley's *Prometheus Unbound*

Shelley observes in the Preface to his *Prometheus Unbound* that to imitate Aeschylus's lost play on the freeing of Prometheus would be to turn Aeschylus into a rival whose precedence would be decisive. In such a case, Shelley's work could only be judged by the example of what has gone before—Greece and its dramatic literature. But, as Shelley also notes, acceptance of Greece as a precedent would run counter to how the Greek dramatists related to each other. Shelley writes that this acceptance would "resign those claims to preference" on which the dramatic contests of Athens were based. Rather than repeat what has already been written, the Greek tragic writers, Shelley observes, "by no means conceived themselves bound to adhere to the common interpretation or to imitate in story as in title their rivals and predecessors."[1] With this remark, the Preface indicates that Shelley's *Prometheus Unbound* will bear a relation to Greece that is not based on either mimesis or the judgment mimesis pronounces whenever there occurs any attempt to emulate antiquity. This distinction between Shelley's *Prometheus Unbound* and any Greek precedent is emphasized further when Shelley states that his play will not offer the kind of reconciliation between Prometheus and Jupiter that would "restore the lost drama of Aeschylus." By refusing such a reconciliation, Shelley rejects what he refers to as a "feeble catastrophe." This refusal suggests that Shelley's rejection of the plot of Aeschylus's lost drama asserts an irreconcilable difference between Greece and the modernity of his own age. Paradoxically, this refusal aligns Shelley more closely with the tragic drama of Greece. However, Shelley's relation to Greece and Aeschylus cannot be contained by so predictable a device as paradox, or, to give this paradox its proper name, so romantic a Hellenism (since Hellenism promotes the paradox from which it arises).

As the Preface unfolds, Shelley's rejection of Aeschylus's "feeble catastrophe" is only given voice after his description of how the Greek tragedians related to each other. In this description, Shelley uses the word "bound" to define precisely how we are not to understand the relation existing between the works of the Greek tragic writers ("by no means conceived themselves bound"). To imitate Aeschylus or to set up Greece as a model is to be bound to Greece in a way that its own writers were not.[2] Hellenism in this light is nothing less than the attempt to invent a Greece that one may be bound to in the same way that one would bind oneself to history whenever history is deemed to judge the present as its effect. Far from being a mere thematic byway in the history of literature, Hellenism represents the attempt to establish, historically, a basis for the judgment of modernity. As the work of Winckelmann already made clear, the recognition of history as a mode of judgment is at stake in this Hellenism.

By rejecting what the Greek tragedy writers have already done, Shelley preserves a past whose history is based on "arbitrary discretion." For this reason Greece cannot be sustained as the representation of a certain content to be affirmed over and over again in each of its examples— if anything is to be affirmed it is perhaps the refusal of such affirmations, of such exemplarity. Although the "arbitrary discretion" of its writers already assured this refusal, subsequent history has sought to negate this discretion in its relation to Greece. Shelley, by adopting this discretion, indicates a conception of Greece not hampered by the mimesis which has defined its place in literary history.

While the emphasis Shelley places on the variation practiced by the Greek tragedians points to a relation in which these writers are always unbound with respect to their predecessors, this does not mean that Shelley subscribes to a past whose defining characteristic is to be inimitable. The past, in the form of Greece, has been defined frequently in this manner—in the name of a modernity that defines its historical telos according to the example of Greece as well as by the rejections of an avenging modernity desirous of its own place in history.³ In both these cases, the past judges the possibility of the future with respect to what should or should not be imitated: what takes place in history is judged either to be repetition or to have no relation to the past. From such a perspective, there can be no variation, no other alternatives.

By authoring a play that takes the title ascribed to a lost play of Aeschylus, Shelley not only signals the relation of his *Prometheus Unbound* to Greece and the past but also indicates that what links his work to the past is precisely what constitutes the past as the past: its being unbound. This does not mean, however, that unbinding is to be understood as some kind of revelation of what Greece was. Rather, Shelley's Preface points out his play as an unbinding from the models of Greece, an unbinding that the political and historical representation of Greece has always sought to deny. In each of these respects, Shelley's play refuses the judgment of time, that is, the judgment pronounced by time measured as history. Within this understanding the mere fact of preexistence, of precedence, does not account for judgment. Of course this does not prevent judgment from taking place. From such judgment we are to be unbound. And it is to such an unbinding that the past must also listen—as the epigraph to Shelley's Preface points out: "audisne hæc Amphiarae, sub terram abdite?" ("Do you hear this, Amphiaraus, in your home beneath the earth?")

While Shelley's Preface raises the question of the past as a source of judgment, the play develops such a questioning by means of a plot that unfolds through the unambiguous relation of justice to time. This relation of time to justice finds its first explicit illustration during the dialogue between Mercury and Prometheus. Prometheus speaks:

> Let others flatter Crime where it sits thron'd
> In brief Omnipotence; secure are they:
> For Justice when triumphant will weep down
> Pity not punishment on her own wrongs,
> Too much avenged by those who err. I wait,
> Enduring thus the retributive hour
> Which since we spake is even nearer now. (1.401–7)⁴

In these lines, Justice and the judgment it pronounces are defined by a time that has no historical existence. Such a justice is therefore distinct from those judgments pronounced by a time that is already known: the judgments of history. For Prometheus, the time of judgment ("the retributive hour") is not the time of the past, but rather a time that has not yet occurred. Here, justice and judgment are conceived as being without history even though any significance they may possess is resolutely historical. (The historical significance of such judgments is thematically present in *Prometheus Unbound* both when Asia recalls the history of first Saturn and then Jove in Act 2, Scene 2, and in the repeated references to the end of Jupiter's reign.) If justice and judgment are only thinkable in terms of a time that has not yet taken place, then justice can only become actual by means of what is categorically different from itself. For this reason justice is always allegorical. Justice first arises as a language that must always be unsaid by history if it is to have any significance. (Even justice is complicit in this unsaying to the extent that it requires history to be its judge.) Yet, even though judgment is unsaid by history as it passes from language to event, the origin of justice persists as what can never be unsaid, since it only exists as justice by preceding the historical. Toward the time of this justice the action of *Prometheus Unbound* tends but in a far more complex way than the distinction between history and prehistorical mythology suggests.

Schematically, Shelley's play presents the persistence of a mythological past that the reign of Jupiter cannot destroy or do without, because it holds the answer to the duration of his reign. This schematic account suggests that the figure of Prometheus may be understood as resisting the tyranny associated with Jupiter's reign. So viewed it is easy to recognize Prometheus as a representative of the very freedom that Jupiter does not espouse—and there are those in the play who subscribe to the "national history or mythology" that sees Prometheus in this light.[5] Shelley's presentation of Prometheus is more complicated than this easy identification of freedom in a figure of opposition. As both Shelley and Hegel knew, such an opposing is only concerned with mastery. If the reconciliation of Jupiter with Prometheus is a feeble catastrophe, then the victory of Prometheus (freedom) over Jupiter will be equally feeble, since freedom's victory can only limit what it stands for by ascending to the position of Jupiter. The play, like Prometheus, is caught in a difficulty it cannot avoid: the question of its own unbinding, a question that makes Prometheus, in the words of Shelley's Preface, "the type of the highest per-fection of moral and intellectual nature, impelled by the purest and the truest motives to the best and noblest ends."[6] For Prometheus to be so impelled does not mean that the play cannot afford some reflection on the difficulty produced by such motives, most notably, the question of a justice whose judgments do not bind, a justice that is free.

The difficulty in which the play places Prometheus is evident from the outset. Just as there is one thing that lies outside the omnipotence of Jupiter (his ability to make Prometheus say the period of his reign), there is one thing that lies outside the power of Prometheus to recall: the curse he pronounced on Jupiter. In each case, there is an event that has no lan-guage in which its occurrence may be recognized. Together these two events mark the history of Jupiter's reign. More than this they mark a powerlessness to command and control history by means of language. As the attempt to recall the curse makes explicit, this powerlessness arises from the inability of language to recall itself. Prometheus himself indi-cates as much when he expresses uncertainty about whether his own words possess the ability to recover the language in which a past event took place—not to mention whether the words of the curse had such a power to begin with. Prometheus says, "If then my words had power / . . . let them not lose it now!" (1.69–72). Jupiter's powerlessness to know the end of his oppressive reign is repeated in Prometheus's powerlessness to know the curse that would define such a reign. Further, in the case of Prometheus, this powerlessness is traced to an inability expressed by the conditional: "*If* then my words had power." What this conditional points to is an inability to know whether or not what is recalled has the power that history would ascribe to it as beginning and end. The question is whether or not the curse commands time and thereby makes history.

By referring to his past words as a curse, Prometheus clearly under-stands these past words as if they possessed a power over time and history. To recall such an understanding—in all senses of recall since one is not capable of revoking what one can neither remember nor repeat[7]—is to re-call a judgment. In this instance, it is to recall a judgment from the time of history, for a curse is always the anticipation of an event of retributive punishment. And, more usually than not, it marks the end of something or someone. Prometheus must thus adopt the power of the curse's language in order to revoke the power of that same curse. But, if Prometheus no longer has confidence in the power of his own language, he can no longer know whether the curse has such power to begin with. Only by recalling the curse, by trying to unbind its words, could such a power be known. But if the curse had no such power, then Prometheus would have no power to know this. The only certain way for the curse to retain its power is never to recall it, never to risk one's own language whenever one desires to know the relation of language and historical event.

Despite such a risk Shelley's Prometheus does not turn from the recall of his curse. As Prometheus points out, such a recall is made less because of doubts about the power of his own language than because of a change in his view of Jupiter. Instead of a curse whose judgment brings punishment, Prometheus would now replace that curse with pity. Prometheus describes this shift as he tells of the fate of Jupiter in a passage that again underlines the extent to which any judgment on the reign of Jupiter is a matter of time:

> And yet to me welcome is Day and Night,
> Whether one breaks the hoar frost of the morn,
> Or, starry, dim, and slow, the other climbs
> The leaden-coloured East; for then they lead
> Their wingless crawling Hours, one among whom . . .
> Shall drag thee, cruel King, to kiss the blood
> From these pale feet, which then might trample thee
> If they disdained not such a prostrate slave.
> Disdain? Ah no! I pity thee.[8]

When considered in the light of the later dialogue with Mercury in which a triumphant justice offers pity, rather than punishment, Prometheus's shift from disdain to pity puts him in the position subsequently attributed to justice. Since the shift that produces the recall of the curse is derived from pity, then this attempt to recall the curse may be associated with the question of justice in *Prometheus Unbound*. In both cases—justice and the recall—no punishment is to be exacted. Rather, both are set in a context that demonstrates the difficulty of establishing one or the other. Prometheus's inability to recall his curse already reflects this difficulty. As for justice, this difficulty becomes apparent in the dialogue between Prometheus and Mercury when Prometheus describes justice as "weep[ing] down /

Pity not punishment on her own wrongs." The pity produced by justice is directed toward what justice has wrought—"her own wrongs." In these words, Prometheus describes a justice that commits the very crimes it is supposed to punish. Since its judgments may commit the wrongs it seeks to right, justice is in the position of being unable to know whether it is correcting a wrong or giving reason for further correction. As the allegorical figure reveals, such a justice is blind, not because it is impartial, but because it cannot tell whether or not it judges in the name of justice. Here, Prometheus describes a justice unable to know the justness of its own judgments until too late. This is the same situation developed by Prometheus's desire to recall the curse: Prometheus is unable to know the effect of the curse (his judgment) until it is beyond the power of his recall. In both cases, judgment errs because it does not yet know justice. Knowledge of justice does not in this instance lead to the correction of a past error. As Prometheus points out, its wrongs will be "too much avenged by those who err." To avenge the wrongs of justice is to recall—or, revoke—justice in the name of the justice that needs to be avenged. Rather than punish justice for its unjustness, Shelley's Prometheus is resigned to pity a situation in which justice can never be recalled or revoked, but can only punish itself for these inadequacies. This is how justice errs.

To the extent that justice and the curse are embroiled in the same difficulty of recall, it is to be expected that their resolution should not result from an act of judging. Prometheus repeatedly asserts that the retribution in which such a resolution will occur belongs to time. This understanding is asserted at the very beginning of Act 1, when Prometheus speaks of one of the crawling hours that shall drag down Jupiter. This understanding is given in greater detail during the dialogue with Mercury, when Mercury broaches the question of Jupiter's reign:

> There is a secret known
> To thee and to none else of living things
> Which may transfer the sceptre of wide Heaven,
> The fear of which perplexes the Supreme . . .
> Clothe it in words, and bid it clasp his throne
> In intercession. (1.371–76)

To Jupiter and Mercury what Prometheus knows is a secret that cannot be conveyed except by the mediation of words.[9] Since such a secret is unknown to Mercury and Jupiter, it does not occupy the place of thought. Rather, it occupies the place of a forethought that can only be known once it has passed into a form different from itself (in this case, language). Only then does it become thought. Tacitly, Mercury confirms the extent to which thought (as the recognition of knowledge) occurs because of language. At the same time, Mercury also confirms the extent to which thought and language are to be traced to a source they cannot present but only speak on its behalf. Both language and thought intercede on behalf of a meaning whose existence neither can affirm. Jupiter, who seeks, by means of language, knowledge of this secret is troubled little by this difficulty. As Mercury states, Jupiter will accept the means of intercession (clothing the secret in words) as an act of intercession. As a result, what Prometheus is being asked in this scene is less to reveal a secret than to affirm that what comes before language and thought (forethought) can be known by language and thought. In other words, language and thought can judge its own secret origin. To give language such a power of judgment is to give the means of knowledge, the clothing, the ability to be synonymous with what it clothes. In Jupiter's terms the means of transfer (language) will define transfer itself. Only through such a language can the secret perplexing Jupiter be allayed; only in this form can such a secret "clasp," or fasten itself, to the throne of Jupiter. Yet, such a clasping, despite taking on the appearance of being a judgment, occurs because it cannot establish any relation between the event it foretells and the means of foretelling that event. It is a judgment without a judge.

As others have documented, Prometheus has also sought to subject language to the kind of understanding that Mercury and Jupiter pursue. This congruence is perhaps nowhere more evident than in the curse, when Prometheus uses the same verb as Mercury used when he described the desired effect of Prometheus's words on the throne of Jupiter:

> I curse thee! let a sufferer's curse
> Clasp thee, his torturer, like remorse,
> Till thine Infinity shall be
> A robe of envenomed agony. (1.286–89)

The curse is to fasten itself to Jupiter with the effect of turning his infinity into a robe that will, like the cloak of Heracles, poison its wearer. The effects are strikingly similar: language is to be capable of a physical act—

clasping; and words that name (secret, infinity) without presenting what they name are to be understood metaphorically as if they were a physical article—clothing. The use of "clasp" in addition to the understanding of language present in these lines clearly casts Jupiter's desire to know the secret of his reign and the Prometheus of the curse into the same realm. On the basis of this similarity, the evolution of Prometheus toward a position different from Jupiter's may be traced.[10] The whole question of establishing a justice in the wake of Jupiter depends on such an evolution, which implies the possibility of a language capable of being both source and means of judgment. For this evolution to occur, recall of the curse is mandatory, because it involves the recall and the revoking of the language of Jupiter.

While the Prometheus who uttered the curse speaks the language of Jupiter, his reply when he hears such language from the mouth of Mercury speaks of temporal necessity. To Mercury's question, "Thou knowest not the period of Jove's power?" Prometheus simply states, "I know but this, that it must come" (1.412–13). The response does not affirm the question. Mercury seeks to know that Prometheus does not in fact know the period of Jupiter's reign. Mercury desires knowledge about an event in time, but Prometheus only offers him the knowledge that judgment will come in time. When Mercury replies, "Thou canst not count thy years to come of pain?" (1.414), he suggests that Prometheus's answer to his question derives from either an inability to count or a period that is too great to be counted. In either case, counting is seen to be inadequate to the task it has been set, namely, defining the period of Jupiter's reign. The inference behind Mercury's question is that judgment and the counting of time can be equated, or, if they cannot, then the end of Jupiter's reign cannot take place. Prometheus's reply reasserts that the time which brings Jupiter's reign to an end cannot be equated with counting but only with itself: "They [Prometheus's years of pain] last while Jove must reign; nor more nor less / Do I desire or fear" (1.415–16). The years of Prometheus's pain, which are bound to the years of Jupiter's reign, can only be counted from the moment that Jupiter's reign ends. Yet, it is precisely this moment that is never said in any historical sense in the course of the play, since the moment in which the retributive hour arrives is announced after its arrival. In the same vein, Shelley makes Asia ask, "When shall the destined hour arrive?" and Demogorgon answer, "Behold!" (2.4.128). If the time can be said to arrive anywhere, then it is in the caesura of line 128. As a result, it is in the passage of time (marked by the rhythm of the poetic line), and not in language, that the hour arrives. Then, as now, the moment of transfer or change from which historical time is measured and counted is missing except as an effect of the history it inaugurates. Change or transfer cannot be measured by the means of measurement it establishes. Within the context of *Prometheus Unbound*, to know this moment of transfer or change is no different than recalling the curse and knowing it as one's own words. In both cases, something is missing but not because it belongs to a past that cannot be recalled—after all the curse is repeated.

Mercury will give voice to what is missing while at the same time expressing the condition that governs any recall of the moment of transfer or change. It is a recall, and not a prophecy, as Mercury makes clear when he makes the following request of Prometheus:

> Yet, pause, and plunge
> Into Eternity, where recorded time,
> Even all that we imagine, age on age,
> Seems but a point, and the reluctant mind
> Flags wearily in its unending flight
> Till it sink, dizzy, blind, lost, shelterless;
> Perchance it has not numbered the slow years
> Which thou must spend in torture, unreprieved. (1.416–23)

Into the "recorded time" of eternity Mercury urges Prometheus to plunge. Since, according to Mercury, what is to happen is already recorded, the knowledge he seeks on behalf of Jupiter may only be disclosed by being recalled. Unaware of how this play has already provided a reflection on such attempts at recall, Mercury would now put Prometheus back into the position he occupied when he attempted to recall his curse: to revoke time by recalling what takes place in time. Defining the former in terms of the latter is the difficulty already faced by Prometheus. Even by desiring to recall the curse, Prometheus must recognize that knowing there was a time when the curse was uttered does not lead to knowledge of what took place in that time. Unable to know what was uttered, Prometheus cannot know whether or not his words were in fact a curse; he has no memory to measure the curse against. Mercury and Jupiter must also face this difficulty, even as they try to evade it in the form of an event that has not yet taken place.

While Prometheus's experience in recalling the curse indicates a difficulty Mercury does not consider, only in the dialogue with Mercury does the difficulty present in Prometheus's attempt to recall the curse find its fullest exposition. As Mercury says, Prometheus must pause in order to plunge into eternity and recorded time; this recall of time must take place in a pause that cannot be a part of recorded time. Given this condition, the knowledge sought by Jupiter requires the interruption of eternity. Even though this constitutes the principal difficulty of Mercury's request to Prometheus, Mercury will direct our attention toward a difficulty that could only arise once the pause in time has occurred. This difficulty is located in a mind reluctant to pursue an unending flight that can only produce its own utter disorientation ("Till it sink, dizzy, blind, lost, shelterless"). From this reluctance, Mercury will conclude that Prometheus may not have counted the years of his punishment. The emphasis Mercury places on counting reflects a desire to know the passing of time, yet the whole argument supporting this possibility derives from the interruption of what is to be known. Like time, the attempt to recall what is recorded is cursed by what it desires to recall. Here, the singularity of an event (such as Prometheus's curse) is not the object of recall; rather, it emerges as what interferes with the desire for knowledge that it promotes.

In his reply to Mercury's request to pause and plunge into eternity, Prometheus appears to locate the precise source of this interference. In his response Prometheus simply states, "Perchance no thought can count them—yet they pass" (1.424). By separating thought and counting from the mere passage of time, Prometheus offers a basis for distinguishing the Promethean from the tyranny of Jupiter while at the same time distinguishing himself from the mythical narrative subsequently related by Asia. According to this narrative Prometheus, as always, is associated with an origin. In the version of this myth that Shelley gives to Asia, Prometheus is the origin of speech and thought as a means of measuring: "He gave man speech, and speech created thought, / Which is the measure of the Universe" (2.4.72–73). If this myth is followed, then Prometheus emerges as the representative of a kind of thought that would stand in opposition to the kind represented by Jupiter. This opposition between Prometheus as thought and the "thought-executing ministers" (1.387) of Jupiter can, however, only be maintained by a limited reading of the dialogue between Mercury and Prometheus. In an echo of Mercury's "Perchance it [the reluctant mind] has not numbered the slow years," Prometheus says that "Perchance no thought can count them." Prometheus repeats the uncertainty that accompanies Mercury's conclusion: it may be that thought cannot count the years. Is this what is at stake in the dialogue? Is it possible to know whether thought can count them? Prometheus's words do not say whether thought can or cannot count the years. All Prometheus will say is that they pass. Even if thought were to intervene in its most rudimentary form—counting—this would still be true. Time passes. What Prometheus does say is that no thought can touch time, since to do so is to bring about the interruption that constitutes knowledge as the destruction of itself. And the pause introduced by this interruption is nothing less than the event of thought, that is, the moment that thought reserves for its own occurrence, the moment in which thought judges itself to take place.

If time, as Prometheus says, is what simply passes, then it does so without the help of thought; even the thought that time passes is coincidental and not instrumental. The irrelevance of thought to the passage of time is nowhere articulated more emphatically than in the scene where Prometheus's curse is repeated—but without recall on Prometheus's part. In his command to the Phantasm of Jupiter, Prometheus recognizes that the curse can only be heard again as sound without thought: "Speak the words which I would hear, / Although no thought inform thine empty voice" (1.248–49). Recall of the curse occurs as the repetition of its sound by the ghost of the figure it was directed at. More precisely, as the dialogue between Earth and Prometheus reveals in this same act, the curse is spoken by a figure belonging to one of two worlds. Earth states:

> For know, there are two worlds of life and death:
> One that which thou beholdest, but the other
> Is underneath the grave, where do inhabit
> The shadows of all forms that think and live
> Till death unite them, and they part no more. (1.195–99)

These shadows, Earth explains, belong to one of the worlds of life and death. (Shelley's syntax clearly states that there are two worlds of life and

death, and not one world of life and one world of death.) Prometheus belongs to the world of life and death known by the living. The fact of being alive separates the living from the other world, in which the world of
the living is repeated as shadow, ghost, phantasm. Since the living only
know the other world as thought, so the shadows only know the living in
terms of their own thoughtless existence. One cannot know the other and
still be in its own world. Only through death does one world join with
the other, but this does not result in some synthesis of the two worlds.
Rather, in death, one world has passed over into the other, and this is why
it can "part no more." To do so is to return across that instance where
neither time nor thought have any place: death.

By having no choice but to listen to his curse spoken by a phantasm, Prometheus is being made to listen to the fate of his own words.
Like Jupiter in Act 1, the recall of the curse is to listen to the empty voice
of the past as the thoughtless reminder that thought (the language of the
living) once took place. Since this past is constituted by the words of the
curse, Prometheus is made to listen to the phantasmatic medium of his
own thought, the medium in which the curse as Prometheus's judgment
on Jupiter took place. If the living inform language with thought or
power only because they are not dead, then Asia's claim that Prometheus
"gave man speech, and speech created thought" is correct in its historical
order but not in its emphasis on speech as the causation of thought.
Speech can only create thought if speech is already capable of thought.
The recall of the curse makes it clear that this is not so. And, as Prometheus points out, thought informs speech (1.249), that is, thought tells
speech what it is thinking. It even tells speech that it is, in Asia's words,
thinking and thereby creating thought. As a result, any historical account
of the relation of speech and thought must make two irreconcilable as-
sumptions: first, that speech, the medium in which thought is expressed,
precedes thought and is therefore not capable of thought by itself; second,
that speech is already thought, that speech is, since its inception, the
thought it already represents. Together these two conditions introduce
the added complication that there must be two kinds of speech: the
thoughtful and the thoughtless. Yet it is from such a complication that
the historical understanding sought by Jupiter and so on has consistently
turned away. Ultimately, this historical understanding is less concerned

with the priority of one over the other than with the establishment of a concept of representation in which the thought of the past will not be revoked by the recall of its origin in the phantasmatic repetitions of the present. Prometheus is uncertain about such a representation from the very outset of the play. Prometheus's reflection on the power of his words to recall the past speaks to this uncertainty, as does his apprehension about the power of words to represent and so judge the future in the form of a curse. In the terms of the play, such uncertainty is developed, first, by Earth's account of there being two languages and, second, when the curse is spoken by the empty, thoughtless voice of the Phantasm of Jupiter. One leads directly to the other.

After the voices describe the effect of the curse spoken by Prometheus, Earth begins to speak in a voice that Prometheus cannot distinguish or identify ("I hear a sound of voices—not the voice / Which I gave forth" [1.112–13]). The dialogue, for it is presented as such, proceeds as two voices that do not understand each other. Throughout this dialogue Prometheus calls out for the repetition of the curse, but he receives no response. The failure of Prometheus's language to possess such power is explained by Earth when she speaks of a language different from that spoken by Prometheus: "How canst thou hear / Who knowest not the language of the dead?" (1.138–37). Prometheus's inability to distinguish the curse from the sounds he hears is emphasized again by Earth just prior to the moment when she changes to a language he can understand.[11] She states at this moment:

> No, thou canst not hear:
> Thou art immortal, and this tongue is known
> Only to those who die. . . .[12]

Since Prometheus's inability to hear is related to his immortality, his language would be the language of the living, the language of those whose speech is informed by thought. Earth goes on to be more specific about what the language of the living is opposed to, but does so by speaking in a language that Prometheus can now hear and understand:

> aye, I heard
> The curse, the which if thou rememberest not
> Yet my innumerable seas and streams,

Mountains and caves and winds, and yon wide Air
And the inarticulate people of the dead
Preserve, a treasured spell. (1.179–84)

The curse is preserved in a medium that cannot speak its meaning. In this respect, the language of the dead is as inarticulate as the natural world: like nature, death is, but it produces no perception and no recall of its own existence that we are able to perceive (to have such perception is always to interpret the language of the dead by the language of the living). Within such a language, no judgment is possible since its inarticulateness precludes the intent to represent what lies at the base of all judgment. The curse, as an historical event belonging to the past, is preserved by not being recalled: its meaning resides in the memory of an event (the uttering of the curse), rather than in the recall of what constituted that event (its content). Through the repetition of the curse by the Phantasm of Jupiter, Shelley presents this discontinuity between the memory of an event and the recall of what took place in such an event. Where memory of an event marks time as the language of history, recall of the curse would present the thought that attempts to control history ever since the speaking of the curse—a curse being one form in which thought offers itself to the judgment of time.

If the purpose lying behind the original uttering of the curse was the expression of Prometheus's thought, then its recall suggests that the curse cannot confirm the thought from which it was produced. Shelley makes Prometheus unable to give voice to his past words and only allows the curse to be repeated by a thoughtless voice in the form of the Phantasm of Jupiter. That Shelley makes Prometheus call upon the ghost of Jupiter as the means to recall the curse is not an act meant to indicate that the Prometheus of the curse is as tyrannical as Jupiter. Rather, it forms a commentary on the attempt of both Prometheus and Jupiter to recall the two events framing the development of *Prometheus Unbound*: the curse and the period of Jupiter's reign.

It is hardly an accident that Shelley should make Prometheus recall the curse through the Phantasm of Jupiter while making Prometheus become the means through which Jupiter seeks to recall (from recorded time) the end of his reign. But, however attractive the symmetry of this situation may appear to be, it is not sustained by the play. In the first case,

Jupiter seeks knowledge of the end of his reign from the living Prometheus, whereas Prometheus seeks the recall of his curse from the Phantasm of Jupiter. What is at stake in this difference may be traced to the purpose of their respective attempts at recall. By requesting knowledge of the period of his reign, Jupiter seeks the relation of what is to what must be. Prometheus, by recalling his curse, would withdraw an utterance that contradicts what he now is and what he would now be. The difference introduced by the failure of an exact symmetry is enacted by the play when the repetition of the curse occurs: when the curse is spoken we hear neither the words of Prometheus nor the words of Jupiter. By this means, the Phantasm becomes a commentary on the attempt to know (by recall) an event (either in the past or in the recorded time of the future). Because the repetition of the curse is linked to the recall sought by both Prometheus and Jupiter, it offers a commentary on the unbinding announced in the play's title: the unbinding that releases Prometheus and Jupiter from both the curse and the reign that occasions the curse. While this unbinding would already be more complex than the feeble catastrophe Shelley renounces in the Preface, it is still a catastrophe that places Prometheus under the aegis of the mythical provider of freedom. The unbinding explored in this play is hardly so straightforward as may be seen in the cases of both Jupiter and Prometheus: Jupiter desires the curse, or forethought,[13] that binds him to a fate that announces the unbinding of his reign; Prometheus would be unbound from such a curse, but the price of such unbinding requires the recognition of the curse as his own words; it requires that the words of the curse be recognized as the expression of his thought. If this were not the case, then there would be nothing from which Prometheus needs to be unbound.

The understanding Prometheus must revoke in order to be unbound from his curse is apparent from the words he utters upon seeing the Phantasm of Jupiter: "Tremendous Image! as thou art must be / He whom thou shadowest forth" (1.246–47). Here, Prometheus gives voice to the understanding that this image from the shadow world of life and death will define the Jupiter of his own world. If this understanding is recast in the words of Earth, then Prometheus states the shadows of all forms that think and live are the unbinding of all that thinks and lives. This understanding clearly contradicts the division between the worlds of life and death that

Earth had spoken of, and it does so by insisting on the ability of the shadow to represent what is to come. Despite the radical and theoretical tendency suggested by this insistence, it is hardly upsetting to historical confidence in the power of representation since these shadows at least represent the living world. As Prometheus indicates this assertion of representation is a matter of necessity ("as thou art *must* be / He") and not a matter of judgment. If necessity binds what is (the shadow) to what must be (Jupiter), then all need to judge this binding is avoided. Necessity arises in the place of judgment, not because judgment has failed, but rather because it has not been allowed to occur. As the phrase used by Prometheus indicates, judgment has been given no time in which to take place. The necessity of "must" allows little room for judgment and still less room for the judgment to be enacted by the time when Jupiter is said to become what his shadow now is. Speech and the necessity to which it alone can give voice would take the place of time.

Both Prometheus's desire to recall the curse and Jupiter's desire to have the secret of the end of his reign clothed in words require this necessity. In each case, speech is to control time by a necessity that is none other than the necessity of speaking. Prometheus's words immediately prior to the repetition of the curse make this clear. In these words Prometheus first presents time as what can be seen; however, this is quickly interrupted by the command to speak[14]:

> I see the curse on gestures proud and cold,
> And looks of firm defiance, and calm hate,
> And such despair as mocks itself with smiles,
> Written as on a scroll . . . yet speak—O speak![15]

Prometheus first sees the curse as if it could be represented in the physical movements as well as in the eyes of the Phantasm. Then, it is again given visual reference as Prometheus describes what he has seen in terms of a written scroll. Yet, such a phenomenal record is not enough. The words of the historical moment must be uttered in an act that replaces the phenomenal with language. Only then can Prometheus confirm the judgment he has made on his own past—the judgment offering pity, not disdain, the judgment giving rise to the desire to recall his past. Only then can Prometheus be truly unbound in the sense of being set free from the judgment that produced the curse. But, if this unbinding turns upon the remembrance and revocation of the curse, then it is another sense of recall that will prevent the historical occurrence of justice. When the curse is repeated Prometheus does not even know it as a repetition, and even less as his own words. He must ask Earth for this knowledge. Here, the unbinding sought by Prometheus meets an obstacle of its devising. To revoke and therefore be unbound from the curse, Prometheus must know it as his own thought and judgment. So defined how can one ever be unbound from a curse or even a thought that one cannot recognize as one's own?

As is evident from the play, Prometheus's expression of his inability to remember is less a failing of memory than a failing to recognize his own words. This is why the curse is spoken by the shadow of his foe, and not what the shadow represents. The curse is spoken by what does not belong to the world of Jupiter and Prometheus. Yet, it is spoken in the language that belongs to that world, the language that would always be informed by thought; otherwise it would not even be recognizable as language. Prometheus is faced with, not an inability to judge language as the representation of thought, but an inability to judge the thought or intent that produced it when he hears his own words in the mouth of the Phantasm. This inability is attributed to a failure to see himself in his own words, despite his initial assumption that he could see the curse written in the features of his face ("gestures proud and cold / And looks of firm defiance"). Armed with such an inability Prometheus is able to proclaim, "It doth repent me" (1.303), when he points to language ("words are quick and vain" [1.303]) as the reason why the curse is able to decide his repentance.[16] To Prometheus, Prometheus is not the forethought of speech. The words of the Phantasm fail to affirm the phenomenal understanding by which they are preceded. Moreover, Prometheus's failure to recognize the curse and the repentance it permits now becomes a failure to affirm the history and meaning of his own name: forethought.

That Prometheus understands his unbinding as an unbinding from his own name is indicated when, in response to the emblem of Christ offered as an example by one of the Furies, Prometheus exclaims, "O horrible! Thy name I will not speak, / It hath become a curse."[17] As the Chorus observes in the passage preceding Prometheus's dialogue with the Fury, the words of Christ "outlived him, like swift poison / Withering up

truth, peace and pity" (1.548–49). To preserve the words of Christ is to
hear those words in the mouth of a thoughtless phantasm, words that
give up the thought from which they arose as the price of expressing that
thought. Now subject to the thought of others, the words of Christ have
turned the name Christ into a curse, the curse of a name no longer thinkable in even its own words. From such a curse Prometheus would be free
as he fails to recognize his own words, because in this failing Prometheus
would no longer know himself, would no longer recognize himself in the
Promethean. But can one be freed from this curse in the same way that
one is separated from the past?

Prometheus's failure to recognize his words no longer points to the
curse as something lying in a past. Rather, it indicates that the curse lies in
an act of recall uttered by a thoughtless phantasm.[18] The Phantasm of Jupiter's repetition of the curse revokes the past by the very means in which
the past continues to claim significance. If the means by which the past
persists is revoked by its recall, then the repetition of the curse takes away
any hope of revoking an event informing not just the language of the living but also the Promethean itself. In this respect, Prometheus, like Jupiter,
will be a victim of his own will even as he wishes to free himself from that
will. As the curse tells us, Prometheus's will is one of only two things over
which Jupiter did not have power. By excepting his will from Jupiter's
power, Prometheus preserves his ability to resist Jupiter. The interpretation
of Prometheus as the hero of humanity against the gods rests on this will,
as does Prometheus's association with freedom. Yet, in Shelley's *Prometheus
Unbound*, this will is not allowed to become a simple source of command.

Prior to the appearance of the Phantasm we are told by Earth that
the figure who will repeat the curse is to be chosen according to Prometheus's will: "Call at will / Thine own ghost, or the ghost of Jupiter /
Hades or Typhon."[19] In order to hear the curse, Prometheus's will can
only call upon the shadow of what his will commands. At this point, Prometheus's will (which remains outside the power of Jupiter) calls upon an
image that is also presented as being outside the power of Jupiter (to the
extent that the Phantasm defines what Jupiter must be and not vice
versa). Prometheus's will has done nothing more than call upon the one
other thing that remains outside of Jupiter's power: the image that will
define Jupiter's self. Prometheus and Prometheus alone describes this

shadow as having no thought to inform its "empty voice." Before the Phantasm even speaks Prometheus has created the condition that will allow him to say about the curse, "It doth repent me." The Phantasm, being thoughtless, would speak a language without intent, without forethought. When Prometheus hears the speech of the Phantasm, he listens to how he has already decided to understand its language. And this understanding frees him from the curse he wishes to revoke. Once repeated, the curse loses its Promethean character as an act of defiance. The play has already demonstrated this aspect of the curse when Shelley makes the Earth describe how the curse has been preserved:

> I heard
> The curse, the which if thou rememberest not
> Yet my innumerable seas and streams,
> Mountains and caves and winds, and yon wide Air
> And the inarticulate people of the dead
> Preserve, a treasured spell. We meditate
> In secret joy and hope those dreadful words
> But dare not speak them. (1.179–86)

The curse possesses significance by not being repeated, by being preserved in what is unable to give it voice. Once given voice by Prometheus's will, this significance would be lost since the curse is set free from what it pronounced. In this understanding of the curse Prometheus describes two languages: a language that gives voice to the will, and a language that revokes that will. For Prometheus, the latter would revoke the former. By this revocation Prometheus would be freed from not only his own past but also from the one thing that still binds him to Jupiter: the will he excepted from Jupiter's power. This will binds Prometheus to Jupiter because it can only be realized through Jupiter. With the repetition of the curse, Prometheus would now free himself from this condition. But he can only do so by actualizing in the Phantasm of Jupiter the possibility of a language without thought. Prometheus's unbinding can now be seen as the result of a will to a pure language. This language without thought forges the possibility of Prometheus's freedom, because it eradicates the defiance associated with the curse.

If the unbinding of Prometheus is to be seen as an act of the Promethean will, then Prometheus may well be unbound from Jupiter. This unbinding, however, causes the return of the question posed by Prometheus at the very beginning of the play. As stated earlier, this question arises when Prometheus reflects on the power of his words to recall the curse: "If then my words had power . . . let them not lose it now." In the present context, this power must now be seen as the power of Prometheus's words to enact his will. Even in this first reflection on the power of his words, the form in which the will is given linguistic expression is present. By means of the imperative, Prometheus calls upon his words to possess the power of recalling the curse. Later, when the Phantasm appears, Prometheus again gives voice to the curse by means of the imperative ("yet speak—O speak!"). And again, at the end of the curse, the imperative appears when Prometheus proclaims the condition that announces the end of Jupiter's reign:

> let the hour
> Come, when thou must appear to be
> That which thou art internally.
> And after many a false fruitless crime
> Scorn track thy lagging fall through boundless space and time.
>   (1.297–301)

These last words of the curse point to the imperative as a will that would exert its power over time and know it as history. It is no accident that Shelley should make the moment announced by this imperative coincide with the moment of self-representation in which Jupiter becomes his own image. At this moment, what is hidden from sight will come into view as Jupiter is seen to be what he is. No longer will Jupiter have to be judged, since in such representation all judgment comes to an end when justice is performed. But, so understood, this moment in which Justice takes place is also the moment in which justice need no longer exist since it has been usurped by the primacy of self-representation, the primacy of the moment in which the image is what it represents. Since judgment becomes irrelevant in this moment, the temporal modality of judgment and the claims of representation are only reconcilable if the latter takes the place of the former. When this occurs language has become the judge of the hour in which Jupiter's power is transferred. At this moment, language would become not just the representation of time, but time itself. Isn't this the curse that Prometheus seeks to recall and revoke? But doesn't the recall of the curse require precisely what it seeks to recall? Can Prometheus's imperatives give power to language in order to take that power away from language? And, can Prometheus revoke the curse without making this revocation become, like Jupiter, the external sign of what he is now internally? Above all else, such a revocation requires that Prometheus be able to recognize the curse as his words, despite his description of them as words whose thoughtlessness would preclude this recognition. In order to become what he now is—the Prometheus who, in pitying Jupiter, is aligned with the figure of Justice—Prometheus must revoke the curse that represents him as he once was. But doesn't this line of argument assume that Shelley's Prometheus only wants to be bound to his own myth?[20] Need one recall that this play is actually entitled *Prometheus Unbound*?

Prometheus's failure to know as his own the words spoken by the Phantasm now appears as his attempt to avoid fulfilling the curse he pronounced on Jupiter: negating what he once said makes these words become the sign of what Prometheus is now internally. His inability to judge whether or not such words are his own refuses to turn judgment into the representation of a time, a temporal event. Earth alone makes this judgment when she pronounces, "They were thine." Here, Earth along with Ione and Panthea would assert the myth of Prometheus in a figure who remains unfallen and unvanquished. Such a figure is dialectically dependent on the tyranny of Jupiter. This dialectical relation not only makes Prometheus the opposite of Jupiter but also means, in the terms of the curse, that Prometheus is a figure who, instead of falling like Jupiter, "through boundless space and time," will rise bound to the space and time of the myth cherished by Earth, Ione, and Panthea. From this myth and from the exact self-representation in which Jupiter will meet his fate, Prometheus is to be unbound. That this unbinding occurs in a question about whether or not the curse is his own words suggests speech should be understood as the means of this unbinding. But can language be judged—or, bound—to such an unbinding? Can its representation of itself be the same as itself? Can it command itself, be its own imperative (Let there be language!)? When understanding, representation, and judgment are at stake there is always one exception to be made.

When Shelley gives the power of recognizing Prometheus's words to Earth, she is made to perform an act of judgment. However, this act only takes place because judgment is effectively removed from the time in which it takes place. Instead, it is turned into a history representing Prometheus as he is seen by Earth. By this act, Shelley shows how judgment is removed from time so that it may be made to represent time as history. By this same act, Shelley also makes clear how removing judgment from time allows judgment to be turned into the representation of an abstract, atemporal Justice. Two contradictory conclusions are supported by an act of judgment understood as being at the same time an act of representation. Prometheus's desire to recall and revoke the curse enacts this contradiction: for Prometheus to recognize the words of the curse is to perform the judgment that at once represents history and makes him the event of justice. Prometheus seeks neither of these alternatives when he is unable to recall his words. This does not mean, however, that he escapes judgment and its inevitable representation.

To follow these consequences, recall that when Shelley gives Earth the role of judging the curse's words, Prometheus appears to avoid its representation of his past self. At the same time, he preserves the possibility of its revocation. But, by questioning whether or not these words are his, he must listen to the curse as a repetition without history, as an empty voice without thought. The dilemma the curse proposes centers on the question of how to account for the transformation (or transfer) of such speech into the representation of thought. This is where judgment is to occur. The dilemma is thus to account for a judgment that links speech to thought and, in so doing, creates thought as the subject of speech. The logic explored by this dilemma has the necessity of a time that cannot be reversed (recalled) but only repeated in a temporally different representation of itself. It is this difference that Prometheus cannot judge when he asks, "Were these words mine?" This inability to judge is also the inability to think of any relation between the utterance of the curse in the present and its occurrence in the past. Thus Prometheus remains unable to judge the curse as the representation of thought. Unable to judge his own history, Prometheus cannot affirm the narrative, given by Asia, that leads from speech to thought. Nor can he affirm, as the curse would, that his will is above the omnipotence of Jupiter—for it is Prometheus's will that calls for the curse whose authority is doubted by its author. Rather than become the representative of justice by the recognition of his former defiance, Prometheus must recognize that there is no triumph in judgment. As Prometheus will say after hearing the curse, "Justice when triumphant will weep down / Pity not punishment on her own wrongs." The triumph of Justice is the transgression of judgment. Judgments made in its name only triumph to the extent that they wrong their authority. Moreover, it is on those wrongs that one perpetuates such triumphs in the name of revenge. Justice arises from a judgment that would trace its origin to what it produces. The time in which judgment takes place cannot be a judgment of time; it cannot be a judgment of what time represents. Prometheus would recall such a time, but in the unrecognized repetition, he hears only the time, the event of the judgment pronounced by his curse, the phantasm of time, the empty voice of the forethought of time. Such is the judgment of time. In this repetition, the past survives as a judgment whose error can only be avenged by a history unwilling to recognize itself except by means of another.

The danger of such a repetition is clearly seen in Shelley's Preface to *Prometheus Unbound*: a Greece always in danger of being entrapped by its own myths despite its dramatic treatment of those myths. As the Preface indicates in conjunction with the treatment of Prometheus in Shelley's play, no more feeble a catastrophe could be imagined than the Hellenism that views Greece as the origin of a tradition to be revoked in the name of a freedom whose imperative affords no protection from its precariousness. To be so unbound is to be bound to the myth of Prometheus, to a past from whose thought we would free ourselves in a will to power that calls upon our history to speak. As this history is, so must we be. As the Earth exhorted Prometheus: Call at will. To recall Shelley's epigraph: Amphiaraus is listening (*sub terram*). But can Amphiaraus hear? Or must we conclude that "this tongue is known / Only to those who die"?

6

The Recall of Thought: Hölderlin

Within Hölderlin's poetic reflection, Greece plays so extensive a role that one can be easily tempted into viewing Hölderlin's oeuvre as wholly subordinate to Greek influence. Indeed, the source of Hölderlin's poetic thought may be traced in many instances to his engagement with Greek poetry and drama, but simply subordinating his work to Greek antiquity runs counter to his statements on the subject of Greece and its relation to modernity. The epigraph to this book, cited from Hölderlin's "The Perspective from which We Have to Look at Antiquity," provides an example of the need to make such a distinction. When Hölderlin speaks in this passage of our attempt to be new—and therefore modern—as "a reaction, as it were, a mild revenge against the slavery with which we have behaved toward antiquity," he clearly views modernity as the continuing legacy of an antiquity to which we can only enslave ourselves.[1] Hölderlin's ability to see this enslavement, not to mention modernity's ideological commitment to it, indicates the possibility of an antiquity no longer enslaved to its legacy. This possibility restores antiquity to us as the source of a question about what our modernity is, rather than an answer to what our modernity is not. Antiquity, to which modernity need no longer be subordinate, emerges with a particular individuality no longer appropriated as a means for our historical definition.

From Schelling's account of Greek tragedy, one can already deduce that the individuality of antiquity is related to the whole issue of our modernity. In Schelling's work, freedom and individuality are joined in a single event that recognizes and rejects fate, just as modernity recognizes and rejects past historical development. Yet, this notion of individuality only arises from a resolutely negative moment: the death in which the individuality of the hero is attained. The question of an individuality that would no longer demand the destruction of what it names as the price for the historical significance it subsequently possesses remains to be posed. Hölderlin frames the question of such an individuality as the question of Greece.

Similarly to both Schelling and Shelley, Hölderlin enacts his most searching exploration of this question in relation to Greek tragedy.[2] Unlike Schelling and more like Shelley in his recourse to Aeschylus's *Persians* and then to the no-longer-extant *Prometheus Unbound*, Hölderlin's exploration involves a translation at whose center lies the lyrical resources of poetry. In Hölderlin, such an exploration is given a literal expression discerned most clearly in his translations of Sophocles. These translations, long regarded, as Walter Benjamin notes, for their aberrant and eccentric treatment of the Greek text (Schiller regarded them as the work of a madman), mark a reflection on Greece centering on its language and on the possibility of that language being translated into modernity (which is to say they raise the question of a language for modernity).[3] Perhaps these translations have been regarded as failing what Winckelmann would call the "noble grandeur" of their original because our modernity demands the kind of accuracy that assigns translation the fate of being, at best, a provisional exercise waiting to be surpassed by yet another translation whose fate is likewise to be subsequently passed over. In this respect, translation and its history follows the pattern that marks the history of modernity in its continual judgment of the past as an inadequate representation of itself.

Hölderlin's focus on the language of Greece indicates a relationship to Greece different from a relation developed through cultural objects— such as that of Winckelmann. Yet, despite this difference, Hölderlin will express sentiments recalling the basis from which Winckelmann develops a historical understanding of culture, most notably, the climate and the body of the Greeks. In a letter written from France to Böhlendorff in

1802, Hölderlin writes, "The athletic character of the southern people in the ruins of the ancient spirit made me more familiar with the true essence ['eigentlichen Wesen'] of the Greeks; I became acquainted with their nature and their wisdom, their body, the way in which they developed within their climate, and the rule by which they protected their exuberant genius against the violence of the elements."[4] Winckelmann also traces the beauty he ascribes to Greek sculpture in the descendants of the Greeks; however, in Hölderlin's case, tracing the "essence of the Greeks" occurs in another country, because this foreignness is essential to how he understands being Greek. Hölderlin continues in his letter:

This determined their popularity, their way of assuming foreign natures ["fremde Naturen anzunehmen"] and communicating themselves through them; this is why they have their own authentic individuality ["darum haben sie ihr Eigentümlich-individuelles"] which appears alive in so far as the highest understanding is, in the Greek sense, the power of reflection ["Reflexionskraft"]; and this becomes intelligible for us if we comprehend the heroic body of the Greeks; it [this power] is tenderness, like our popularity.[5]

Despite an apparent affinity these remarks share with Winckelmann's themes, the relation to Greece described in these words departs from the sense of identity so crucial to Winckelmann's *History of Ancient Art*. This distinction becomes clear when Hölderlin speaks of both the popularity of the Greeks and our popularity. For Hölderlin, how the Greeks related to and communicated through what was foreign to them determines their popularity. Such a relation determines popularity according to an ability to assume, rather than turn away from or reject, what is foreign. Popularity, then, in its most essential and straightforward form is a relation to others. But, in Hölderlin, this popularity must also account for why the Greeks have "their own authentic individuality." Hölderlin's understanding of individuality in the passage just cited indicates a paradox in this respect: the Greeks possess popularity by their ability to assume a non-Greek identity, but from this ability they derive their individuality as Greeks. An understanding of this paradoxical account of individuality is essential if our relation to the Greeks, as Hölderlin sees it, is to be explained.[6]

Hölderlin also speaks of the popularity of our modernity. In his words, this popularity is rooted in a tenderness that, through the heroic body of the Greeks, makes intelligible to us, not beauty as is the case in Winckelmann, but the power of reflection ("Reflexionskraft"). Since, for Hölderlin, popularity is a way of assuming foreign natures, this passage indicates the extent to which we experience the individuality of the Greeks by assuming not simply their nature but the foreignness of their nature. (Hölderlin's language is precise on this point; one does not assume the nature of another, but rather the foreignness of that nature: "fremde Naturen anzunehmen.") As Hölderlin also points out, more is at stake than the mere question of an identity or a nationality. Assuming the foreignness of another nature gives rise to an individuality in which the highest power, the highest understanding comes into existence ("haben sie ihr Eigentümlich individuelles, das lebendig erscheint, sofern der höchste Verstand in griechischen Sinne Reflexionskraft ist"). Through our popularity, Hölderlin argues, we both assume and recall the foreignness of the Greeks. In so doing, we call thought into existence in a way that does not subordinate us to the Greeks (since in our taking on the foreignness of the Greeks, our individuality and hence our power of reflection arises).[7]

In a curious and Winckelmann-like gesture, Hölderlin states in a letter he writes from France that this individuality is derived from the climate in which a people resides. In France, Hölderlin writes that he not only became familiar with the "authentic essence of the Greeks" but also "became acquainted with . . . the way in which they developed within their climate, and the rule by which they protected their exuberant genius against the violence of the elements." Although, for Hölderlin, the climate influences how the Greeks developed, it is not simply a beneficent force leading to the noble beauty so important to Winckelmann. The climate is also the source of elements from which the Greeks had to protect themselves. As a result, the climate evoked by Winckelmann, Montesquieu, and others must also be seen as a threat to the Greeks, rather than the simple source of what is Greek.

This sense of threat is crucial to how Hölderlin thinks the "authentic individuality" of the Greeks. From this threat arises what Hölderlin calls the "rule," by which the Greeks protected their "exuberant genius." As a means of protection, this rule marks the moment at which the Greeks separate themselves from the climate within which they develop. Through this separation Hölderlin discloses the difficulty Winckelmann would avoid by historicizing our relation to Greece so that the individuality of Greece is folded into a historical epoch modernity feels compelled to either emulate or reject. Only by closing off Greece as an historical epoch can Winckelmann preserve an individuality *for Greece* while evading the consequence of attributing the origin of this individuality to the climate. If the climate were the decisive influence on the development of the Greeks, then only classical Greeks should emerge from that location. Here, the account of origin possesses a logic running counter to the historical frame where it is subsumed by Winckelmann.[8] In contrast to Winckelmann, Hölderlin speaks of a rule protective of Greek development.

By its nature, such a rule cannot belong to the climate but rather to what Hölderlin calls the "reflective understanding." As the product of the understanding through which the Greeks are protected from the climate and the violence of its elements, this rule cannot be separated in Hölderlin from the appearance of their "authentic individuality," from the means by which they sought to limit and define themselves. In this case, individuality arises from a rule that guides and enables reflection. This rule demands the separation of the Greeks from the violent elements, thereby distinguishing reflection from the influence of the climate. While Winckelmann explores neither the origin of any such rule nor the separation it demands (preferring to give climate primary if not absolute influence), his historicization of antiquity does recognize such a separation in the form of a modernity fated to reject repeatedly its past as well as itself. Hölderlin, however, recalls such a separation to the place of its origin in reflective understanding. With this move, his remarks on the Greeks transform Greece from the reference point it became within Hellenism. Now Greece becomes available as the example of a reflection whose individuality is destroyed by this same Hellenism, precisely because it defers to judgments made in the name of political, historical, and cultural reference.

Having distinguished Greece from the historicizing and ideological tendencies of Hellenism, Hölderlin poses the question of Greek individuality as well as the question of how to conceive of this individuality. Hölderlin broaches these questions in a November 1802 letter to Böhlendorff:

Beholding the ancients has given me an impression which renders intelligible to me not only the Greeks but, generally, the highest in art which, even in the highest movement and phenomenalization of the concepts and of everything that is meant seriously, still sustains everything upright and for itself ["dennoch alles stehend und für sich selbst erhält"], so that security ["Sicherheit"] of this sense is the highest form of the sign ["die höchste Art des Zeichens"].[9]

These remarks can be framed within a Winckelmann-like perspective if care is not taken to read the movement of thought. Hölderlin notes that beholding the Greeks makes two knowledges available to him: first, a knowledge of the Greeks; second, a more general knowledge concerning the highest in art. But as this sentence proceeds, emphasis falls not on what distinguishes the Greeks, but rather upon the precise nature of the impression ("Eindruck") that leads to a knowledge of the Greeks and the highest in art. This impression arises, as Hölderlin states, from what should be translated with all its literal force as a "look towards the an-cients ['Der Anblick der Antiken']." Keats's reflection on the meaning of such looking in his sonnet, "On First Looking into Chapman's Homer," should be recalled here, because this sonnet also poses the question of what constitutes Greece when it can no longer be known within the in-dividuality of its historical moment. But to recall Keats here is also to in-dicate the difference Hölderlin brings to the question. More explicitly than Keats, Hölderlin emphasizes the extent to which his "look towards the ancients" allows the emergence of art as the place in which everything that distinguishes itself by being both upright and for itself is sustained. In other words, such an art reveals everything that would be known by the name of individuality. Hölderlin also emphasizes that this ability per-sists even when art is called upon to give a phenomenal existence to the concepts generated by thought. Although Hölderlin ascribes such an ability to art, this ability is only guaranteed (remains secure) because of the nature of the sign. Unlike Winckelmann, for whom the body of the Greeks provided such a guarantee, Hölderlin not only gives language the task of safeguarding the highest achievement of art but also equates this property of language with the nature of art whenever the sign is expressed in its highest form.[10] If art, in its highest form is where Hölderlin locates individuality, then the appearance (or phenomenal existence) of such an individuality is linked to this property of the sign (which Hölderlin sees as its ability to secure the highest achievement of art).

Clearly Hölderlin is not proposing a biological and phenomenal understanding of individuality. As a result, this understanding cannot be restricted to the example offered by the mere existence of one person, as Hölderlin emphasizes in a remark about Achilles at the end of "On Different Forms of Poetic Composition." There Hölderlin states, "The individuality of Achilles, which surely is made for this purpose, imparts itself to everything and anybody, to what surrounds him and not just to the circumstances but to the characters as well."[11] The effect of Achilles, which is the effect of his individuality, is duplicated in those who surround him. By taking on the individuality of Achilles, others take on a nature that is foreign to themselves. The individuality of Achilles, and not Achilles himself, is duplicated here. This asserts quite a different effect than the phenomenal cloning implied by a more impressionistic reading of these sentences. This impressionistic reading is not entirely wrong, however; it merely lacks the will to overcome its desire to see Achilles as nothing more than a concept manifest in the separate phenomenal existence of those who surround him. This would signify an understanding that can only conceive of individuality by deducing its existence from its representation in another.

Hölderlin's remarks on Achilles point to the way in which individuality occurs within the duplication of Achilles's phenomenal existence, and not as a result of some conceptual existence that has been viewed as its historical precedent. Hölderlin speaks of individuality in this kind of duplication when he describes how Achilles becomes manifest in others: "At the contests that are being held in honor of the dead Patroklos, almost all other heroes of the Greek army wear more or less noticeably his color, and finally the old Priam in all his suffering appears to rejuvenate in front of the youth who, after all, was his enemy."[12] The individuality of Achilles is not experienced by Achilles, but rather by what others see as his appearance. Because of this phenomenal aspect, Achilles has an individuality. This indicates for Hölderlin that individuality cannot exist as the singular possession of one person. Only when others take on the attributes of Achilles can his individuality be recognized. But this recognition can only occur on condition of a separation present either in those who observe the duplication of Achilles on themselves, or in those who observe Priam and the Greeks. In both cases, an insurmountable difference returns as the condition of both individuality and the individual who conceives such a concept. This difference alone guarantees individuality; neither Hölderlin, the Greeks, nor we can claim exception from it.

The shift initiated by Hölderlin's remarks helps explain why, in his own words, "We must not have anything identical equal with [the Greeks]."[13] To do so would be to deny the difference that makes individuality by trying to adopt an example of individuality represented by the Greeks. The one thing modernity will never assume is Greek individuality, because it is the precise characteristic of such identification to destroy its own purpose: to take the individuality of another. When Hölderlin says "It is so dangerous to deduce the rules of art for oneself exclusively from Greek excellence," this sense of individuality is also at stake. But it is accompanied by a clarification of what distinguishes the Greeks for Hölderlin:

They excel in their talent for presentation ["Darstellungsgabe"], beginning with Homer, because this exceptional man was sufficiently sensitive to conquer the western *Junonian sobriety* for his Apollonian empire and thus to veritably appropriate what is foreign. With us it is the reverse. Hence it is also dangerous to deduce ["abstrahieren"] the rules of art for oneself exclusively from Greek excellence. I have labored long over this and know by now that, with the exception of what must be the highest for the Greeks and for us, namely, the living relationship and destiny, we must not have anything *equal* with them.[14]

The modern can only have anything equal to or like the Greeks where the highest is involved. For Hölderlin, however, to have what the Greeks had does not mean the modern is dependent on the Greeks for what is highest. Indeed that would entail a relationship of subordination, thereby condemning the modern to the kind of perpetual failure that Hellenism feeds upon. What Hölderlin indicates here is a relationship with antiquity that can only be attained when modernity possesses what the Greeks also possessed. Yet, this possession cannot in any way be determined by an act of mimetic derivation.

Hölderlin describes what the Greeks possessed and what must also be the highest possession for modernity as "the living relationship and destiny." Despite the obscurity invited by the vagueness of this phrase, Hölderlin's words indicate that wherever the relationship attained by modernity is to be living it cannot be subordinate to the historical specificity or moment of Greek art. If it were so subordinated, then it would be dependent on a living relationship that does not belong to itself, but rather to a past it can never surpass. (Here, the model of history fostered by Winckelmann can be most easily discerned.) Since modernity must possess equally the living relationship Hölderlin accredits to the Greeks, this relationship must in every case be specific to modernity. This is why in an earlier section of the same letter Hölderlin speaks of no longer pursuing the Greek talent for presentation, but instead of pursuing the one aspect they did not master: "beautiful passion."

Hölderlin introduces this as the concluding statement to a chain of thought that situates the whole subject of modernity's relation to the Greeks within the question of nationality: "We learn nothing with more difficulty than to freely use the national. And, I believe that it is precisely the clarity of presentation that is so original and therefore so natural to us as is the fire from heaven to the Greeks. For exactly that reason they will have to be surpassed in beautiful passion . . . rather than in that Homeric presence of mind and talent for presentation."[15] Hölderlin observes that as long as modernity labors under the legacy of the Greeks, it will likewise labor under a mode of presentation whose originality and naturalness will be perceived by us in the same way as fire from heaven was perceived by the Greeks. The analogy warrants attention, because it describes what the Greeks would have regarded as original and natural but which modernity would see as just the opposite. Here, the Greeks become the source of an example that contradicts the clarity of the presentation they bequeathed to modernity, thereby allowing this ability to be viewed as modernity's fire from heaven. The Greek talent for presentation now becomes for modernity what fire from heaven was to the Greeks: an external determining force. If modernity is ever to attain what is equal to the Greeks, then it must renounce this talent as its defining characteristic otherwise its history and any nationality it asserts within this history will be secondary to Greece.

As a means of avoiding this secondary relation, Hölderlin speaks of the need to pursue the "beautiful passion," which he will subsequently refer to as the "sacred pathos." Hölderlin refers to "sacred pathos" as the one thing Greeks did not master to the same extent as their talent for presentation. The reason for this failure is attributed to the fact that such a pathos was "inborn" ("es ihnen angeboren war") to the Greeks; therefore, they had no need to develop it. By focusing on the what the Greeks failed to develop, Hölderlin turns from a talent that he had described as becoming, in the hands of Homer, an ability "to appropriate what is foreign." Since such an appropriation defines for Hölderlin the development of Greece as a nation, his turn from this talent insists on an intention to preserve a sense of nationality that does not depend on the precedence of the Greeks. Rather, the possibility of a nationality free from this talent for presentation—this ability to appropriate what is foreign—is at stake.[16] Freeing nationality from the historical dominance of Greece means liberating nationality from that which appropriates the foreign. But, more importantly, it points to a path of thought in which the possibility of freedom within an historical existence, our modernity, is to be conceived. Yet, as Hölderlin's thought provides testimony, such freedom is not obtained by the easy rejection of either Greece or this talent—as if modernity were simply a refusal of the past and this refusal an act of freedom. Hölderlin writes, "What is one's own ['das Eigene'] must be learned as well as what is foreign. This is why the Greeks are so indispensable to us. It is only that we will not follow them in what is our own, our national [spirit] since, as I said, the *free* use of *what is one's own* is the most difficult."[17] In these concluding sentences to Hölderlin's 1801 letter to Böhlendorff, what is to be learnt first is the movement by which nationality and individuality occurred for the Greeks. But how can this movement (described earlier as "their way of assuming foreign natures and communicating through them") be understood as indispensable ("unentbehrlich") to securing the free use of one's own individuality? If one merely follows the example of the Greeks, then what the Greeks saw as their own determines and confines the modern individual. But what the Greeks saw as their own must be foreign to the modern individual. The refusal of this foreignness takes two forms, either it accedes to the example of a nation whose history has already been written (as is the case in Hellenism), or it rejects this example on ideological grounds. In both cases, the foreignness or difference of Greece is never considered as the essential legacy of Greece. This legacy imposes upon modernity the difficult task of attaining the free use of what is its own: its individuality. When Hölderlin links this task to the national, the link between the national ("unserm Eigenen, Nationellen") and the individual is not just present in the phrasing that places *Eigen* in apposition to *Nationell*; rather, it arises because, by achieving its own identity, the national individualizes itself and thus attains for itself the difference Hölderlin accords to the Greeks.

While such individuality remains closely linked to the national for Hölderlin, its occurrence does not rely solely on political or historical causes. This individuality is also to be found in the highest art or, as Hölderlin put it, in that art where the highest form of the sign is expressed (it is in such art that everything "upright and for itself is sustained"). Here, the significance Hölderlin attaches to Homer as the poet whose talent for presentation "conquered Junonian sobriety for his Apollonian empire" returns as art is designated the place where the free use of one's individuality is most at stake. That Homer provided the means of presentation through which Greece as a nation is formed underscores the way in which Hölderlin conceives of art as the place where reflection on the national and the individual occurs. At the same time, since Hölderlin insists we should not deduce the rules of art from "Greek excellence," the individuality of his modernity must seek such rules in an art that no longer imitates or subordinates itself to Greek art. Rather, it must equal the achievement of that art. Hölderlin locates such achievement in the individuality of the highest in art. In this way, Hölderlin envisages a relation to Greece no longer based on identity and the ideological relations it fosters, but rather on the difference that the highest in art attains and which the sign secures for it. Since this relation sustains how Hölderlin understands individuality and the national, it provides a basis for reading much of his poetry, in particular, the poetry in which Greece and Germany are ever present. Indeed, in the resources of his poetry Hölderlin not only explores the individuation, or formation, of the national but also locates the highest understanding of such formation. However, rather than resort to those poems of Hölderlin in which one nation or another is thematized, two poems on memory, "Andenken" and "Mnemosyne," present the poetic consequences of his letters, or, more accurately, find the causes of the theoretical reflections presented in his letters.[18]

Despite taking memory as their common subject, these two poems are named in a way that invokes the whole question of translation between Greek and German in Hölderlin's work. "Mnemosyne" is mythological and Greek in provenance; "Andenken" is German (it is written from the perspective of the poet's return to Germany from France). While both poems can be said to address the same subject across the linguistic and historical difference presented by their titles, the sense in which this subject is understood in these poems has little in common with the task that Winckelmann defined for art at its inception: "Art was already employed very early to preserve the remembrance of a person through their figure" ("Die Kunst wurde schon sehr zeitig gebraucht, das andenken einer Person durch seine Figur zu erhalten").[19] In the case of "Mnemosyne," this claim may be feasible at least to the extent that a single figure is named in its title. In the case of "Andenken," this claim is harder to sustain even on such a superficial level. By its title, this poem, rather than remember an individual, recalls what memory or remembrance is. Hölderlin's understanding of memory tends in a whole other direction, which is explicit in "Andenken." This will also be seen in "Mnemosyne," where individuality will be located within the movement of memory, rather than serve as the object toward which it is directed. Indeed, as "Andenken" makes clear, what remains crucial to Hölderlin is not the preservation of an individual, but rather the centrality of memory to both thought and poetry. Here, by linking memory to thought and poetry, Hölderlin recognizes how the relation of thought to language (or even concept to form) must be faced before subordinating itself to an individuality lodged in the past—whether in the form of a person's body or the singularity of an event.

The treatment of this relation in "Andenken" will be examined first even though the context of this reading would appear to insist that "Andenken" with its modern topical reference should be read as a reflection on a poem such as "Mnemosyne," which takes its subject from antiquity. That the mythological or Greek subject probably comes later in Hölderlin's oeuvre does not however require us to see this as a valorization of antiquity over the modern. Instead it requires us to consider the extent to which "Andenken" opens up the possibility of writing a poem such as "Mnemosyne," whose opening line, "Ein Zeichen sind wir" ("A sign we are"), indicates how closely Hölderlin's poetic reflections on memory are linked to his reflections on antiquity and the highest in art—whose "security" is "the highest form of the sign."

With its recall of France, "Andenken" begins in an analogous way to the November 1802 letter to Böhlendorff. Then, as now, what is foreign to the poet becomes a guide to his thought. However, in "Andenken" this foreignness is not located in the example of individuals from a particular region of France. Instead of an individual, Hölderlin offers a landscape. After noting the presence of a propitious wind for the sailors who will only be mentioned again in the final stanza once they have already departed, Hölderlin turns from the prospect of a voyage and focuses the first part of this poem by means of an imperative that exhorts us to greet a river:

> Geh aber nun und grüsse
> Die schöne Garonne,
> Und die Gärten von Bourdeaux
> Dort, wo am scharfen Ufer
> Hingehet der steg und in den Strom
> Tief fällt der Bach, darüber aber
> Hinschauet ein edel Paar
> Von Eichen und Silberpappeln;[20]

> But go now and greet
> The beautiful Garonne
> And the gardens of Bordeaux,
> There, where, along the steep bank,
> The footpath goes, and into the stream
> Deeply falls the brook, but above it
> Looks out a noble pair
> Of oaks and silver poplars;

The turn from the description of the wind and the sailors in the opening four lines of "Andenken"—the first of many in this poem—is signaled, as it will be again later, by the conjunction "aber." The importance of this conjunction to the poem has been commented on by Heidegger in his essay on "Andenken" where he emphasizes its role in signaling the question around which Hölderlin's poetic writing revolves.[21] While this aspect of Hölderlin's writing cannot be avoided—it is what Adorno calls his "paratactic style" but in a reading with an emphasis quite different from Heidegger's—its significance must also comprehend the points between which the turning takes place. Otherwise what Hölderlin writes will be reduced to a poetry limited to those words that Aristotle chose to describe as without meaning (λογος ασεμος), namely, conjunctions.[22] In this first stanza, the turn occurs with a command to greet the Garonne River at a specific location ("There, where"). While this evocation of place—to be repeated later in the poem—could already indicate, as Dieter Henrich has suggested, the importance of this evocation of Bordeaux to the structure and the content of the poem, the line that begins the second stanza cautions against any easy reading of this poem in the context of the landscape it evokes.[23]

The second stanza begins by reflecting on what the first has just described. Hölderlin writes, "Noch denket das mir wohl." A translation that signals the interposing of the poet, but does not quite catch the active role of the verb in this line, would read, "Still the thought of that returns to me." Before taking up the significance of *denken* in this line, one should first note that this interjection by the poet qualifies the evocation of landscape in the first stanza. The command to go and greet the Garonne and the topographical details to which it leads are now recognized as details owing their presence in the poem to not only memory but also, as the diction of this line indicates, to thought: "Noch *denket* das mir wohl." Such a memory, as thinking, is now recognized as the mode in which experience takes place. As a result, the poet's command to go and greet the Garonne becomes a command to go and greet thought, rather than displace oneself into the physical landscape of the Garonne.[24]

Even after starting the second stanza with such a recognition, Hölderlin will take up once again the description of physical aspects of the landscape, thus posing the question of why memory persists even after it is recognized as thought:

> Noch denket das mir wohl und wie
> Die breiten Gipfel neiget
> Der Ulmwald, über die Mühl';
> Im Hofe aber wächset ein Feigenbaum.
> An Feiertagen gehn
> Die braunen Frauen daselbst
> Auf seidnen Boden,
> Zur Märzenzeit,
> Wenn gleich ist Nacht und Tag,

Und über langsamen Stegen,
Von goldenen Träumen schwer,
Einwiegende Lüfte ziehen.

Still that thought returns to me, and how
The broad crowns of the elmwood
Bend above the mill,
But in the courtyard grows a fig tree.
On festive days walk
The brown women in that very place
On the silken ground
In the month of March [At the time of March]
When equal is night and day
And over slow footpaths,
Heavy with golden dreams,
Lulling breezes move.

The paratactic movement of this stanza offers four points of focus: first, the elms above the mill on the stream; second, the fig tree in the courtyard; third, the courtyard as the place of activity; and fourth, the lulling breezes. Of these four, the first continues the sense of place evoked in the first stanza, however, the second introduces a different place: the fig tree in the courtyard, which forms the focus of the second stanza. Despite this shift, both the reference to the elms and the courtyard occur in the sentence beginning in the first stanza with the poet's command to go and greet the Garonne. By introducing the courtyard within a sentence whose significance is defined by the place evoked in the first stanza, Hölderlin interrupts the movement of that sentence, but he does so by a phrase that belongs to it both syntactically and grammatically. Here, the relation between syntax and thought comes to the fore in a way that indicates a noncoincidence between a formal structure, such as the sentence and our assumption, since at least Plato, that such a structure guarantees both thought and understanding.

Within the structure of this sentence the courtyard with its fig tree stands like a foreign element, because the subject it introduces belongs, properly speaking, to the sentence that follows. Hölderlin gives us a grammatical disjunction in a passage where its occurrence can easily be overlooked or subordinated to a mere evocation of place (the courtyard and its fig tree). We learn in the third focus of this stanza that Hölderlin harbors no intention to subordinate the courtyard in this way: the image of brown women who walk on the "silken ground" of the courtyard. Already in the phrase "silken ground" Hölderlin's language marks a conjunction that strains the analogical basis of metaphor, but the focus toward which Hölderlin moves is still more important. The festive days when these women walk in the courtyard occur at the time of the equinox, as Hölderlin writes, "When equal is night and day." The second stanza comes to focus on this moment when night and day are exactly paired, but here the example offers no moment of joining, but rather it emphasizes a difference: night does not become day. It is this difference that must now be read within the context of the courtyard.

The courtyard is first introduced in a syntax belonging to the place by the Garonne to which Hölderlin commands us to go; therefore, it is formally paired with that place as if it contained an analogous understanding. Yet, the courtyard's foreignness within that syntax assaults the understanding with all the force of a non sequitur. The courtyard is where it does not belong syntactically, at least whenever syntax is defined as the development of a single idea. This effect is reinforced when the courtyard provides the setting for the descriptions of the festive days given in the next sentence. Syntactically, it would make more sense to place the introduction of the courtyard at the beginning of the second sentence. Interpretively, it is also attractive to proceed as if this were indeed what Hölderlin wrote, but then we must ignore the specific relation of thought to the language and syntax offered by this poem.

The introduction of the courtyard at the end of the first sentence's references to the Garonne and the physical features surrounding it indicate emphatically that the courtyard with its fig tree is to be read in conjunction with the descriptions and the command made in the first sentence. The courtyard and its fig tree thus appear as a thought that has not been taken into account. This failure is signaled by the use of "but" as the pivotal conjunction. What such a thought could be is traceable in the second stanza, when the significance of the courtyard is defined in terms of a temporal event, the equinox. By defining the courtyard as the place where this temporal event occurs, the second stanza indicates, as Shelley's reflection on judgment in *Prometheus Unbound* also did, that a temporality is to be taken into account. In Hölderlin's case this temporality takes the form of remembrance—such is the purpose of the "festival days" ("Feiertagen") with which the courtyard is associated. This remembrance is complicated by the equinox, and these days celebrate a temporal point with no actual moment in time assigned to it. In this respect, the point that defines the equinox (Hölderlin writes, literally, "In the time of March / When equal is night and day") is the point that differentiates night and day. By emphasizing this moment, Hölderlin draws our attention to a point that has only conceptual existence, even though it is spoken of as if it could be experienced in the same way that we experience time. As such, this emphasis makes the courtyard become the location where the relation of a concept (the moment when day and night are equal) and a phenomenon (the experience of time as day or night) are brought into this poem. By these references, the second stanza associates the courtyard with a temporal question and does so in a form that recalls Hölderlin's remarks on the ways in which the highest in art may occur. In the 1802 letter to Böhlendorff, Hölderlin wrote that the highest in art also occurs "even in the highest movement and phenomenalization of the concepts." In the example of the equinox offered by "Andenken," the rendering of a concept in terms of what can be seen, as experience, repeats this movement, but it does so by recalling a moment in which the concept (the point of equality) cannot attain the phenomenal existence (in time) it requires. In short, the problem introduced through the courtyard takes the form of a concept that refers to time for its meaning, but which leads to inconsistency and contradiction if time is to be used as a measure of that meaning.[25]

Recognition of the way in which such a problem is introduced into this poem allows the topical details presented in both the first and second stanzas to be read as already crucial to the development of Hölderlin's reflection on remembrance, rather than a record of this poet's topical remembrances (and against which such a reflection subsequently develops). The courtyard stands out among these details because of the way it figures as the pivotal point between the descriptions of place given in the first stanza and the emphasis given to events in the second stanza. By first introducing the courtyard in the context of these descriptions or remembrances of place and then making the courtyard become the place in which the problematic relation of concept and phenomenon is presented, Hölderlin is already showing how this initial context is marked by what his thought has not yet subject to reflection. That the courtyard possesses this significance because of the event described in the second stanza (the time in which the women walk there) indicates that within this poem the movement of remembrance takes place. Such remembrance, as the title and first line of the second stanza insist, is the work of thought and interpretation. Hölderlin's refusal to follow the anticipated relation of thought and syntax is central to originating this movement. But, as will be seen, it is also an inevitable effect of the movement of thought being recalled to itself.

While the syntactic placement of the clause introducing the courtyard reveals an essential aspect of how Hölderlin's thought moves in this poem, the focus on the courtyard has obscured an equally important detail, one that, if we follow the word order of this line, is emphasized more than the courtyard itself. Hölderlin writes, "Im Hofe *aber* wächset ein Feigenbaum" ("In the courtyard *however* grows a fig tree").[26] After seeing how this poem deliberately introduces an element whose significance can only be returned to after reading subsequent lines and then recalling the intrusion of this element, we are drawn back to what this courtyard also contains: a fig tree. Unlike the descriptions that follow of the activities occurring in the courtyard, this detail, by itself, gives no direct indication of its signification. We must turn to the later of Hölderlin's two poems on memory, "Mnemosyne," to trace a significance for this detail and its relation with what the courtyard is subsequently associated.

The final stanza of "Mnemosyne" not only refers to a fig tree but associates this tree with Achilles.[27] While this association brings Hölderlin's remarks on individuality into play once more, it does so in a way that centrally places individuality within how we conceive of our relation to the past, in general, and to Greece, in particular. By means of this relation, individuality emerges as a crucial element within what Hölderlin understands as thought and remembrance. The final stanza of "Mnemosyne" begins:

> Am Feigenbaum ist mein
> Achilles mir gestorben,
> Und Ajax liegt
> An den Grotten der See,
> An Bächen, benachbart dem Skamandros.
> An Schläfen Sausen ist, nach

Der unbewegeten Salamis steter
Gewohnheit, in der Fremd' ist groß
Ajax gestorben.
Patroklos aber in des Königes Harnisch. Und es starben
Noch andere viel.

By the fig tree is my
Achilles dead to me,
And Ajax lies
By the grottoes of the sea,
By streams, beside the Skamandros.
Of a roaring in his temples, according to
Unwavering Salamis' persistent
Custom, in a foreign land, is great,
Ajax dead.
But Patroklos [died] in the king's armour. And there died
Still others, many.[28]

Hölderlin's short prose text, "On Achilles," an earlier elegy, "Achill," and his use of Achilles as an example of individuality in "On Different Forms of Poetic Composition" each mark the singular importance Hölderlin accords this Homeric hero.[29] "Mnemosyne," by identifying the fig tree with the death of Achilles, suggests that the reference to the fig tree in "Andenken" may be read in relation to the significance Achilles has within Hölderlin's poetic thought. As a result of this association in "Mnemosyne," we are forced to recognize that our interpretative venture—our thought about "Andenken"—will follow the path of remembrance as we recall this poem through the reflection offered by "Mnemosyne."[30] Through "Mnemosyne" recall takes a singular form, not just because it centers on the individual figure of Achilles, but because it raises the question of how memory, thought, and reference are related to one another as a source of poetry within Hölderlin's writing. This question will be posed explicitly by the closing lines of "Andenken," when Hölderlin writes, "Was bleibet aber, stiften die Dichter" ("But what remains, the poets establish"). Through the elaboration of this question, the historical issue raised and then evaded by both Hellenism and its ideological critique will be given its most searching commentary. This issue, as Hölderlin is acutely aware, involves the possibility of an individuality for modernity. Such individuality, as the terms adopted by these two poems indicate, is inseparable from the possibility of a thinking no longer subordinate to the recalling of the past, to a history or individuality not our own.

To read the fig tree of "Andenken" through the final stanza of "Mnemosyne" implies that when this tree first appears in the earlier poem we have nothing to recall in its place. Indeed, before being recalled in "Mnemosyne," the fig tree could easily be dismissed as another example of the "meaningless sign" Hölderlin writes about in the opening lines of the stanza with which the second version of "Mnemosyne" begins: "Ein Zeichen sind wir, deutungslos / Schmerzlos sind wir und haben fast / Die Sprechen in der Fremde über Menschen" ("A sign we are, meaningless / Painless we are and have almost / Lost our language in foreignness"). Set in the context of this later poem, the fig tree of "Andenken" would appear to have lost its meaning in the same way that a language does when it is spoken in a foreign country where it remains unknown: the fig tree means something, but its context does not indicate what that is in terms of a history susceptible to recall. In "Andenken" this foreignness is present on two levels: first, the fig tree belongs to a phrase that occurs as a foreign element in the syntax of the first sentence of "Andenken"; second, it remains foreign to the activities taking place in the courtyard in the second stanza of "Andenken." To recover meaning for this sign, in effect, to reclaim it from its foreign "journey," we must turn to "Mnemosyne." In effect, we must turn to a poem recalling in the figure of Mnemosyne both the source of memory and, as one of the Muses, a source of poetry. Or to emphasize both the title of "Andenken" and the first line of its second stanza ("Noch denket das mir wohl" ["Still that comes well to mind"]) we must turn to a poem recalling the thought in which this source is externalized and thus made foreign for the first time.

This recall takes a singular form in "Mnemosyne," where it is centered on the figure of Achilles, who more than Ajax and Patroklos is the hero who died for the poet and the hero the poet claims for his own ("Am Feigenbaum ist *mein* / Achilles *mir* gestorben" ("By the fig tree did *my* Achilles die to *me*"). While these pronouns indicate identification, they also, and more importantly, indicate possession.[31] The poet's Achilles has died. The possessive pronouns point to Achilles as the form in which the poet experiences a death, not his own death but the death of an individuality that the poet has taken as if it were his own. Given Hölderlin's remarks on the individuality of Achilles in his essay "On Different Forms of Poetic Composition" this individuality is, as we saw earlier, what others see as the appearance of Achilles. When Hölderlin speaks of the death of his Achilles, he records the death of this appearance, that is, he records the death of how the individuality of Achilles is known.

In "Mnemosyne," Achilles is singled out by these pronouns, even though Hölderlin refers to Ajax, Patroklos, and "many other" Greek heroes. While this distinction would again emphasize the particular place held by Achilles in Hölderlin's thought, its significance cannot be limited to the kind of identification suggested by this thematic presence. Indeed, this poem's reference to Achilles has to be read in the context provided by Ajax and Patroklos. Ajax brings to this context a Greek hero who, in an act of madness preceding his suicide, attacks a flock of sheep, believing them to be the Greek warriors who cheated him of the armor of Achilles. Ajax's anger at being cheated of Achilles armor reveals a common element; Achilles is also a hero distinguished by his anger. Patroklos is another matter, an exception noted by Hölderlin, who introduces Patroklos in the third stanza of "Mnemosyne" in the same way that the courtyard and its fig tree are introduced in "Andenken": "Patroklos *aber* in des Königes Harnisch" ("*But* Patroklos in the king's armor"). Neither anger nor even the wrath of Achilles (even if Patroklos is its indirect victim) are the point here. Rather, the point is that Patroklos appears in the form of Achilles at the moment of his death. This is what Hölderlin emphasizes. As a result, the armor of Achilles, the form in which Achilles appears and in which his individuality is made known, provides the element linking the deaths of Ajax and Patroklos to Achilles.[32]

While such a link takes a physical form in the fates of Ajax and Patroklos, this same expression of individuality is repeated by Hölderlin when he speaks of *his* Achilles. As the opening lines of the third stanza of "Mnemosyne" reveal, the individuality of Achilles (in the sense Hölderlin gives to this word) no longer takes the form of his armor, but rather the form of his name. The subsequent references to Ajax and Patroklos help clarify this possession of the name Achilles: as Ajax would possess the armor and Patroklos did possess it, so would Hölderlin possess the name of Achilles ("my Achilles"). When Hölderlin writes that his Achilles has died to him, he is not referring to the mere death of Achilles but to the death of his ability to appropriate the name of Achilles. No longer can he simply say "my Achilles" because what has died is the relation of this phrase to him. The fateful difficulty toward which Hölderlin's thought leads is implicitly present here: at its most essential, individuality is a sign whose possession, or desire to possess, either involves a death or, in the case of Hölderlin's Achilles, is met with a death.

With such a fatefulness in mind, the lines in which Hölderlin describes the death of Ajax take on considerable importance.

> An Schläfen Sausen ist, nach
> Der unbewegten Salamis steter
> Gewohnheit, in der Fremd' ist groß
> Ajax gestorben.

> Of a roaring in the temples, according to
> Unwavering Salamis' persistent
> Custom, in a foreign land, did great
> Ajax die.

If these lines are simplified, then Hölderlin is saying no more than the fact that Ajax's death occurred in a foreign land. But, when the middle phrase of this sentence is considered, the event of this foreign death is described as resulting from a custom ("Gewohnheit"), which not only persists but also originates for Hölderlin with Salamis. Hölderlin's reference to Salamis is first and foremost a reference to Ajax's origin. Still, mythological biography does not account for why Hölderlin describes Salamis as being both unwavering and the source for a persistent custom. To understand why Salamis is given this role requires that we give proper emphasis to Ajax's death in a foreign land. The persistent custom from which Salamis does not waver requires such a death; the Greek hero Ajax must die in a land not his own. This is also the fate of Achilles, Patroklos, and the "many others" (Und es starben / Noch andere viel") who die at Troy. In the case of Ajax, this shared fate is traced to Salamis, which, if considered in the context provided by a text such as Aeschylus's *Persians*, can only refer to a Greece given existence by what is foreign to it.[33] When Greece comes into existence in this way, it is individualized. Here, Hölderlin's remarks in his 1802 letter to Böhlendorff return. In that letter, the popularity of the Greeks (which, as previously discussed, means their relation to others) is spoken of by Hölderlin as "their way of assuming foreign natures and communicating themselves through them." Following this observation, Hölderlin goes on to say, "This is why they have their own authentic individuality." For the Greeks to obtain what Hölderlin describes as the most difficult thing of all—to come into their own, their authentic individuality—they must do so by means of what is foreign. In the context of these remarks the significance of the reference to the three Greek heroes (and many others) in the final stanza of "Mnemosyne" can be read. All die in a foreign land and all die in a way that allows them to be individualized. Even in the case of Patroklos, this is true because his death allows the Trojans to know they did not fight against Achilles despite appearances. This would also be true in the case of the "many others" Hölderlin does not single out in this poem.

While the relation of heroism to popularity (and thus individuality in Hölderlin's understanding) can be clearly seen in the examples Hölderlin offers in "Mnemosyne," this poem develops the remarks made in the letter to Böhldendorff. Now, foreignness becomes what these heroes cannot return from. The custom of Salamis, that is, the custom of what is Greek is both persistent and unswerving in this respect. Salamis requires that the hero become a hero, individualized through two related risks: foreignness and death. By emphasizing the death of the hero in a foreign land, Hölderlin again stresses that individuality is communicated through foreignness. More to the point, he signals that such individuality can only be preserved in death. Why this is so reveals the reason a poem exploring this issue is also a poem about memory.

The individuality of each hero is affirmed in a death that takes away any personification of individuality through their living bodies. At this point, they become what the opening line of "Mnemosyne" says we already are, a sign. The tense is emphatically placed in the poetic line: "Ein Zeichen *sind* wir." If the fate of Achilles, Ajax, Patroklos, and many others is also to be our fate, then reflection on the sign's role in the formation of individuality becomes crucial.

In the 1802 letter to Böhlendorff, such a connection between the sign and individuality is already present in Hölderlin's thought. Hölderlin writes in this letter that the sign secures art at its highest, when art "sustains everything upright and for itself." To return to these words in the context provided by "Mnemosyne" is to emphasize the extent to which individuality is not only secured by the sign but also the extent to which this securing occurs at the same time as the highest in art. Although, in the case of art, Hölderlin's language describes this point as an example of singularity, the perception of this point in terms of individuality is easily grasped: since the highest is without equal it can only exist in its individuality. However, if it is to be preserved, or rather secured in its individuality, then it must become a sign—like Achilles, Ajax, Patroklos, and many others. Hölderlin will state that the highest sense of art is secured in this form. Nevertheless, what is being secured has little to do with the protection of a past to which one must continually refer in order to judge the present or future course of art. This sense of the highest becomes clearer when it is remembered that its individuality, as Hölderlin's language indicates, finds security in the sign, rather than in any passive reflection offered by the sign. The distinction is important if Hölderlin's work is to be read as more than a simple glorification of the Greeks (and which the letters already indicate would be a gross error). The distinction underscores the crucial role of the sign in any account of Hölderlin's relation to Greece, its heroes, and, more generally, any relation to what we call the past, whether it be actual or mythical.

When Hölderlin states that we are a sign in the opening lines of the first stanza of "Mnemosyne," language can no longer be a simple mediation between ourselves in the present and the others populating the past. The subject who would know the past can only be known in the same way that the past is known: as a sign. This situation was already present in Hölderlin's account of the individuality of Achilles when he spoke of the way in which others would take on the individuality of this hero. By wearing the same color as Achilles during the contests held after the funeral of Patroklos, the Greeks turn themselves into the sign of his individuality. Since this individuality is derived from withdrawal and separation in the course of Homer's *Iliad*, the wearing of Achilles color becomes the sole means by which his individual significance can be given (Patroklos's wearing of his armor is another example of this). But, as the opening lines of the final stanza to "Mnemosyne" reveal, this mediation has consequences for those who would possess individuality by means of a reflection: Hölderlin in the name Achilles ("my Achilles"); Patroklos in

Achilles's armor; as well as Ajax and all those who participated in the contest for this armor. In the case of the named heroes a loss is recorded, all are dead. Here, we discover the importance of the heroes given as examples: those who take on the armor of Achilles or else define their existence by the need to take on this armor become the sign of an individuality that can only be possessed by a sign whose meaning is fatally beyond their grasp and beyond our possession. The same is also true of Achilles in this poem although it occurs on the level of the poet's relation to this hero. When Hölderlin first indicates his possession of Achilles, this possession is immediately followed by the death of the hero for him: "ist mein / Achilles mir gestorben" ("is my / Achilles to me dead"). So runs the word order. Death comes to the poet's possession, as the name "Achilles" becomes a sign for the poet who may no longer possess such signs. By tracing Hölderlin's thought through to the final lines of "Mnemosyne," this situation can be understood. At that point, we may return to "Andenken" and its fig tree.

When the poet's attempt to possess the name of Achilles is met with death, the name becomes a sign whose fate, as the opening lines of the first stanza of "Mnemosyne" states, is to be without meaning and without pain: "Ein Zeichen sind wir, deutungslos / Schmerzlos sind wir" ("A sign we are, meaningless / Painless we are"). While this state of being without meaning and without pain can be related to Achilles, Ajax, and Patroklos, this state's relation to us is less clear. Unlike these heroes, we are presumed to be alive. Yet, this distinction, based on the difference between the living and the dead, holds little weight here; in fact, it contributes to a lack of clarity. The poet and the Greek heroes he lists are both subject to the same persistent habit whenever their individuality is at issue. Just as the individuality of Achilles is known through others who become the sign of that individuality, so too our individuality is recognized in a sign; that is the form in which it becomes known to ourselves and to others. To know oneself as an individual is to know oneself under the sign of individuality, and this sign is not within one's possession. Rather, in Hölderlin's words, it dies to oneself.

Such a condition is referred to by Hölderlin continuing his description of our painless and meaningless state as a sign: "und haben fast / Die Sprechen in der Fremde über Menschen" ("and have almost / Lost our language in foreignness"). Cast abroad in the sign, our individuality risks loss in the foreignness it requires if it is to possess meaning (if it is to be the sign of an individual, rather than the fate of individuality). The sign, as Hölderlin understands it, marks the presence of a foreignness, which arises because of the way we are fated to think of individuality. The foreignness in this case is not what has to be opposed to the sign or to the Greeks. Rather, as Hölderlin indicates in both his letters and "Mnemosyne," it is a condition of the sign and of being Greek. In each case, individuality is sought, and this search leads invariably to the foreign. Here, to be individualized is to be assigned a particular significance. Since this significance can only be attained through foreignness, the risk that it will be lost and will therefore always be the subject of recall, of remembrance, persists. In this context, memory would appear as the means to preserve an individuality that takes the form of the highest in art ("everything upright and for itself"). But it may equally be present in the sign as well as in any attempt to attain "the free use of one's own."

If memory is to take on this role, then the lines with which "Mnemosyne" closes introduce a complication that has long posed considerable difficulty for the interpretation of Hölderlin's poetic thought. After recalling the many others who died in addition to Achilles, Ajax, and Patroklos, Hölderlin writes:

> Am Kithäron aber lag
> Elevtherä, der Mnemosyne Stadt. Der auch, als
> Ablegte den Mantel Gott, der abendliche nachher löste
> Die Loken. Himmlische nemlich sind
> Unwillig, wenn einer nicht
> Die Seele schonend sich
> Zusammengenommen, aber er muß doch; dem
> Gleich fehlet die Trauer.

> But near Kithairon lay
> Eleutherai, city of Mnemosyne. She also, when
> He put down his mantle the god, the evening afterwards loosened
> Her locks. The heavenly are
> Angry if someone,
> Saving his soul does not
> Gather himself together, but still he must; for him
> Equally mourning errs.[34]

Quite apart from the difficulties posed by what constitutes Hölderlin's text in this stanza, the queen of the Muses, Mnemosyne, must also be read in the context introduced by Hölderlin's lines on Achilles.[35] As with the Greek heroes, little is specified with respect to Mnemosyne. We are simply told of two acts and both are presented as what belongs to the West ("abendlich"): the putting down of a mantle and the loosening of locks of hair by a god, who is described in the form of evening.[36] In this context, the act of putting down the mantle appears as the divestment of the divine equivalent of the armor of Achilles. By this act, the gods give up the appearance by which they are known. Mnemosyne's hair is loosened only after this act, as if the divesting of the mantle signals a loss that invites this other act. The subsequent lines express why this act takes place, why it is performed by a god who is figured as not only the West but also its evening: we are told of a failure to gather oneself together ("sich zusammennehmen"), a failure that angers the gods.

This anger is not, however, addressed to Mnemosyne, at least not directly. Rather, this anger is directed at a subject revealed as masculine in the phrase "aber er muß doch" ("but he must still"). This revelation emphasizes the change in the address of this poem to an unspecified, yet singular, subject who comes after Mnemosyne, the Greek heroes, and their gods. The reference to "saving his soul" confirms this historical change by describing the present in a characteristically Christian phrase. From this standpoint, the putting off of the mantle and the loosening of the locks of Mnemosyne can be read as the sign of the fall of an antiquity whose failure is now interpreted by its Christian successor.[37] For this reason the god is figured in the word "abendlich," as both evening and the West, since the moment Mnemosyne puts off her mantle is the moment when the gods will begin to fade. Their last significant act is to loosen the hair of the one who guaranteed not just the story of their existence but also the story of Achilles, Ajax, Patroklos, and many others. But what will remain?

If Hölderlin were to adhere to the kind of Hellenism initiated by Winckelmann, then a mourning for antiquity would remain. Such mourning simultaneously subordinates the modern to what can no longer have any living presence (to what in Jean-Luc Nancy's phrase can no longer be born to presence).[38] But to mourn for such figures of antiquity, as the presence of the verb *fehlen* in the final phrase of "Mnemosyne" points out, is to err. Rather than invoke a faulty mourning, such as Freud's melancholia, to explain this erring, mourning is always directed at an individual.[39] Such mourning arises because death has revealed individuality to be, quite literally, a sign we can no longer wish to put on without recognizing its inability to embody the significance we wish to recall (as the figure of Patroklos teaches us by his death, Ajax by his madness, and the poet by his inability to possess Achilles). As the attempt to recall the individual, mourning, like memory, must already err, because it cannot return individuality to the individual. In mourning, the sign of the individual faces its source in a body that has become a sign. However, mourning persists as our only witness to an erring that originates within mourning and also memory. Accordingly, such an erring is the direct result of mourning's attempt to overcome errancy in the first place. Mourning produces the errancy it sets out to overcome.

Only through such a movement does mourning go amiss and only then can it be said to have gone astray. This movement also makes clear that mourning, like all things that go astray, must experience a foreignness as the fundamental sign of its errancy.[40] In this respect, mourning repeats the language Hölderlin describes in the opening lines of one of the versions of "Mnemosyne." This language seems "almost lost in foreign lands," almost because mourning as memory never quite lets go. Instead, it is always attempting to recall its signs from the foreign land or foreign body in which it is fated to misplace them. Here, mourning follows the fate of the signs through which it would recall the past. To become meaningful such signs must be sent abroad in the same way that Hölderlin's remembrance of the Garonne and Bordeaux is sent abroad in "Andenken." To become foreign is the requirement that attaches itself to every sign as they take on meaning and are thereby individualized. But death and madness, both examples of the return of language to its starting point, haunt this individualization of the sign. For this we mourn, for this we go astray once more.

Just as mourning carries with it the errancy it seeks to overcome, so too the sign can only be read as the foreignness it is meant to overcome. In each case, a going astray (the movement of *fehlen*) remains in discord with the "gathering together" the heavenly are said to demand in the final lines of "Mnemosyne." In this context, *fehlen* appears to be opposed to the movement of *zusammennehmen*; however, this does not mean that *fehlen* is to be understood as another mode in which the fading of antiquity takes place—as if *fehlen* were to repeat both the putting off of the god's mantle and the loosening of Mnemosyne's locks. Rather, *fehlen* is the relation through which the poet recognizes not just antiquity but also its end. To understand this relation, both senses of *fehlen*—failing and erring—must be kept in mind, but not in order to resume a Hellenism in which our failure to imitate antiquity becomes the error of our modernity. Hölderlin writes that mourning is what goes astray or fails; he is not mourning for the failure or errancy of antiquity, but rather for the failure or errancy present within whatever tries to "gather together." As Hölderlin's syntax indicates, such a mourning is to be understood in analogy to the gathering together described in the preceding phrase: "dem / *Gleich* fehlet die Trauer" ("For him / *Likewise* mourning errs," or "For him / Mourning errs *in the same way*"). Following this analogy, the poet's relation to the subject of this poem, Mnemosyne, must now be known in a mourning that goes astray as it fails to gather together the sign (Mnemosyne) with its individual meaning. This meaning, as the choice of Mnemosyne reveals, is concerned with the figure through which antiquity is gathered together. The queen of the muses, Mnemosyne, is that figure from which flows the ability of antiquity to represent itself to itself. To mourn for such a figure is truly to err. Mourning, as an act through which one would gather oneself together, must in this instance mourn for what failed to achieve the very goal of mourning, namely, the "gathering together" through which antiquity reveals and recalls itself.

The difficulty Hölderlin explores in these lines is nowhere more present than in the sentence whose language suggests the advent of a Christian era. This sentence speaks of one ("einer") who would save his soul without gathering himself together. As the anger of the gods reveals, this saving of the soul is not enough if this "one," this individual, does not gather himself together ("sich zusammennehmen"). In the end, as the incomplete phrase preceding the observation that mourning errs indicates, such a gathering together can only be recognized as an unavoidable necessity: "aber er muß doch." The presence of "aber" and "doch" in this phrase highlight a necessity that must be asserted, because the gathering together demanded by the "heavenly" has not taken place. Why this gathering together occurs under the sign of necessity is subsequently explained by the final phrase: "dem / Gleich fehlet die Trauer" ("for him / likewise mourning errs"). The failure to achieve this "gathering together" is equal (also the meaning of "gleich") to mourning in the sense that such a "gathering together," like mourning, is the source of the failure it sets out to overcome. By attempting to overcome this failure, both err equally. Thus in the errancy of mourning the necessity of "gathering together" arises from the failure to effect such a "gathering together." As Hölderlin points out in the phrase "aber er *muß* doch," there is no choice but to attempt such a gathering together, even if it must go astray because of such an attempt. Since the attempt to gather oneself together always produces the need to perform this attempt, "sich zusammennehmen" is truly a necessity one cannot avoid.

One undeveloped aspect of "Mnemosyne"—which will return us to "Andenken"—lies in its implication that mourning for antiquity must also be a mourning for Mnemosyne, for a memory that has gone astray because it can never return to the place from which it has been recalled.[41] In this case, memory must mourn for its inability to gather together both what it recalls to itself and what is being recalled.[42] The descriptions of the Garonne in the opening stanza of "Andenken" fall within the operation of such a memory as Hölderlin makes clear at the beginning of this poem's second stanza when he writes, "Noch denket das mir wohl." As we have already seen, this phrase underlines that what Hölderlin recalls is now a landscape belonging to thought, or, more precisely, belonging to *andenken*, to a "thinking toward" in which the object of this thought does not play a predetermining role.[43] Only the calling to mind of the poet remains significant. This is why the poem is about remembrance itself, rather than the remembrance of a specific event or location and its significance in the past.[44] In this context, the fig tree first appears when it is singled out in a place where an event (the women walking and the repeated festival) marks a time that can have no phenomenal existence of its own ("When equal is night and day"). The metonymic relation of the fig tree to what is described in the courtyard is precisely what the final stanza of "Mnemosyne" explores in terms of a relation to antiquity. In both cases, the fig tree figures as a sign and does so over and above any symbolic or thematic significance derived from literary history, even if it is powerless to prevent the recall of such significance.[45] Yet, given the relation to Achilles provided by "Mnemosyne," if one were to seek such a significance, then one could do no worse than turn to Homer's *Iliad* where a fig tree appears as a marker on the battle landscape.[46] In the *Iliad*, however, the fig tree serves as no more than a reference point whose significance remains undeveloped even though it is always there, albeit to one side of the events described by this epic. This metonymic role recurs in "Mnemosyne" where the fig tree operates as the reference point beside which the whole question explored in the final stanza of this poem unfolds. This role is made explicit by its positioning at the outset of this stanza: "Am Feigenbaum ist mein / Achilles mir gestorben." In this instance, the fig tree introduces no additional significance; it only serves to mark the place beside which the relation of the poet to Achilles is articulated. This relation, as discussed above, is essentially concerned with the place of the sign within memory and the recognition of individuality. In "Andenken," the fig tree also specifies a place, this time a courtyard, rather than the place of a death. But again, as the syntax emphasizes in "Andenken," the fig tree remains disconnected to what occurs in the courtyard, it simply grows there ("In Hofe aber wächset ein Feigenbaum" ["But in the courtyard a fig tree grows"]). In this way, the fig tree marks the place of a memory but does so without embodying a significance that individualizes or determines this memory. This is demonstrated across the syntax of "Mnemosyne" when this poem moves from the place, the "Stadt" of Mnemosyne to the presence of Mnemosyne. In both cases, the fig tree functions as a sign marking the place of a memory, without accounting for why a particular memory (death of Achilles, the festive days) should be associated with it. As a result, the fig tree preserves its metonymic role. In this role the tree will define the subject of "Andenken" and "Mnemosyne," as well as the poet's relation to this subject.

The nature of this subject is continually threatened by the tendency to transform the fig tree into a metaphor and then gather the poem around the symbolic or conceptual meaning this metaphorical value allows to be introduced. Indeed, if anything needs to be remembered in both of these poems, then it is the metonymy through which the fig tree is introduced and through which it relates to the subsequent development of each poem. In the example of "Andenken," this relation allows the full significance of what occurs in the courtyard to be perceived.

In "Andenken" the fig tree is metonymically placed in a context that emphatically marks the passage of time and history (time in the form of the equinox and history in the form of the festival celebrated during the "festive days"). In "Mnemosyne," such a passage is also present when the fig tree is used to mark the place where Achilles died: a time and a history are marked by what has no influence on that time and history. The fig tree merely survives and, in so doing, marks the place of a time and history that have no other sign. In this respect the fig tree acts as a kind of memory, but not in the sense that it recalls an event to which it was witness. Rather, it recalls the means of memory by emphasizing that the reference point for memory exists to one side of what it is meant to recall. Hölderlin's poetry places this metonymic aspect before us as both the means by which memory operates and the result of memory's operation. What is remembered is that memory takes the place of what it has commanded us to recall. What is remembered is the imperative to remember. That memory is related to such a command in "Andenken" is clear from its first stanza since it is from an imperative that the poem's recall of the Garonne landscape evolves: "Geh aber nun und grüsse . . . " ("But go now and greet . . . "). When we recall how this command is met with the recognition "Noch denket das mir wohl" (what comes to the poet's mind in the form of thought) then, it is evident that Hölderlin is commanding us to go and greet not the landscape of the Garonne, but rather thought as it arises from the remains of memory.

In the case of the fig tree in "Andenken," memory is both expressed and arrested in the same utterance. Thought arises from this, but not as something that stands in opposition to memory. Rather, thought emerges from memory at the moment memory faces the sign through which it is expressed. In "Mnemosyne" the fig tree's position as a marker for what is to be remembered represents this process. In "Andenken," the fig tree also functions as such a sign, again marking the place of an experience to which it has no other relation than contiguity.[47] Through this contiguity, the fig tree points to, but must at the same time be recognized as separate from, the event with which it is associated. This double relation is repeated, quite literally, in the course of the poem when its streams and rivers are followed to their destination. Like the fig tree, this destination takes and gives. Hölderlin writes:

An Traubenbergen, wo herab
Die Dordogne kommt,
Und zusammen mit der prächt 'gen
Garonne meerbreit
Ausgehet der Strom. Es nehmet aber
Und giebt Gedächtniss die See,

By the hillsides of grapes, where downward
The Dordogne comes
And together with the splendid
Garonne, wide as an ocean,
The stream goes forth. But the sea
Takes and gives memory

The sea is viewed as both the source and destination to which all memory tends. Described in this way, the sea becomes the element that makes memory possible, but at the same time, it takes possession of the memory it bears. In this role, the sea must take what it gives. To this double role, "Andenken" directs its course as it presents its own attempt to recall memory.

In "Andenken," the sea's significance far outweighs any other single aspect of the landscape Hölderlin evokes. Indeed, the sea is where the landscape goes.[48] As before with the fig tree, the significance of the sea is not located in any external symbolic source. To read the significance Hölderlin attaches to the sea requires a step back into the fourth stanza, where Hölderlin first refers directly to the sea. Here, the sea is understood as a place whose promise of wealth offers an alternative to those who do not accompany the poet to the source:

Wo aber sind die Freund? Bellarmin
Mit dem Gefährten? Mancher
Trägt Scheue, an die Quelle zu gehn;
Es beginnt nemlich der Reichtum
Im Meere.

But where are my friends? Bellarmin
With his companion? Many
Are shy to go to the source;
Wealth begins, namely,
In the sea.

Without his friends, the poet goes alone to the source; those who are shy seek the wealth that begins in the sea. Here, the wealth offered by the sea seems to be literal, but when the remainder of this stanza is read, this wealth is not merely commercial. Those too shy to go to the source are like painters:

Sie,
Wie Mahler, bringen zusammen
Das Schöne der Erd' und verschmähn
Die geflügelten Krieg nicht

They,
Like painters, bring together
The beauty of the earth and disdain not
The winged war

Like the sea that takes and gives, the painters are engaged in an activity that involves a contradictory movement: they are concerned with both bringing together and the war that pulls apart. This comparison to painters emphasizes the visual in a way that reiterates the descriptive form in which memory occurs in this poem. However, the comparison also serves to introduce a distinction between, on the one hand, the painter and those who are too shy to go to the source, and, on the other, the poet.

In this distinction between the poet and the painter one can begin to read the precise point of Hölderlin's difference from the Hellenism developed by Winckelmann (namely, the Hellenism that grows out of Winckelmann's unquestioned confidence in the ability of the linguistic to take the place of the visual). By separating the poetic task from that of the painter, Hölderlin insists on an element that exceeds the grasp of the visual. This element is indicated in the remaining lines of this stanza when Hölderlin describes the fate of those who seek wealth in the sea:

Zu wohnen einsam, jahrlang, unter
Dem entlaubten Mast, wo nicht die Nacht durchglänzen
Die Feiertage der Stadt,
Und Saitenspiel und eingeborener Tanz nicht.

To live alone, yearlong, beneath
The leafless mast, where the festive days of the city
Do not shine through the night,
Nor the play of strings, nor native dance.

They must forsake the festive days celebrated in the courtyard where the fig tree grows and also substitute a "leafless mast" for this tree. To seek wealth in a sea that takes and gives memory is to turn away from what the course of this poem has led us through. Such a turning away is equivalent to embarking upon the voyage promised by the northeast wind at the beginning of the poem. Hölderlin does not go on such a voyage—as if the foreign could only be experienced in this way. Instead, the voyage is interrupted by the command to go and greet a landscape. In the opening line of the final stanza, this command appears to have been heard when the departure of sailors is recorded in words that repeat those through which this command is first given ("Geh aber nun"). Hölderlin writes:

> Nun aber sind zu Indiern
> Die Männer gegangen
>
> But now to the Indies
> The men are gone[49]

Here, the men do not go to greet the Garonne. Nor do they go to greet what the poet refers to as "what comes well to mind." Rather, they are carried along by the confluence of the Garonne with the Dordogne and the onward sweep of this confluence into the sea. In this respect, the sailors are subordinate to the forces present in the actual landscape, and, as such, they are caught within a realm that can only take what it also gives—in the sense that the landscape is both the source of a memory and the place that would take back such a memory. That Hölderlin aims at another understanding becomes apparent in this final stanza as memory gives way to thought.

With the departure of both the sailors and the friends of the poet we are left to anticipate the infamously gnomic final line of "Andenken." The men have left for the sea where wealth begins, but the poet, alone, stays behind to go to the source ("an die Quelle zu gehen"). As the last sentence of "Andenken" reveals, this source is to be distinguished from what the sea offers, but this is not all it is to be distinguished from:

> Es nehmet aber
> Und giebt Gedächtniss die See,
> Und die Lieb' auch heftet fleissig die Augen,
> Was bleibet aber, stiften die Dichter.

> But the sea
> Takes and gives memory,
> And love also diligently fixes our eyes
> But what remains, the poets found.

Just as the sailors leave and are caught within a sea that takes and gives memory, love also has the effect of catching those who fall within its reach. In the case of love, this catching centers on eyes now diligently fixed. This fixing, as Hölderlin's syntax indicates, is not a fixing of the eyes on some object ("heften die Augen auf . . . "), but rather a fixing or fastening restricted to the eyes. In short, the eyes through which the landscape first enters memory become fixed in a way that arrests this source at the end of the poem. This arrest reiterates the single prior mention of love in the third stanza of this poem. After remarking in this third stanza, "It is not good / To be soulless with / Mortal thoughts," Hölderlin speaks of love as one of the good things:

> Doch gut
> Ist ein Gespräch und zu sagen
> Des Herzens Meinung, zu hören viel
> Von Tagen der Lieb',
> Und Thaten, welche geschehen

> But dialogue
> Is good and to speak
> The heart's meaning, to hear much
> About days of love
> And deeds which are done.

Here, love is to appear within a dialogue that will speak about not just the "heart's meaning" but also "deeds which are done." This dialogue effectively takes the two elements present in the last sentence of "Andenken," namely, love and memory, and holds them up as the subject of a dialogue in which the poet will turn from thinking about mortality ("sterblichen Gedanken"). But this dialogue fails, as the beginning of the fourth stanza makes clear, when the poet asks after his absent friends ("But where are my friends? Bellarmin / With his companion?"). Left without his friends and therefore without the dialogue of love and memory, the poet remains. What then does this remainder found? What does the poet call to mind? Hölderlin uses the verb *stiften* to describe what the poets do. This word indicates not only the activity of founding and establishing but also, through *ein Stift*, a pencil, the activity of writing. While this sense is to be heard in *stiftung*, it is not essential since the founding that the poets do can be nothing more than the writing of their language. In Hölderlin's works, this writing becomes the form in which an individuality is founded. As we read earlier, Hölderlin defined individuality in the context of his remarks on Greece as "the free use of one's own." In "Andenken" the poet possesses as his own what the poet is left with, and this, as the course of the poem reminds us, survives the absence of the friends, the departure of the sailors, and the effect of love. Viewed from this position, what remains in "Andenken" is what would either be lost or obscured by dialogue, memory, and love's fixing of sight. What remains does so because it does not become subordinate to another person or object. In this respect what remains must also be understood in terms of an individuality that cannot be separated from the sign that poetry helps to found. Since such individuality is recognized through a foreignness in Hölderlin's writings, the question about what poets found becomes a question about the foreignness that poets bring to language. But, how does this individuality arise in "Andenken"? By what means is it founded and to what end is it directed within Hölderlin's poetic thought?

At each of the major turning points of "Andenken," the poet remains alone: first, when the command to go and greet the Garonne is made; second, when the command is made to pass the cup of wine so that he may rest;[50] third, when the desire for dialogue is expressed; and fourth, when the sailors who first appear in the opening four lines of the poem have departed. The return of the poet's words persists, so that these words become the subject of the poet's reflection. This is nowhere more emphatically present than in the opening lines of the second stanza when the descriptions of the Garonne given in the first stanza are recognized as thought, rather than memory. Here, memory is recalled as thought, or to be more precise, thought is recalled from memory when Hölderlin writes "Noch denket das mir wohl" ("Still the thought of that returns to me"). Instead of greeting the landscape, the words of memory are recalled to the poet as thought, they are neither absorbed (taken) by the landscape nor are they recognized as being given by the landscape. The attempt to recall the landscape brings the poet to thought that would otherwise remain concealed within memory, particularly when the significance of that memory is restricted to a specific place, event, or person. What Hölderlin recalls is then thought, but this thought, as the movement of this poem amply demonstrates, is not separable from the attempt to recall (implying that what we are concerned with here is not an opposition of thought and memory in which one must exclude the other). Rather, thought remains once memory has run its course. The moment at which this remainder occurs (when memory gives way to thought) is the moment at which the individuality of the poet emerges—that is, the moment when the poet emerges *as* a poet.

How the poet becomes a poet can be traced to a memory that, within the course of "Andenken," returns to the poet without the familiar and comforting presence of what it describes. Here, the *Andenken* of this poem is distinguished from the more familiar *Angedenken* whose usage has more in common with the love that "diligently fixes eyes," namely, the fond remembrance of a loved one. This turn from a memory so fixed upon a preexisting object or person is precisely what the poem demonstrates on a syntactic level. The phrase at the beginning of the second stanza, when the poet turns from further evocation of the landscape and introduces the fig tree in the courtyard, provides a primary example of such a turn. This phrase does not continue the descriptions of the Garonne scene, but instead arrests them even as it appears to continue them. The fig tree in the courtyard stands against these descriptions in a way that no longer simply calls upon memory. Rather, the fig tree calls upon thought in a way that effectively recalls it from the course of memory as it is mapped out in "Andenken" through the course taken by the Garonne and Dordogne Rivers. What the fig tree establishes in this poem is a sign that has to remember (the "aber er muß" of "Mnemosyne") that it is a sign. This is the precise point of contact between "Mnemosyne" and "Andenken." In "Mnemosyne" such a recognition occurs at the moment when Achilles dies for the poet and at the moment when the mantle of the god is put down. The memory of this putting down of the mantle and the memory of this death are what remain for the poet, but such memory remains only in what is placed to one side (in the case of Achilles, it is again the fig tree; in the case of Mnemosyne it becomes both her hair and the city of Eleutherai through which she is known as a god[51]). This placing of the sign as a sign becomes in "Andenken" the moment around which the poem, as a poem about memory, is organized.[52] Here, it is crucial to keep in mind that "Andenken" is a poem about memory and not a poem of memory. As a reflection on the course of memory, rather than the presentation of images and evocations in the form of memory, "Andenken" is, as its title indicates, a poem in which the relation of memory to thought remains.

This relation of memory to thought is most apparent in the scene following the introduction of the fig tree, in which the women's walking is used to mark the place of a time only thought can approach. (Here, the sense of *an-denken* as "thinking toward" emphasized by Heidegger cannot be avoided.) As is the case with the fig tree, this walking marks the place of what is to be remembered. But here, memory, like the god, must put off its mantle and stand revealed like the fig tree, unavoidably present yet always to one side of what it stands for, like a sign that must recall its source in thought and not in the landscape or event it gives to sight. In the end, "Andenken" establishes this recall as the source of its poetry and thought—its *Andenken*. But this recall, as both "Andenken" and "Mnemosyne" remind us, marks an individuality that has nothing to do with subjectivity (in the sense that one could say that every memory is personal and therefore its significance is restricted to the individual as a subject). Nor is this individuality a figure for some universal condition. If it were, then it would be nothing more than a synecdoche, the mere memory of everything different from itself. Instead, this individuality recalls the difference allowing every sign to promise what it can never fulfill: its meaning is another sign. Such a difference, such a promise, is a fact of language. Hölderlin's poetry returns to this fact, because it recalls thought from the memory that would engulf it as it sweeps toward the sea in "Andenken." Such an engulfing is nowhere more present than in those moments when the fig tree becomes the occasion for an intertextual reading whose aim is nothing less than the overcoming of the individuality of Hölderlin's thought. This aim is apparent wherever the classical or Christian tradition is evoked (just like the Garonne) and thereby established in the place marked by the fig tree. Such an intertextuality and the traditions it calls upon would forget by remembering too much, would forget what remains in Hölderlin's "Andenken," would mourn for a past, for the mantle of a past that Hölderlin explicitly describes in "Mnemosyne" as having been put down by the past. To seek this mantle is to err, since mourning, in seeking to possess what it does not own—the mantle of the past, not to mention the mantle of a Greece—as an act of memory belonging to the present, goes astray, seduced by the promise of a memory that the sea (as well as the fig tree) endlessly takes and gives. To remain, as the poet does, is to establish the free use of what the poet possesses apart from the past: to recall from memory the sign of thought. In such a sign Hölderlin not only secures art from the memory of Greece but also secures Greece from a memory it could never have recalled.

REFERENCE MATTER

Notes

PREFACE

1. Homer, *Odyssey*, trans. Richmond Lattimore (New York: Harper, 1965), 12.189–91.

2. Franz Kafka, "The Silence of the Sirens," in his *Kafka: The Complete Stories* (New York: Schocken, 1976), 431. Despite its reliance on a different account of this mythical incident, Kafka's emphasis on the silence of the Sirens opens a question not entertained by Horkheimer and Adorno in their readings of this incident from Homer's *Odyssey*. In "Odysseus, or Myth and Enlightenment" (in *Dialectic of Enlightenment* [New York: Herder and Herder, 1972]), silence is the effect of Odysseus's trick (58–59). The unfolding of this trick is compared to tragedy and the inevitable silencing that the mythic figure is made to succumb to in this form: "The epic says nothing of what happened to the Sirens once the ship had disappeared. In tragedy, however, it would have been their last hour, as it was for the Sphinx when Oedipus solved the riddle" (59). On this incident, and for two strong unpublished discussions of Horkheimer's and Adorno's reading of it, mention must be made of the papers delivered by Rebecca Comay and Albrecht Wellmer during a conference devoted to the *Dialectic of Enlightenment* ("From Enlightenment to Dialectics," New York City, February 26–28, 1998).

3. Homer, *Odyssey*, 12.192–94.

4. Letter 236, in *Friedrich Hölderlin: Essays and Letters on Theory*, trans. and ed. Thomas Pfau (Albany: SUNY Press, 1988), 150.

5. Ibid.

INTRODUCTION

1. Despite its emergence in Winckelmann, this relation will not find popular expression until Schiller's *Letters on the Aesthetic Education of Man*.

2. Frederic Jameson has provided the most significant of recent accounts of a dialectically pervasive political unconscious (see, for example, *The Political Unconsciousness* [Ithaca, N.Y.: Cornell University Press, 1980]), but it is Adorno who

first links this understanding directly to a consciousness of modernity, specifically, to that consciousness we now describe historically as modernism (see, for example, *Aesthetic Theory*, trans. Robert Hullot-Kentor [Minneapolis: University of Minnesota Press, 1997]).

3. The unrealizable aspect of this modernity—its fantastic character—has been adopted by Orrin Wang in his study of the relation of romanticism to postmodern theory (see *Fantastic Modernity* [Baltimore: Johns Hopkins University Press, 1996], 2–4). What remains to be seen is whether the characterization of modernity as a phantasmal historical category (in effect, a trope in Wang's book) can evince a critical position in relation to modernity, or whether such a fantasy is an integral part of a modernity that survives by luring its critics into this same fantasy. In the case of the latter, the postmodern is aptly named, because it has been programmed to repeat the founding gestures of modernity by its desire to separate itself from modernity. Modernity is not excluded from its own modernization; indeed, that is how it defines itself as a project. On this aspect of modernity, see also Jürgen Habermas, "Modernity versus Postmodernity" (*New German Critique* 22 [winter 1981]: 3–22)—an essay first presented as a lecture entitled: "Modernity—an Unfinished Project." For a recent example of how a lack of awareness of this incompletion as a general aspect of modernity remains essential to fostering a critique of modernity as a purely western concept, see Gregory Jusdanis, *Belated Modernity and Aesthetic Culture* (Albany: SUNY Press, 1991).

4. What we refer to as the "Western tradition" is a subject that has only been taught in American universities since just after World War I. See Lawrence W. Levine, *The Opening of the American Mind* (Boston: Beacon, 1996), 54–74. Although Levine sees the emergence of Western civilization courses as a response to the need to establish the values at stake for the United States in the First World War, it should not be overlooked that such a thing as a "Western tradition" begins its institutional life at the moment of modernism. In this historical conjunction, it is possible to see the extent to which modernity and tradition may possess a common critical project.

5. In this sense Jean-Luc Nancy speaks of myth when he writes, "The tradition is suspended at the very moment it fulfills itself. It is interrupted at that precise and familiar point where we know that it is all a myth." ("Myth Interrupted," in *The Inoperative Community*, trans. Peter Connor [Minneapolis: University of Minnesota Press, 1991], 52).

6. This critical relation does not, of course, exclude modernity from periodization. Indeed, this relation is itself a device of periodization since what precedes modernity is always known in terms of a period or era. On modernity and history, see Nietzsche's "On the Uses and Disadvantages of History for Life," in his *Untimely Meditations*, as well as de Man's "Literary History and Literary

Modernity," in his *Blindness and Insight*, 2d ed. (Minneapolis: University of Minnesota Press, 1983).

7. The former has received its most recent and extensive expression in Martin Bernal's *Black Athena* (Ithaca, N.Y.: Cornell University Press, 1987–). One of its earliest expressions may be found in the writings of Diodorus of Sicily. For an account of the relation between history and myth amongst the Greeks, see Paul Veyne, *Did the Greeks Believe in Their Myths?* (Chicago: University of Chicago Press, 1988).

8. Here, if one speaks of Greece as the first example of modernity, then one can only speak of the first extant example. This, in turn, raises the question of why Greece became, for us, such an example—an issue that will be taken up in Chapter 4 on Shelley's *Hellas* and Aeschylus's *Persians* with regard to why the latter is our first extant and complete Greek tragedy.

9. What more convincing evidence could be found than in the use of funeral orations as a means to articulate the historical significance of Greece? In such orations what survives the death of Greeks would be Greece. On this genre and its political and historical uses, see Nicole Loraux's admirable study, *The Invention of Athens: The Funeral Oration in the Classical City* (Cambridge: Harvard University Press, 1986).

10. On Greek texts and the Renaissance, see N. G. Wilson, *From Byzantium to Italy: Greek Studies in the Italian Renaissance* (Baltimore: Johns Hopkins University Press, 1993). Despite the rediscovery of Greek learning that helped fuel the Renaissance, this rediscovery is not accompanied by the development of a concept of culture in which politics and aesthetics are related as the basis of such a concept. With the development of such a concept in the eighteenth century, the stage is set for an extended interpretation of the significance of Greece to the Renaissance and subsequent history.

11. Excavations at Herculaneum began in 1738 and at Pompeii in 1748. The dissemination of what the Herculaneum excavations yielded began in the 1750s with accounts published in both Italy and France, some of which were translated quickly into English. More scientific accounts with engraved plates appeared after the founding of the Academia Ercolanese in 1755 (for this and other details, see B. H. Stern, *The Rise of Romantic Hellenism in English Literature 1732–1786* [1940; reprint, New York: Octagon Books, 1969], 10–11).

12. For an account of Winckelmann's reception, see Henry Hatfield's still useful study *Winckelmann and his German Critics 1755–1781*, Columbia University Germanic Studies, no. 15 (New York: Columbia University Press, 1943). As Hatfield details, the academic reception of Winckelmann's work did not always follow its popularity, yet even when critical, this reception does not dispute the significance attributed to antiquity.

13. On the authenticity of classical art in the mid- to late eighteenth century, see Alex Potts's "Greek Sculpture and Roman Copies I: Anton Raphael Mengs and the Eighteenth Century," *Journal of the Warburg and Cortauld Institutes* 43 (1980): 150–73.

14. An early example of this can be found in Matthew Arnold's call for criticism to pursue "a disinterested endeavour to learn and propagate the best that is known and thought in the world" (*Selected Criticism,* ed. Christopher Ricks [New York: Signet, 1972], 115). If the situation of criticism in the late nineteenth century is taken into account (in particular, the insularity of British literary criticism vis-à-vis Europe), then within its limitations Arnold's appeal reflects the critical situation of the late twentieth century. Arnold's call is, however, accompanied by a vision in which the culture of Europe is given a political mission: "the criticism which alone can much help us for the future . . . is a criticism which regards Europe as being, for intellectual and spiritual purposes, one great confederation, bound to a joint action and working to a common result; and whose members have, for their proper outfit, a knowledge of Greek, Roman, and Eastern antiquity, and of one another" (115). In these words, Arnold envisages a history in the form of the future of Europe, as the embodiment of a cultural development to be produced by criticism. In the most modern version of this vision, Europe must now become part of a larger confederation as our understanding of culture once again becomes the site of history, the history of the future.

15. The crisis of humanism in which the human subject confesses an inability to ground its centrality to the world can be read within the academic disciplines that form the modern history of the humanities. More than any other division of knowledge, the humanities has invested in the inquirer as the subject and ground of its inquiries. Once this investment becomes constitutive of the humanities as it has in contemporary thought and critical writing (of which the current penchant for memoir is an effect) a self-induced sense of crisis is produced. The significance of this sense of crisis lies, not so much in the promise of a new era no longer predicated on the human subject, but rather in its ability to prolong the centrality of this subject in the face of its own deconstruction. In this regard, when all is said and done, the human subject is in crisis as it becomes the human subject who now grounds its humanism in this sense of crisis. Suffice it to add that our ability to experience this crisis is a direct effect of our belief that the traditional guiding assumption of humanism remains in force even when no longer tenable. On the meaning and fate of humanism in the twentieth century, see Martin Heidegger's "Letter on Humanism," in his *Basic Writings,* ed. and trans. David Farrell Krell (New York: Harper, 1977), 189–242; and Gianni Vattimo's "The Crisis of Humanism," in his *The End of Modernity,* trans. Jon R. Snyder (Baltimore: Johns Hopkins University Press, 1988).

16. Gotthold Ephraim Lessing, *Laocoön*, trans. E. Allen McCormick (Baltimore: Johns Hopkins University Press, 1984), 138–57.

17. Levin's study is actually the senior thesis he wrote at Bowdoin College; it was subsequently published by Harvard University Press in 1931. Prior to Levin, mention should be made of Louis Bertrand's earlier study, *La fin du classicisme et le retour à l'antique dans la seconde moitié du XVIIIme siècle* (1897; reprint, Paris: Hachette, 1971). The 1930s and early 1940s witnessed the emergence of Hellenism as a subject of academic literary discourse. In addition to Levin's study, this period saw the publication of what became two of its canonical critical texts, E. M. Butler's *The Tyranny of Greece over Germany* (Cambridge: Cambridge University Press, 1935); and B. H. Stern's *The Rise of Romantic Hellenism in English Romantic Literature 1732–1786* (1940; reprint, New York: Octagon, 1969). Despite their historical proximity the interpretation of Hellenism pursued by these books remains quite distinct. In the preface to the 1958 American edition of her book, Butler recalls Nazi Germany of the 1930s (in particular the listing of her book on the Nazi Index) and then traces the misreading of myth that founds the tyrannical ideal in which an era as abhorrent as that of Nazi Germany seeks an aesthetic justification for its assault on history. As Butler notes, the myth of Hellenism is the site of a danger that does not necessarily have to take the form of a return to Greece. Stern makes no such historical claims for his study; indeed, his book is directed more toward establishing an origin for a British romantic Hellenism that remained independent of continental influence and independent of political significance. Not until the 1980s is there a significant return to publication on romantic Hellenism, beginning with Timothy Webb's anthology, *English Romantic Hellenism 1700–1824* (Manchester: Manchester University Press, 1982). Removed from the context of Europe in the 1930s, this return did not, at least initially, emphasize the political consequences of Hellenism. But, with the exception of Reinhold Bichler's *"Hellenismus." Geschichte und Problematik eines Epochenbegriffs* (Darmstadt: Wissenschaftliche Buchgesellschaft, 1983), it has been content to view Hellenism either as an historically limited thematic presence within the literature of the period (celebrating, of course, a mythical Greece) or as a phenomenon that produced a copious travel literature. In addition to Webb and Bichler, other publications from this period include: David Constantine's *Early Greek Travelers and the Hellenic Ideal* (Cambridge: Cambridge University Press, 1984); G. W. Clarke's *Rediscovering Hellenism: The Hellenic Inheritance and the English Imagination* (Cambridge: Cambridge University Press, 1989); Seymour Howard's *Antiquity Restored: Essays on the Afterlife of the Antique* (Vienna: IRSA, 1990); Olga Augustinos's *French Odysseys: Greece in French Travel Literature from the Renaissance to the Romantic Era* (Baltimore: Johns Hopkins University Press, 1994); and, most recently, Louis A. Ruprecht's *Afterwords: Hellenism, Modernism, and*

the Myth of Decadence (Albany: SUNY Press, 1996). This later period has also seen the publication of studies focusing on the relation of particular authors to Hellenism, notably, Martin Aske's *Keats and Hellenism: an Essay* (Cambridge: Cambridge University Press, 1985). More recently, Jennifer Wallace's *Shelley and Greece: Rethinking Romantic Hellenism* (London: Macmillan, 1997) provides an example of a serious attempt to come to terms with the legacy of Hellenism as she attempts a rereading of Shelley's Hellenism from a perspective in which the ideologies of our critical modernity are much in evidence.

18. While such a difficulty allows criticism to have a history (in the form of recording its attempts to sustain a ground for judgment), the mere existence of such a history does not itself constitute in any way an account of judgment. In such a case, criticism has still to confront Kant's confession that the aesthetic idea is the best we can do when it comes to a ground for judgment. That Kant must turn to the aesthetic as a means of accounting for judgment should not be lost on modern criticism and its tendency to criticize the aesthetic as a turning away from the historical world it cherishes so dearly. Here, the price modern criticism pays for its insight is an amnesic response to its own history. A paraphrase of Marx is only too appropriate in this context: material history has become the opium of our critical modernity.

19. How we have defined the present era is also a symptom of this. As postmoderns we are still defined by reference to what we would refuse as the image of our age. Yet, in an age when crisis of one thing or another abounds, we are merely perpetuating the crisis that modernity uses to announce its arrival. In this case, it would be more accurate to speak not of the crisis of modernity but of its crises. This is why modernity can be viewed as being already postmodern: it established a crisis it could only refuse if a sense of modernity is to be preserved. And, when modernity enters into crisis with itself, it perpetuates itself in the name of historical progress: postmodernism.

20. To consider Winckelmann's history as a model for an aesthetic form of history should not be confused with the aestheticization of history from which Alex Potts wishes to keep Winckelmann separate. In making this distinction, Potts turns Winckelmann's history into a "map" and, in so doing, downplays the role of the aesthetic as a mode of perceiving "a larger history" (*Flesh and the Ideal* [New Haven, Conn.: Yale University Press, 1994], 35).

21. René Wellek gives a rather different account of the origin of literary history, tracing its first true example to Thomas Warton's *History of English Poetry* (1774–81). Wellek judges Warton such an example; he argues that Warton represents the first attempt to write a systematic account of English poetry from the conquest to revolution of 1688. (René Wellek, *The Rise of English Literary History* [1941; reprint, New York: McGraw-Hill, 1966], 133 ff., 166 ff.) A systematic his-

tory of literature does not exist before Warton; however, Wellek and Warton, unlike Winckelmann, do not judge the advent of a systematic account of art according to the moment when the aesthetic becomes both the subject and medium of artistic history. From this step modern literary history derives a significance for the task it has set itself: it inaugurates the possibility of its own theorization, a possibility most fully realized within German romanticism through the writings of Freidrich Schlegel.

22. At the beginning of his incisive essay, "Anacoluthon: On Cultural Studies" (*Modern Language Notes* 112 (1997): 366–84), Timothy Bahti remarks, "To study cultural studies seems to risk entering a hall of mirrors—a place familiar, but no less uncanny—where the object of study and the method become images of one another." Placed in this context, cultural studies may be the best witness to the dilemma no modernity can escape.

23. Significantly, the relation of academic study to these questions arises within romanticism for the first time most notably in Fichte's *Some Lectures Concerning the Scholar's Vocation*, trans. Daniel Breazeale, in *Early Philosophical Lectures* (1794; reprint, Ithaca, N.Y.: Cornell University Press, 1988); and Schelling's *On University Studies*, trans. E. S. Morgan; ed. Norbert Guterman (1802; reprint, Athens: Ohio University Press, 1966).

24. As Henry Hatfield recalls in his study of Winckelmann, the teaching of Greek in the German university curriculum was no longer confined to the study of the New Testament, but rather became a subject of historical interest in its own right only in the years following publication of Winckelmann's work. This historical footnote underlines the larger question from which this study proceeds: Why does the literature and language of classical Greece become a subject within the university curriculum only after the development of aesthetics as a branch of human knowledge in the eighteenth century? Indeed, what is there in Winckelmann's account of ancient art that could foster not only a return to its literature and language but also would eventually lead to the establishment of classics and philology as academic disciplines? (See Hatfield, *Winckelmann and his German Critics 1755–1781*, 3–4). On Winckelmann's importance to the development of archaeology, see Ulrich von Wilamowitz-Moellendorff, *Geschichtede Philologie* (Berlin: Teubner, 1921), 96–97.

25. This need for a paradigm is recognized at the very beginning of a discourse on the political within the West. In Plato's *Statesman*, the possibility of obtaining an adequate definition of what a paradigm is, is taken up as a step that necessarily precedes any definition of the politician. Here one can observe the centrality of paradigms to the articulation of political thought at its very inception.

26. The principal documents of this debate are A. O. Lovejoy's "On the Discrimination of Romanticisms" (1924) and "The Meaning of Romanticism for the

Historian of Ideas" (1941); René Wellek's "The Concept of Romanticism in Literary History" (1949) and "Romanticism Re-examined" (1963); and Morse Peckham's "Toward a Theory of Romanticism" (1951). The continuation of this debate may also be read in works such as McGann's *The Romantic Ideology,* which continues this debate about the definition of romanticism while attempting to bring it to an ideological conclusion. For McGann's own account of the relation of *The Romantic Ideology* to Wellek's articles, see "Rethinking Romanticism," *ELH* 59 (1992): 735–54.

27. Need one add that it is only during the romantic period that the critical notion of a literary period comes into currency?

CHAPTER I

1. For a full account of the fortunes of antiquity up to the beginning of the eighteenth century, see the first two volumes of the still-useful history written by J. E. Sandys, *A History of Classical Scholarship,* 3 vols. (London: Cambridge University Press, 1908). On the transmission of Greek learning through the Italian Renaissance, see N. G. Wilson's *From Byzantium to Italy: Greek Studies in the Italian Renaissance* (Baltimore: Johns Hopkins University Press, 1993).

2. This persistence is documented by Richard Jenkyns in *The Victorians and Ancient Greece* (Cambridge: Harvard University Press, 1980); and by Frank M. Turner in *Greek Heritage in Victorian Britain* (New Haven, Conn.: Yale University Press, 1981).

3. Winckelmann was already faulted in 1766 by Lessing for wrongly dating certain works of Greek art and therefore wrongly assigning them within his periodization of the development of art. See *Laocoön: An Essay on the Limits of Painting and Poetry,* trans. E. Allen McCormick [Baltimore: Johns Hopkins University Press, 1984], 138–57) for the first criticism of Winckelmann's dating (as well as other inaccuracies). These errors did not affect acceptance of the basic historical structure of his account of art; they only affected how that structure had been represented.

4. In this respect, cultural study extends the project of interdisciplinary study to its widest possible reach. On the difficulties produced by this goal, see Janet Wolf, "Excess and Inhibition: Interdisciplinarity in the Study of Art," in *Cultural Studies,* ed. Laurence Grossberg, Cary Nelson, and Paula Treichler (New York: Routledge, 1992), 706–18.

5. To the extent that this concept of culture "keeps alive . . . the possibility of a unified mode of being," it is open, as Geoffrey Hartman states in a continuation of this remark, to adoption by the much less benign tendencies of ethnic politics. See *The Fateful Question of Culture* (New York: Columbia University Press, 1997), 127.

6. Lamentably, the only accounting so far undertaken has been in the form of a parody, namely, Alan Sokal's "Transgressing the Boundaries: Toward a Transformative Hermeneutics of Quantum Gravity" (*Social Text* 46–47 [1996]: 217–52). If Sokal's article is to have any significance beyond that of a hoax, then it lies in the article's appropriation of the generic character of modern criticism. Only in a field where generic characteristics have come to define methodology and thought could such a parody be published as an example of thought and methodology. Given this situation, Sokal's article inadvertently poses another question, a question concerning the difficulties that arise once judgment is no longer a mimetic exercise seeking to confirm a conceptual language whose rationale, as Nietzsche has already observed, cannot be remembered. (On the constitutive role of forgetting in the process of conceptualization, see Friedrich Nietzsche, "On Truth and Lie in an Extra-Moral Sense," in *Friedrich Nietzsche on Rhetoric and Language*, ed. and trans. Sander L. Gilman, Carole Blair, and David J. Parent [New York: Oxford University Press, 1989], 246–57.)

7. Although Winckelmann is not the only example of the attempt to negotiate this relation in the eighteenth century—Diderot's writings on art also reflect a concern with this relation—Winckelmann is alone in developing this relation into a systematic historical account of culture in general.

8. In his study of Winckelmann, Alex Potts distinguishes between "what we might call today an aestheticization of history" and making the aesthetic a source of historical knowledge (*Flesh and the Ideal*, [New Haven, Conn.: Yale University Press, 1994], 35). Potts's distinction is made in order to preserve a difference between the political and the aesthetic, a distinction Winckelmann also needs in order to ensure that the aesthetic represents something other than the merely beautiful. This commitment to a political dimension underlines a complicity between the aesthetic and the political: through the former the latter comes to have a history in the sense of possessing a significance other than the sheer singularity of an event or action. In remarks on Leopold von Ranke's *Französische Geschichte*, Hans Robert Jauss examined the early role of the aesthetic as the source of a model for historical understanding. See Jauss's "Geschichte der Kunst und Historie," in his *Literaturgeschichte als Provokation der Literaturwissenschaft* (Frankfurt am Main: Suhrkamp, 1974), 222–25.

9. Hegel, in the Introduction to his *Lectures on the Aesthetic*, commends Winckelmann as someone who, "in the field of art, opened up for the spirit a new organ and totally new modes of treatment." Although Hegel will go on to say that Winckelmann's view has had less influence on "the theory and philosophical knowledge of art" (*Hegel's Aesthetics*, 2 vols., trans. T. M. Knox [Oxford: Oxford University Press, 1975], 1:63), Hegel's own development of the aesthetic follows the pattern laid out in Winckelmann's *History of Ancient Art*. The differ-

ence being that Winckelmann did not develop his history as a dialectical movement of spirit, that is, as a mode of appearance for philosophic thought. This distinction determines Hegel's assessment of Winckelmann's influence.

10. See Potts, *Flesh and the Ideal*, 54–56.

11. Mention has already been made in the Introduction to Nicole Loraux's
study of the Greek funeral oration and its role in establishing the state through
the individual (whose image is nowhere better represented than by a corpse).
Here, it would be suggestive to read Winckelmann's invention of Greece as an
extended example of this genre. The difference being that Winckelmann laid
the groundwork for transforming this genre into what we now recognize as the
humanities.

12. On these works in Winckelmann, see Potts, *Flesh and the Ideal*, 38, 60–64;
and, "Greek Sculpture and Roman Copies I: Anton Raphael Mengs and the
Eighteenth Century," *Journal of the Warburg and Cortauld Institutes* 43 (1980):
150–73.

13. The text cited here is from the first edition of Winckelmann's *Geschichte
der Kunst des Altertums* (Vienna: Phaidon, 1934), 9. Unless otherwise indicated,
all citations of this text are to this edition. Subsequent references will be given
parenthetically and will include the short title, *Geschichte*; page reference to the
German text is followed by reference to where the cited passages may be found
in the only complete English translation, which dates from the 1840s. This translation (*History of Ancient Art*, 4 vols., trans. G. Henry Lodge [reprint, New York:
Ungar, 1968]) includes material added to Winckelmann's 1764 text. Prior to the
appearance of the *History of Ancient Art* in English, his earlier work, *Reflections
on the Imitation of Greek Works in Painting and Sculpture* (1755), had appeared in
London in Henry Fuseli's translation in 1765. All translations from both of these
works are my own.

14. Although a pedagogical ambition is more explicit in *Lehrgebäude* than in
System, both share a scientific character particularly in their desire to have their
representations regarded as descriptions of what is. In this respect, one can speak
of a systematic intention in Winckelmann, even if this does not yet approach the
understanding of systematicity we inherit from German Idealism.

15. In typography *cliché* names a group of frequently recurring letters, such as
"th" in English, which are available as a unit rather than having to be composed
of two letters when type is being set. From this origin, one can easily perceive its
extension to the plate from which multiple copies may be produced. The rhetorical figure of the cliché remains true to this history since, as a figure, one is dealing with a reproducible pattern of words, which in this case derives its meaning
from its repetitiousness.

16. In this respect, Winckelmann is already developing a tendency that would

dominate the philosophically oriented aesthetics of the romantic period. The first full critical account of this tendency within romanticism is provided by Walter Benjamin in his dissertation *Der Begriff der Kunstkritik in der deutschen Romantik* (1920), now translated in *Selected Writings*, ed. Marcus Bullock and Michael W. Jennings (Cambridge: Harvard University Press, 1996), 116–200. Subsequent accounts of the systematicity present in romantic thought and aesthetics may be found in Phillipe Lacoue-Labarthe and Jean-Luc Nancy, *The Literary Absolute* (Albany: SUNY Press, 1988); and Jean-Marie Schaeffer, *L'art de l'âge moderne* (Paris: Gallimard, 1992). See also Heidegger's reflection on systematicity in this period in *Schelling's Treatise on the Essence of Human Freedom*, trans. Joan Stambaugh (Athens: Ohio University Press, 1985), 42–61.

17. Here, Winckelmann's *History of Ancient Art* already establishes the pattern Hegel will follow in his *Lectures on the Aesthetic* when he describes the end of art as the moment in which art no longer continues as a representation of spirit (this being the moment when art, in the medium of language, gives up its aesthetic purpose and becomes what Hegel describes as the prose of thought). The difference between Hegel and Winckelmann lies in this development of the medium of art: in Winckelmann an account of the historical persistence of art after its downfall is expressed, whereas in Hegel art is subsumed into a philosophical-historical project that would determine all social, aesthetic, and political history with regard to the development of spirit (see note 16 above). Since Hegel's pronouncement in the Introduction to his *Lectures on the Aesthetic*, the end of art has become an inescapable motif in the history of the aesthetic. The recurrence of this motif in various guises during the twentieth century, notably in the work of Benjamin, Adorno, Marcuse, and, most lately, Vattimo, indicates the necessity of its presence whenever a significant form of art appropriate to our modernity is being described. Through its insistence on the persistence of art enabled by changes in the perception of what art is and what function it serves, this recurrence expresses a resistance to the Hegelian subjugation of art to a philosophy based on the development of the spirit. This resistance frequently appeals to technological developments in order to account for a fundamental change in the nature of art and, in particular, its adoption of the rise of electronic media and its cultivation of a mass market as the unequivocal sign of such a change. Yet, the end result is an art that has merely extended its reach by conferring aesthetic significance on objects and media previously regarded as inartistic. If this is modernity's best defense against Hegel's determination of the aesthetic, then modernity has made little advance beyond what Winckelmann founds as the history of art. Indeed, it has merely transformed the moment of failure of high art into the advent of mass art, thereby preserving the original purpose of art as the historical medium in which social, political, and cultural changes may be read. Another Athens will arise, electroni-

cally. In the end, it is uncertain whether such a change in the form of art is really that different from the development Hegel describes, particularly if we regard spirit as the *techne* of art and philosophers such as Hegel as one more figure seeking a technological resolution of art. Of the twentieth-century figures mentioned above, Vattimo has elaborated to the fullest extent a modernity of art in which the continued perception of the decline of art becomes our only means to experience an aesthetic that would no longer fall within the metaphysically determined history so present in Winckelmann and Hegel. In this sense, what Vattimo envisages through the decline of art (in effect, an aesthetics of decline and failure) is, in his words, "an announcement of an epoch of Being in which—in the perspective of an 'ontology of decline'—thought may open itself up to the only partially negative and 'fallen' meaning . . . which the experience of aestheticity has acquired in the era of mechanical reproduction and mass culture" ("The Death or Decline of Art," in *The End of Modernity*, trans. Jon R. Snyder [Baltimore: Johns Hopkins University Press, 1988], 64). For Vattimo, only in its downfall can art give to thought an understanding of Being; as a result art must be continually preserved in its decline but must never actually die if this understanding is to be accessible. This state of affairs produces an art that still belongs to the era of a traditional philosophic aesthetic (since it is such an aesthetic that is in decline), but through this aesthetic another understanding of Being different from the one that gives rise to traditional aesthetics is to be perceived. By refusing to relinquish traditional aesthetics Vattimo avoids the trap into which the assertion of modernity frequently falls. At the same time, this refusal runs the risk of being no more than a radical version of traditional aesthetics in which the essence of art, its relation to Being, can only be thought as a function of its decline. However radical such a thought is, it must still remain an effect of the metaphysics it *would* overcome.

18. Even though Winckelmann's *History of Ancient Art* does refer to at least one example of art that is originally Greek, the intent of this reference is to establish a periodization of art through which the essence of art may be systematically presented. This development of art through different stages requires a systematic account so that those surviving examples, whether Greek or presumed so, may be given a place of historical significance.

19. Although the use of *Umkreis* to define *Figur* represents a striving after a neutral description devoid of any coloring, there can be no neutral figure here since the outline described by *Umkreis* is indistinguishable from shape or form in the sense of *Figur* or *Gestalt*. Winckelmann's distinction depends on there being different degrees of representation within representation: the aesthetic can be more or less aesthetic.

20. While the section dealing with the origin of art in general speaks of the last stage of art in terms of *Überflüssig*, the discussion of Greek art describes this de-

cline as an age of mechanical art (*Geschichte*, 129; *History*, 1.176). Such a view runs counter to Walter Benjamin's thesis in "The Work of Art in the Age of its Technical Reproducibility," unless this latter essay is read as the example of a modernity now limited to the repetition of its failure (to possess aura, for example).

21. In establishing such a form of judgment Winckelmann has already determined the internal structure of the discipline associated with his name, that is, art history. The division of this discipline between art historians and those who engage in the critical judgment of art cannot be avoided when the former see no need for the latter when history already performs the latter. A similar relation between history and judgment can be discerned in the development of modern literary study as it reforms itself after the event of deconstruction.

22. If the canonical account of romanticism is accepted here, then the modern era is ushered in by the refusal of a literary and artistic past defined by mimesis. Later chapters will discuss how romanticism—and, above all, the romanticism that took up the Hellenic—is not as naive as the critical paradigms produced in its name, but, in fact, undertakes a reflection upon these paradigms and their relation to politics, judgment, ideology, and the aesthetic.

23. Winckelmann, *Reflections on the Imitation of Greek Works in Painting and Sculpture* (La Salle, Ill.: Open Court, 1987), 5. Subsequent references to this edition of Winckelmann's text will be given parenthetically. For an account of the problematic role of Renaissance art within the historical division of antiquity and modernity adopted by Winckelmann in this text, see Michael Fried, "Antiquity Now: Reading Winckelmann on Imitation," *October* 37 (1986): 87–97.

24. E. M. Butler, *The Tyranny of Greece over Germany* (1935; reprint, Boston: Beacon, 1958).

25. In the case of Kleist this has been recognized by what critics refer to as his "Kant crisis." A full account of Kleist's relation to Kant has been given by Ludwig Muth in his *Kleist und Kant* (Cologne: Kölner Universtäts-Verlag, 1957). Despite the exhaustive treatment Muth gives this topic and despite his observation that for every interpretation of Kleist a different meaning is given to the "Kant crisis" (16), why the idea of such a crisis has so great an appeal for Kleist criticism still awaits interpretation. The event of this crisis may have less to do with Kleist than with the relation of modern criticism to Kant. An initial step in this direction has been made by Andrzej Warminski, who locates Kleist's Kant crisis in a crisis of reading (see "A Question of an Other Order: Deflections of the Straight Man," *Diacritics* 9 [1979]: 76–77).

26. For an account of romanticism as the moment in which crisis is produced as part of a critical project, see Lacoue-Labarthe and Nancy, *The Literary Absolute*, 29ff. Another account of the response to such a crisis may be found in Schaeffer's *L'art de l'âge moderne*.

27. Eagleton may be singled out in this respect, because much of his work is animated by an insistent critique of the aesthetic. See his *Ideology of the Aesthetic* (Oxford, Eng.: Blackwell, 1900). Eagleton's work does raise the question of what is at stake in the determination of the aesthetic as ideology. If the stake is political and historical understanding as a source of critical judgment, then Eagleton argues not for the cure but for only one more symptom of the critical crisis inaugurated by Kant's *Critique of Judgment.* By conflating the aesthetic and the ideological one merely repeats Kant's own solution to the antinomy of judgment. In a vein not so different from Eagleton's, Ian Hunter, in his essay "Aesthetic and Cultural Studies" (*Cultural Studies*, ed. Grossberg, Nelson, and Treichler, 347–72) argues for a project of "politicizing aesthetics" so that it too may submit to the force of the political, economic, and popular realms that traverse the field of cultural studies.

28. Winckelmann refers to this tradition when, in support of his own argument, he cites Polybius as saying that "Climate shapes the morals, the form, and the complexion of a people" (*Geschichte*, 35; *History*, 1.52).

29. The pursuit of this question requires a development beyond the scope of this context, even though much of what can be said here can be taken as preparing a path through the complications that such a question involves.

30. This is why, in Winckelmann, art does not immediately end with the loss of freedom. When Winckelmann states, "The beautiful style of Greek art continued to flourish a long time after Alexander the Great in different artists of renown and this can be inferred from works in marble . . . and likewise in coins" (*Geschichte*, 225; *History*, 2.142), he defines a period in which the style continues but no longer acts as an expression of what fostered that style. Alex Potts makes reference to this asynchrony as a displacement (*Flesh and the Ideal*, 57–60). What Potts views as displacement becomes the sign of "an incipient rupture" that Winckelmann "plays out, almost unconsciously" in "the idea of a utopian fusion between great art and political freedom" (57). The occurrence of such a rupture contradicts, of course, such utopian fusions. But we also need to ask the question of whether Winckelmann's understanding of history and the aesthetic does not require such ruptures and whether the failing associated with such moments of rupture (of which modernity would be a telling example) is not an intrinsic part of the history he articulates, rather than (and here Potts reveals a significant hesitancy when he writes "almost") its unconscious contradiction.

31. Even when Winckelmann writes, "Finally, at the time when the highest degree of refinement and freedom appears in Greece, art also became freer and nobler" (*Geschichte*, 216; *History*, 2.130), such separation can be discerned in the use of a superlative for the historical condition and a comparative for the aesthetic.

32. The congruence between Winckelmann's description of this moment and

a modern tendency, after Foucault, to view the development of history according to ruptures indicates a necessity within historical argument, rather than a necessarily historical fact, is actually being described.

33. What prevented the Egyptians and the Etruscans from achieving the ideal Winckelmann sees in the Greeks was in the end the unsuitability of their bodies for the highest art. In his discussion of Egyptian art, Winckelmann mentions the form of the Egyptian body as the first liability: "The Egyptians have not moved far from their earliest style of art. This same style could not easily climb to the height it acquired amongst the Greeks. The cause may be sought partly in the formation of their bodies, partly in their mode of thought, and not less in their customs and laws especially their religious customs and laws, and also in the esteem and knowledge of their artists" (*Geschichte*, 46; *History*, 1.63). The emphasis that the initial placing gives to the physical body is made explicit in the sentence that opens the actual discussion of Egyptian art: "The first of the causes of the specific character of the art of the Egyptians lies in their formation; it did not possess those excellences that could stimulate the artist by ideas of high beauty" (*Geschichte*, 46; *History*, 1.63).

34. Although Winckelmann only refers to dramatic works ("theatralischen Stücke"), his description of these works as proceeding through a downfall to their end clearly indicates that he is referring to tragedy.

35. The role of tragedy as an example cannot be confined to history, but rather appears, for example, as a means of defining, in Plato's *Laws*, the political state and, in particular, the relation of the individual to the law. The pervasiveness of tragedy as an example suggests that the aesthetic performs the task of reconciling the questions and difficulties that arise within the separate discourses of history and politics—a role that will be read in Chapter 3, which is devoted to Schelling.

36. To argue for a nonteleological model of history is to ignore the reason why a discourse such as history exists at all. As an organization of past events according to a narrative that reveals their significance, history displays its commitment to an end (and an existence) that will produce knowledge. In this case, to argue that history may be understood according to a nonteleological model is tantamount to saying that there is no reference, no meaning, and so on. If this were really the case, then no one could ever have argued for a nonteleological model of history in the first place, except as an example of bad faith.

37. By coming nearer to the art of the Egyptians, it does not become the art of Egypt once again, but rather it becomes in outline form the medium in which a nation may again fail to preserve itself. If this were not the case, then the fate of all art is to become Egyptian, which, according to Winckelmann's remarks on Egyptian art, is to be unable to develop the highest beauty he associates with Greek art.

38. Such an emphasis is repeated in phrases that turn the name Athens into a figure for what had flourished there: "Art, whose fate had always been the same as that of Athens" (*Geschichte*, 319; *History*, 2.212).

39. See, for example, Adorno's "Lyric Poetry and Society," trans. Bruce Mayo, *Telos* 20 (1974): 56–71. In his *Aesthetic Theory*, Adorno will also define the history of the aesthetic in terms of a failure from which the future social and political significance of art may be traced. It is surely not an accident that the moment at which historical consciousness of this failure occurs is modernism (see Adorno, *Aesthetic Theory*, trans. Robert Hullot-Kentor [Minneapolis: University of Minnesota Press, 1997], 338–40).

CHAPTER 2

1. Aske sees Keats's relation to Greece in a way that transforms the terms of Winckelmann's understanding of the inimitability of Greek art: "Keats appeals to antiquity as a supreme fiction, that is, an ideal space of possibility whose imaginative rehabilitation might guarantee the authority of modern poetry," and "Keats's Hellenism . . . can be read . . . as the site of a problem which has to do with the modern poet's vocation, with the poet's search for a viable identity at a moment in history . . . which the poet himself knows to be belated" (*Keats and Hellenism* [Cambridge: Cambridge University Press, 1985], 1, 3). Like Winckelmann's Greeks, a supreme fiction must be considered inimitable if it is to be at all supreme. In this respect, and in his insistence on the problem such inimitability poses for modernity, Aske's reading of Keats's Hellenism adheres closely to both the historical paradigm fostered by Winckelmann and the aesthetic source of that paradigm.

2. Winckelmann's *History of Ancient Art* makes clear that from this failure the possibility of historical periodization arises, but it does so in such a way as to allow the end of art to be experienced as a repeatable historical phenomenon. According to this history, one era's modernity is condemned to assert itself in the place of a preceding assertion of modernity. (*History of Ancient Art*, 4 vols., trans. G. Henry Lodge [reprint, New York: Ungar, 1968].)

3. A topos of not only literary history but also those prefatory justifications of literary movements that inform such a history can be discerned in this pattern. Each affirms the aesthetic mode of the past as having come to an end, of having deteriorated into the imitation of its formal properties, and each views the moment of modernity as a moment of revitalization in which the historical meaning of artistic production is discovered anew. The occurrence of a literary period such as modernism provides no exception to this history. Indeed, the emphasis on the formal properties of art as a means of distinguishing this period within literary history points to modernism as the moment when the means of determining a

history for art (giving it an end) defines the art that such a history is meant to record. By making the form, in which the end of a historical period of art is signaled, become the defining characteristic of all modern and all future art, modernism would effectively be the form in which literary history becomes the subject of art and literature. In modernism, literary history thinks itself in terms of the end through which it records the development of literature. This is why the period that follows modernism must be known as the postmodern if it is to be thought within such a history at all. Having made its own end the subject of literature and art, the only mode in which modernity can survive its downfall is by the continual reenactment of that downfall in the guise of a history that marks the end of all other histories.

4. While romanticism provides the first historical example of such a refusal in modern literary criticism, the paradigm at work within this example can hardly be restricted to romanticism, but rather finds itself repeated throughout the modern reading of the history of literature.

5. In this vein Marilyn Gaul describes the image of Greece as it emerges in the eighteenth century: "Greece was a counter-culture, an alternative to what we now call neo-classicism, the reason, order, decorum, and abstraction that dominated European thought during the early days of the eighteenth century" (*English Romanticism* [New York: W. W. Norton, 1988], 183). Now that the "counter-culture" of the eighteenth century can be attacked for its conservative reactionary tendencies, the founding gesture of such tendencies is being prepared once again.

6. Nowhere has this been more clearly shown during this century than in Adorno's *Aesthetic Theory* (trans. Robert Hullot-Kentor [Minneapolis: University of Minnesota Press, 1997]). On the use of this fall as a point of historical and philosophical reference in Hegel and Vattimo, see above Chapter 1, n. 17.

7. While such a mode of determination is given its most extensive and systematic development in Hegel, Spinoza provides the insight this development relies upon, namely, his statement, frequently cited by Hegel, "omnis determinatio est negatio." See, for instance, Hegel, *Geschichte der Philosophie*, in *Werke in zwanzig Bänden*, ed. Eva Moldenhauer and Karl Markus Michel (Frankfurt am Main: Suhrkamp, 1971), 20:164.

8. That this history is a philosophic one does not in any way free materialist and politically oriented histories from what such a philosophic history represents: history as the means of producing meaning remains the same whether that meaning is characterized as philosophical, political, or materialist.

9. McGann writes, "The Hegelian synthesis is a form of self-representation: it describes the idea of Hegel's philosophy and not Romantic art, nor even the Romantic ideology of art" (*The Romantic Ideology* [Chicago: University of Chicago Press, 1983], 47).

10. Ibid., 47. McGann's scare quotes around "pure" indicate some hesitation about the purity of Hegel's *Aesthetics* while at the same time asserting the necessity of this purity for the critical position McGann wishes to articulate.

11. In the Introduction to the *Lectures on Aesthetics*, Hegel refers to sound as the last external material of poetry and then states this last external characteristic is "in poetry no longer the feeling of sonority itself, but a *sign* that is meaningless by itself ['ein für sich bedeutungloses Zeichen']. . . . Sonority in this way becomes a *word* as a sound articulated in itself, the meaning of which is to indicate ideas and thoughts . . . at this highest stage art now transcends itself" (*Werke*, 13:122–23; translation mine).

12. McGann expresses this hope when he applauds the "method" of Heine as a method that "may be usefully examined if we wish to understand the limits of the Hegelian and Coleridgean models, and perhaps to go beyond them" (*Romantic Ideology*, 49). McGann's fixation with limiting Hegel and Coleridge already suggests that the problem McGann's critical stance does not want to face, at least in *The Romantic Ideology*, is the problem of limitation, of determination, of negation. Orrin Wang's reading of McGann's use of Heine has shown that even when one practices the textual and historical scholarship advocated by McGann in the wake of *The Romantic Ideology*, Heine is hardly an unproblematic source for establishing such limits (see Orrin Wang, *Fantastic Modernity* [Baltimore: Johns Hopkins University Press, 1996], 102–4). In his later reflection on *The Romantic Ideology*, McGann will speak of the need to recognize limitation but only in order to secure a freedom over and above such a limit. McGann writes, "As I see it, criticism should be seeking a dialectical philology that is not bound by the conceptual forms it studies and generates. The paradox of such a philosophy is that its freedom would be secured only when it accepts the historical limits of its own forms of thought. It is not bound by its theoretical forms because it holds itself open to the boundary conditions established by other conceptual forms." Here, a telling example of the rhetorical gesture underwrites McGann's critical project and the distinctions it wishes to uphold. This dialectical philology becomes historical through the paradox that such a philology is said to bring upon itself (McGann asserts, "when it accepts"). But the recognition this philology brings upon itself in one sentence (recognition of the historical limits of its form of thought) becomes in the next sentence a recognition of other conceptual forms. Where history is to be discovered here remains unclear unless it is recognized under the sign of a paradox or through yet more conceptualization.

13. In this way the aesthetic originates in Hegel with the symbolic. Even at the classical stage of its development, when the spirit has found a form most adequate to itself, the aesthetic still remains an external form to which the spirit is

related by adequation. Take away this difference and there is merely the abstraction of nature.

14. In this respect, the aesthetic is structurally the same as allegory, at least in Walter Benjamin's definition: it is constituted by the noncoincidence of itself with its object. See Benjamin, *Ursprung des deutschen Trauerspiels,* in *Gesammelte Schriften,* ed. Rolf Tiedemann and Hermann Schweppenhäuser, 7 Bände (Frankfurt am Main: Suhrkamp, 1974–1989), 1.1:403, 406.

15. In order to avoid this confusion Winckelmann's history adopts both a delay between the highest art and the moment of greatest freedom in Greece (the highest point occurring for Winckelmann under the reign of Alexander the Great) and a separation at the moment of its downfall. In the latter, history continues as the loss of freedom. At the same time, art's turn toward the imitation of itself is understood as a negative representation of this loss.

16. "Walter Benjamin," Introduction to *Illuminations,* ed. Hannah Arendt (New York: Schocken, 1969), 49.

17. Winckelmann, *Geschichte der Kunst des Altertums* (Vienna: Phaidon, 1934), 319; *History of Ancient Art,* 2.212.

18. The cultivation of a more journalistic mode of writing—as the recent tendency of academic critics to produce memoirs reflects—may be read as a response to this institutionalization of critical discourse. It could also be read as evidence of an anti-intellectualism growing out of this same institutionalization. Either way, the ability of literature to question the very activity to which it now plainly owes its existence (and has since the advent of romanticism) tends to get lost.

19. See Marjorie Levinson, *Keats's Life of Allegory: The Origins of a Style* (Oxford, Eng.: Blackwell, 1988). Although Levinson will try to establish Keats as a poet who maintains a dialogic, rather than a dialectic, relation to poetic tradition, this account of Keats is indebted to a resolutely dialectic method, which transforms the "pronounced badness of Keats's writing" (13) into its most important critical insight. Thus Levinson can conclude, "[the] contained badness of 'Chapman's Homer' constitutes its goodness" (15). Here, recognition of Keats's poetry as "bad" becomes the basis for making an issue of Keats's social class; this, in turn, becomes the basis for admitting historical and political significance into Keats's poetry. Already in the example of Levinson's reading of Keats, the difficulty as well as the precariousness latent in any decision about the historical and political significance of literature can be gauged from its reliance on an inherently negative moment.

20. Lest this remark be dismissed as merely the understanding of a reader of literature, the distinction it points to is made by the historian G. M. Trevelyan, who writes, "Unlike dates, periods are not facts. They are retrospective conceptions that we form about past events, useful to focus discussion, but very often

220   *Notes to Pages 65–70*

leading historical thought astray" (cited by Malcolm Bradbury and James Mc-
Farlane, *Modernism*, ed. Bradbury and McFarlane [Harmondsworth, Eng.: Pen-
guin, 1976], 19).

21. Two examples of this tradition, as Alex Potts points out, may be considered precedents for the systematic presentation of Winckelmann's *History of Ancient Art* (see Potts's *Flesh and the Ideal* [New Haven, Conn.: Yale University
Press, 1994], 72). This precedence indicates how, at the very beginning of our attempt to come to terms with the rhetorical dimension of our language, a systematizing tendency is already at work in the form of history. One of the last examples of this tradition and its ability to focus on issues of central significance
can be seen in the debate on inversion, which can be traced through Condillac
and Diderot during the first half of the eighteenth century.

22. See Kant, *Critique of Judgment*, trans. Werner Pluhar (Indianapolis, Ind.:
Hackett, 1987), §40. The necessity of an account of judgment has been little recognized within the project of critical interpretation despite the unrelenting practice of judgment within criticism. It would seem illogical to make judgments
about the ideology of certain poetic practices without at least accounting for a
nonideological form of judgment. Kant's *Third Critique* could be said to concern
itself with precisely this form of judgment, which it is unable to ground without
resorting to an aesthetic idea. Given the difficulty Kant faces in grounding judgment, it would be instructive to read the *Critique of Judgment* carefully before
rushing to pass ideological judgments on the aesthetic. (In passing, it should be
noted that McGann's *Romantic Ideology* provides no evidence that Kant's *Third
Critique*, one of the most important works in our critical and aesthetic traditions,
has been looked into, never mind read carefully. The omission is glaring when one
realizes we owe the first deduction of the necessity of an aesthetic idea to Kant.)

23. Byron's dismissal of Keats's poetry as an aestheticism that is sexually and
urologically inadequate may be read in a letter to John Murray, dated November
9, 1820.

24. For an account of the different sources that can be traced for Keats's urn,
see Ian Jack, *Keats and the Mirror of Art* (Oxford, Eng.: Clarendon, 1967), 214–24.

25. Aristotle, *Poetics*, 49a15.

26. See Hegel, *Ästhetik*, *Werke* 13:25.

27. Ibid., 13:123.

28. It is difficult to know whether one should attribute the critical tendency
to read this poem as an example of conventional Hellenism to the subtlety of
Keats's argument in this sonnet, or to criticism's unmitigated desire for something from which to disassociate itself. One notable and recent exception to this
tendency may be found in Forest Pyle, "Keats's Materialism," *Studies in Romanticism* 33 (1994): 76, n. 28.

29. Unless otherwise noted, the text established by Jack Stillinger in *John Keats: Complete Poems* (Cambridge, Eng.: Belknap, 1982) will be cited in all references to Keats's poetry.

30. While the drama of having Keats read Chapman in the "breach between the two parts of the sonnet" (*Keats's Life of Allegory*, 14) is a rhetorically significant assertion in Marjorie Levinson's reading of this poem, Keats's words give little credence to such a breach. Syntactically, there is no major break between the octet and the sestet, the latter following directly upon the former with the narrative and temporal conjunction "then." Through this conjunction, the sestet is marked as a reflection upon what has preceded.

31. See Charles and Mary Cowden Clarke, *Recollections of Writers* (1878) cited by John Barnard, *John Keats: The Complete Poems*, 546n. Lattimore's translation of this same passage is considerably more prosaic: "Now he flexed both knees / and his ponderous hands; his very heart was sick with salt water, / and all his flesh was swollen, and the sea water crusted stiffly / in his mouth and nostrils, and with a terrible weariness fallen / upon him he lay unable to breathe or speak in his weakness" (*The Odyssey of Homer*, trans. Richmond Lattimore [New York: Harper, 1965], 5.453–57).

32. The sense of "sur" in the word Keats uses to describe this response to silence should not be overlooked. This silence invites the idea that something should be placed over it as an account of what such silence represents. But as Keats's sonnet records, the translation of this silence into a text, such as Chapman's or even Keats's, does not escape the necessity of looking to which Cortez is brought.

33. The tendency to view these questions as if they were literally questions seeking knowledge about an urn goes hand in hand with the tendency to read this ode alongside a material simulacrum of the urn, which remains a distinct yet unresponsive subject, invisible yet there. Rather, our attention should turn to the role these questions play in creating such an urn. Such questions are not simply literal demands to know what is on the urn, but instead the means by which such a knowing is simultaneously produced and denied without us ever seeing the urn in the question. The questions perform a rhetorical function within the "Ode." This aspect of the ode's questions is in direct contrast to the lyrical significance they are said to represent when read as the utterance of a single poetic voice. Orrin Wang has recently called upon such a reading of the questions in his construction of a tension between public and individual spheres within the poem, in particular, its last lines (see *Fantastic Modernity*, 21–22). Since this tension is deduced from an aesthetic object, Wang's reading actually suggests the significance of Keats's "Ode" does not lie in a reflection on the museum and the social history of art collection and access. Rather, it can be located in a drawing

out of the central problem broached by Kant's *Critique of Judgment*, namely, the possibility of deriving a universal (collective) principle of judgment from individual acts of aesthetic judgment. In other words, the "Ode" and its questions do not simply replay "the options of the poet as cultural critic gazing on the urn" (19), but they afford a reflection on the role of those options in determining the questions asked by a cultural critic.

34. This aspect of these questions has been noted by both Susan Wolfson in *The Questioning Presence* (Princeton: Princeton University Press, 1986); and A. W. Phinney in "Keats in the Museum: Between Aesthetics and History" (*Journal of English and Germanic Philology* [1991]: 208–29). In both cases, however, these questions are reappropriated quickly into an aesthetics of subjectivity without pursuing how this poem examines a rhetoricity of knowledge within the form of the question. To emphasize a subjectivity here is not only to privilege ourselves as the poser of such questions in Keats's ode but also it is to preserve this poem within the long history of an ekphrastic tradition traceable to Greece. This tradition, as Simon Goldhill's essay indicates, arises by producing a self-awareness of interpretation (see "The Naive and the Knowing Eye: Ecphrasis and the Culture of Viewing in the Hellenistic World," in *Art and Text in Ancient Greek Culture*, ed. Simon Goldhill and Robin Osborne [Cambridge: Cambridge University Press, 1994], 197–223). By situating such an awareness within this ode, Keats has made it a subject for reflection, rather than the repetition of the subject before the poem. As a result, before appropriating such a response into the subjectivity of a viewer, the function of Keats's questions within the development of this ode must first be read.

35. Walter Benjamin, in a letter written to Martin Buber in July 1916, offers a definition of the political in language that points to the political as a theory of objective representation, of language and act. See *The Correspondence of Walter Benjamin 1910–1940*, trans. Manfred R. Jacobson and Evelyn M. Jacobson (Chicago: University of Chicago Press, 1994), 79–81.

36. I have used John Barnard's edition, *John Keats: The Complete Poems*, for these lines. This edition assumes that the last two lines of the poem are spoken by the urn, hence, the shift in address from "thou" (used by the poet to address the urn) and "Ye." To regard the "Ye" as the poet's address to the urn raises the question of why the urn has just been addressed as "thou." Even if the "Ye" is read as the poet's generalized address to the subsequent readers of the poem, the question developed in this reading does not change, because *the poem* directs our attention toward the necessity of the understanding performed in the voice of the urn.

37. The operation of this critique can be seen most clearly whenever the specter of a linguistic nihilism is raised and then overcome by asserting that if it is too nihilistic, then it must refer to something and therefore is not really ni-

hilistic. This argument is not recent; it originates with Plato's *Sophist* where it provides the Stranger with the means of defining sophistry. In Plato, at least, the dialectical method employed by such a critique is openly admitted.

38. Immanuel Kant, *Critique of Pure Reason*, trans. Norman Kemp Smith (London: Macmillan, 1982), 344, A366.

39. As stated in Chapter 1, within Winckelmann's presentation, the highest art (whose achievement is tied to the political fate of Athens) continues after the loss of freedom. The aesthetic is thus understood as the mode in which freedom persists as a quasi-historical phenomenon even after its downfall.

CHAPTER 3

1. Winckelmann's *Geschichte der Kunst des Altertums* (Vienna: Phaidon, 1934), 207; and *History of Ancient Art*, 4 vols., trans. G. Henry Lodge (reprint, New York: Ungar, 1968), 2.116. That tragedy is meant by Winckelmann's reference to dramatic works ("theatralischen Stücken") is clear from the five aspects he views as the basis of tragedy's five-act development, namely, "beginning, progress, position of height, decline, and end."

2. On the place of the potential and the possible in Aristotle's *Poetics*, see my "The Possibility of Literary History: Aristotle," in *Theory and the Evasion of History* (Baltimore: Johns Hopkins University Press, 1993), 1–36.

3. In his remarks on Greek tragedy from *The Philosophy of Art*, Schelling refers to his earlier work as follows: "This, as presented here as well as in my own *Philosophical Letters on Dogmatism and Criticism*, is the innermost spirit of Greek tragedy" (*The Philosophy of Art*, trans. Douglas W. Stott [Minneapolis: University of Minnesota Press, 1989], 254). Unlike Nietzsche's *The Birth of Tragedy*, Schelling's remarks on tragedy have generated little critical or interpretive attention even though Schelling is the first to shift tragedy away from an affective and into a properly philosophical aspect. Only Peter Szondi has recognized this watershed. See Szondi's brief remarks on Schelling's understanding of tragedy in his "The Notion of the Tragic in Schelling, Hölderlin and Hegel" (in *On Textual Understanding and Other Essays* [Minneapolis: University of Minnesota Press, 1986], 43–46). Only in the lectures of 1804–1805 does Schelling introduce the concept of indifference that he will emphasize as the ground of his account of freedom in 1809. Such an indifference does not figure in the remarks on tragedy present in the Tenth Letter even if its necessity is implied.

4. See, for example, Schelling's *System of Transcendental Idealism*, trans. Peter Heath (Charlottesville: University of Virginia Press, 1978), 229–33.

5. F. W. J. Schelling, *Philosophische Briefe über Dogmatismus und Kritizismus*, ed. Hans Michael Baumgardner et al. in *Historische-Kritische Ausgabe* (Stuttgart: Frommann, 1982), 1.3.47–112; quote found on page 106. References to this edi-

tion of Schelling's text will be given parenthetically in the text and will be to the page number only.

6. This elimination is offered as a solution to the antinomy of taste in §57 of the *Critique of Judgment*. Since judgments of taste make an appeal to universal assent, they lay claim to a universal principle even though such judgments are judgments of taste precisely because they do not follow any such principle. Kant needs to eliminate this contradiction in order to account for judgment according to a universal principle. But as Kant confesses here, if such an account were attained, then there would be no such thing as a judgment of taste and therefore nothing for the universal principle to account for. He writes, "It is absolutely impossible to provide a determinate, objective principle of taste that would allow us to guide, to test, and to prove its judgments, because then they would not be judgments of taste" (*Critique of Judgment*, trans. Werner S. Pluhar [Indianapolis, Ind.: Hackett, 1987], 213).

7. Martin Heidegger, *Schellings Abhandlungen über das Wesen der Menschlichen Freiheit (1809)* (Tübingen: Niemeyer, 1971), 54.

8. Heidegger spells out what this means in the realm of art in his "The Age of the World Picture" when he remarks, "A third equally essential phenomenon of the modern period lies in the event of art's moving into the purview of aesthetics. That means that the art work becomes the object of mere subjective experience ['Erlebnis'], and that consequently art is considered to be an expression of human life" (*The Question Concerning Technology and Other Essays*, trans. William Lovitt [New York: Harper, 1977], 116).

9. Heidegger, *Schellings*, 45.

10. In the first preface to the *Critique of Pure Reason*, Kant announces that self-knowledge will be the defining object of thought for himself and subsequent philosophy. He speaks of this work as "a call to reason to undertake anew the most difficult of all its tasks, namely, that of self-knowledge" (*Critique of Pure Reason*, trans. Norman Kemp Smith [London: Macmillan, 1982], 9). This call, as the history of philosophy confirms, is essentially Greek, because it is Socrates who first formulates this as the primary task of philosophy in the imperative Γνῶθι σεαυτόν. On this imperative in the romantic period, see David S. Ferris, "The Ghost of Aristotle (Coleridge)," in *Theory and the Evasion of History* (Baltimore: Johns Hopkins University Press, 1993), 37–134.

11. This is at work even at those moments when Greece is viewed as a model to which modernity aspires, because such an aspiration can only arise from the recognition of a past that one no longer can possess. Hellenism in its classic form preserves this unattainability of the past by desiring to imitate its inimitability. This is why Hellenism is less an expression of Greece than the determination of a modernity in which the past is always brought to its tragic, sacrificial completion.

12. Heidegger, *Schellings*, 45.

13. For Hegel's remark on the relation of Winckelmann's work to his own, see above, Chapter 1, n. 6. Since Winckelmann's history is primarily an account of Greek art, it would seem to be about an art and culture that have objective existences. This cannot be confuted, but Greek art and culture are only the particular forms in which Winckelmann's real subject occurs: "the essential, the interior of art."

14. In the same way that Kant's thing-in-itself is not purely a negation of knowledge. As Hegel asserts, this negation is already a knowable property of the thing-in-itself.

15. Schelling, *The Philosophy of Art*, 249.

16. What Schelling describes as freedom underwrites the sense of history elaborated by Frederic Jameson in *The Political Unconscious* when he asserts, "History is the experience of Necessity," and then goes on to say, "Necessity is the inexorable form of events" ([Ithaca, N.Y.: Cornell University Press, 1980], 132). In both cases, necessity is the means through which freedom is to be experienced (this history, for Jameson, is a history free from its "thematization or reification as a mere object of representation" [132]). On the formal and, therefore, aesthetic category Jameson must evoke here (and which Schelling already recognizes as essential to such an experience of freedom), see Samuel Weber, "Capitalizing History," in his *Institution and Interpretation* (Minneapolis: University of Minnesota Press, 1987), 49–54.

17. In this respect, Schelling's remark gives a more philosophical interpretation of Winckelmann's desire to write a history of art, one which would no longer be a history of individual artists.

18. Schelling, *The Philosophy of Art*, 107.

19. As this sentence implies, what is at stake in freedom is its experience and, above all where its aesthetic representation is concerned, the stake is the imitability of freedom. Here, the question Winckelmann broaches in relation to Greece (how its inimitability is to be imitated) can be seen as a formulation of the essential problem of freedom posed by art. On freedom and its experience, see Jean-Luc Nancy's superb reflection *The Experience of Freedom* (Stanford, Calif.: Stanford University Press, 1993), especially 205, n. 9, for remarks addressed specifically to the relation of art to freedom.

20. Schelling, *The Philosophy of Art*, 107.

21. Here, the "thou" address to the urn reveals an issue discussed above in reference to the question, "Who are these coming to the sacrifice?" The urn, as an example of singularity, is addressed as an individual, and yet it is made to speak on behalf of us all (the "ye" of the last two phrases).

22. In *The Philosophy of Art*, Schelling is also emphatic on this point: "This is

the most sublime idea and the greatest victory of freedom: voluntarily to bear the punishment for an unavoidable transgression in order to manifest his freedom precisely in the loss of that very same freedom, and to perish amid a declaration of free will" (254). Schelling's use of the word "perish" emphasizes the finality that must accompany the protagonist's acceptance of guilt.

CHAPTER 4

1. This is true historically speaking, although of late this play has received more attention. Prior to the significant critical discussions centered on this play during the 1980s is Earl Wasserman's *Shelley: A Critical Reading* (Baltimore: Johns Hopkins University Press, 1971); Carl Woodring's *Politics in English Romantic Poetry* (Cambridge: Harvard University Press, 1970); Jerome McGann's "The Secrets of an Elder Day: Shelley after *Hellas*," *Keats-Shelley Journal* 15 (1966): 25–41; and Timothy Webb's "The Greek Example," in his *Shelley: A Voice not Understood* (Manchester, Eng.: Manchester University Press, 1977), 191–227. Since 1980 there have been a number of articles, the best of which have tended to focus on the political questions posed by this play. See, for example, Constance Walker's "The Urn of Bitter Prophecy: Antithetical Patterns in Shelley's *Hellas*," *Keats-Shelley Review* 33 (1983): 36–48; Mark Kipperman's "History and Ideality: The Politics of Shelley's *Hellas*," *Studies in Romanticism* 30 (1991): 147–68; and Mark Kipperman's "Macropolitics of Utopia: Shelley's *Hellas* in Context," in *Macropolitics of Nineteenth-Century Literature: Nationalism, Exoticism, Imperialism*, ed. Jonathan Arac and Harriet Ritvo (Philadelphia: University of Pennsylvania Press, 1991), 86–101; and William Ulmer's "*Hellas* and the Historical Uncanny," *ELH* 58.3: 611–32. The most extended account of the relation of Shelley's *Hellas* to Aeschylus's *Persians* may be found in Michael Erkelenz's "Inspecting the Tragedy of Empire: Shelley's *Hellas* and Aeschylus's *Persians*," *Philological Quarterly* 76, no. 3 (1997): 313–37.

2. That the *Persians* is the earliest extant tragedy we possess may not be completely attributable to chance, since the survival of this drama relied upon its selection as a text for school reading. This occurred first toward the end of the Roman empire and then during the Byzantium empire. Such a choice indicates the exemplary status this play was already accorded as an historical and aesthetic document.

3. All references to Shelley's *Hellas* are to the text presented in *Shelley's Poetry and Prose*, ed. Donald H. Reiman and Sharon Powers (New York: W. W. Norton, 1977). Subsequent references to this edition will be given parenthetically (the text of the play will be referred to parenthetically by line numbers and the Preface by page number). One difference to be noted here between Shelley's play and Winckelmann is that Shelley's Chorus envisages a new Athens arising

in the place of the classical Athens, whereas Dresden is Winckelmann's chosen location.

4. As can be anticipated, Shelley's *Hellas* is an easy target for a critic such as Jerome McGann, who can summarize Shelley's intentions in this play under the banner of "ideas [that] are typical philhellenist illusions and, as such, were open to a political exploitation by Europe's imperialist powers" (*The Romantic Ideology* [Chicago: University of Chicago Press, 1983], 125). If the fact that this summary is based on the citation of two paragraphs from the Preface were not enough to raise suspicions about precisely what McGann reads whenever the discovery of ideology is at stake, then one can also turn to history (always the source of Mc-Gann's critical ambition) which, as Mark Kipperman's essay "History and Ideality," demonstrates is not on McGann's side in 1821 when he speaks of Shelley's exploitation by imperialist powers.

5. Shelley, *Hellas*, 408.

6. Implicit in this movement toward the historical is a renunciation of the reflection on judgment initiated by Kant. What could be more appealing than a source of critical judgment that would no longer require the need to exercise judgment? Here, the materiality of history hopes never to have to ask for the agreement of others, because the facticity of the real would be persuasion enough. Even here, do we not have to recognize that history, despite its origin in the factual occurrence of an event, is itself neither a fact nor an event? Like aesthetic judgment in Kant, history cannot refuse to make its claim for our agreement.

7. This does not mean that Shelley is making a hard and fast distinction between lyric and history, a distinction that leads easily to the overdetermined aestheticism of Emil Staiger's understanding of lyric, or sets up the dialectical recuperation of the political and social significance from this aestheticism in Adorno. See Emil Staiger, *Grundbegriffe der Poetik*, trans. as *Basic Concepts of Poetics*, trans. Janette C. Hudson and Luanne T. Frank (1951; reprint, University Park: Pennsylvania State University Press, 1991). (Staiger also summarizes the understanding of lyric given in this book in his "Lyrik und lyrisch," in *Der Deutschunterricht. Beiträge zu seiner Praxis und wissenschaftlichen Grundlegung* 2 (1952): 7–12. See Adorno's "Lyric and Society," in his *Notes to Literature*, trans. Shierry Weber Nicholson (New York: Columbia University Press, 1991), 1:30–36.

8. Shelley, *Hellas*, 409.

9. This will be true for the Hellenism practiced from the end of the reign of Alexander the Great in 323 B.C. until the first century B.C., as well as for the Hellenism of the eighteenth century.

10. As the apocryphal story goes, Aeschylus fought in the battle of Salamis, Sophocles sang in the chorus celebrating the Greek victory, and Euripides is born on the date of its occurrence.

11. That the historical, political, and cultural significance of Greece was an issue for Greece is made clear in the study by Nicole Loraux referred to in the Introduction.

12. Peter Euben has explored this aspect of the Athenian appropriation of Salamis in "The Battle of Salamis and the Origins of Political Theory" (*Political Theory* 14, no. 3 (1986): 359–90). Euben points out that Aeschylus's *Persians* cannot in the end be an historical play since it actively misrepresents the historical record. Euben notes, "Aeschylus misrepresents Darius as a prudent king who never left Asia, exaggerates the importance of the minor action on Psytallia, portrays Xerxes's retreat from Salamis as the hasty flight of a totally shattered monarch, and virtually invents the disaster at Strymon" (363). The act of pointing out these representations exposes a mythologizing tendency toward Salamis; however, the role of these misrepresentations within Aeschylus's drama remains to be read, otherwise this work will be simply subsumed into the political self-representations of Athens.

13. Line references to Aeschylus's *Persians*, given parenthetically, are to the Greek text. The edition referred to is *The Persae of Aeschylus*, ed. H. D. Broadhead (Cambridge: Cambridge University Press, 1974); the translation is from Edith Hall's edition of the *Persians* (Warminster, Eng.: Aris & Phillips, 1996). This particular quote is found in lines 140–47.

14. This aspect also appears in its language, in particular, when the Chorus invokes the ghost of Darius. See Broadhead's Introduction to *The Persae of Aeschylus*, xxx.

15. *The Persae of Aeschylus*, 185–86.

16. This detail should already cause some hesitation, if not resistance, to the tendency to cast Aeschylus's *Persians* as the first text of European Orientalism. This tendency has most recently been given expression by Edith Hall when she writes that Aeschylus's "*Persae* represents the earliest full-blown expression of orientalism in extant Greek literature" ("Asia Unmanned: Images of Victory in Classical Athens," in *War and Society in the Greek World*, ed. John Rich and Graham Shipley [London: Routledge, 1993], 116). In this remark, Hall is essentially informed by Edward Said, from whom she quotes the following comment on Aeschylus's *Persians*: "Asia speaks through and by virtue of the European imagination, which is depicted as victorious over Asia, that hostile 'other' world across the sea" (Hall, 109). Leaving aside the historical question of what constitutes the European imagination in fifth-century Athens, there remains the need to distinguish between a reading of Aeschylus's play that seeks to affirm such an imagination (from which Said and Hall cannot be exempted if their critical positions and identification of ideology are to be sustained) and a reading directed toward the understanding of such an imagination within this play. In other terms, one

should hesitate before defining a work according to its thematic content, lest it turn out that such a content is what the work reflects upon, rather than what it merely reflects.

17. *The Persae of Aeschylus*, 355–60.

18. The later defeats of the Persian Army at Plataia and of its remaining fleet at Mykale in 479 B.C. are also referred to by Dareios as a prophesy of events already known to the play's audience.

19. An account of the full political and historical consequences of this myth, which is in effect the myth of myth, is presented by Philippe Lacoue-Labarthe in "The Fiction of the Political," in his *Heidegger, Art and Politics*, trans. Chris Turner (Oxford, Eng.: Blackwell, 1990), 93–99.

20. Shelley, *Hellas*, 408.

21. On change in Kant, see *Critique of Pure Reason*, trans. Norman Kemp Smith (London: Macmillan, 1982), 76–77, 216–17.

22. Dareios's comparable statement is, "Leaving Hades is especially difficult, and the gods of the underworld are better at taking than releasing" (687–90).

CHAPTER 5

1. Preface to *Prometheus Unbound*, in *Shelley's Poetry and Prose*, ed. Donald H. Reiman and Sharon B. Powers (New York: W. W. Norton, 1977), 132. Unless otherwise noted all subsequent references to Shelley's work will be to this edition.

2. This resistance to Greece as model is not only evident from Shelley's *Hellas* but also in the play on which Shelley's drama is based, Aeschylus's *Persians*.

3. The prevalence of both of these relations to Greece is documented, even within the romantic period itself, by Timothy Webb in *English Romantic Hellenism 1700–1824* (Manchester, Eng.: Manchester University Press, 1982). At the end of his Introduction, Webb also defines and thereby limits the place of Greece within the romantic period as "an ideal toward which one might aspire or as a false example which must be repudiated" (32). Symptomatic of the literary treatment of this theme, Webb's collection must focus on those prose reflections of Greece that reinforce the critical clichés of romantic Hellenism. As the poetry of the period indicates more clearly, the critical view of what Hellenism is should not be substituted for the way it is treated in the works to which criticism should direct its attention.

4. This passage is also cited early in Susan Hawk Brisman's essay ("'Unsaying His High Language': The Problem of Voice in *Prometheus Unbound*," *Studies in Romanticism* 16 [winter 1977]: 51–86), to which almost all modern readings of *Prometheus Unbound* are in some way indebted. Brisman discusses the passage as an example of Prometheus's continuing scorn for Jupiter and his flatterers. Rather, the reading pursued here seeks to explore the question of a justice no

longer based on deed or event—unlike a justice based on punishment. Although little has been written on the question of judgment and justice in Shelley's *Prometheus Unbound*, the close relation of this question to the play's treatment of language incurs a special indebtedness to Susan Brisman's essay as well as to the Carol Jacobs essay, "Unbinding Words," in her *Uncontainable Romanticism* (Baltimore: Johns Hopkins University Press, 1989).

5. One could even go so far as to say that the entire thematic treatment of the figure of Prometheus subscribes to a national history or mythology of history wherever it is evoked. This suggests that in the figure of Prometheus the negation of freedom is at stake.

6. Shelley, *Prometheus Unbound*, 133.

7. On these senses of recall and their importance throughout *Prometheus Unbound*, see Jacobs, "Unbinding Words," 19–57.

8. Shelley, *Prometheus Unbound*, 1.44–53.

9. Brisman refers to this understanding as "Hermetic," which she opposes to the Orphic, or "new language," of Prometheus as it emerges in the course of the drama ("'Unsaying His High Language,'" 56–60). As this essay will indicate, the difficulty of sustaining such an opposition defines any possibility of another language, and still less a language of the sublime that is no longer directed toward defiance.

10. Of all interpretations of this play, the most persistent is the tendency to see Prometheus as developing toward a new understanding that distinguishes him from Jupiter. The persistence of this tendency reflects the supremacy of the Promethean myth, rather than Shelley's treatment of that myth.

11. As Jacobs has most recently pointed out, the occurrence of these two languages on a page that makes no distinction between the language of the dead and that of the living has a been a source of considerable critical consternation. She also reminds us that we are clearly not meant to read the words of Earth as if we cannot understand them: that is, we are not meant to read this play from the perspective of Prometheus (*Uncontainable Romanticism*, 206–7, n. 15). The difficulty this dialogue poses for criticism may be attributed to the critical tendency to side with a Prometheus whose role is to produce a language that leads to knowledge, a tendency that would recall the curse in order to avoid the curse of recall.

12. Shelley, *Prometheus Unbound*, 1.149–51.

13. As I have indicated in several instances already, speaking of the curse as forethought is appropriate, because it proclaims what is to be worked out through time and history. The meaning of Prometheus's name—forethought—and what it is made to represent are parts of this history.

14. Brisman places much emphasis on this shift as a movement from the

tyranny of visual images, represented by Jupiter and his Furies, to Prometheus's assertion of freedom in speech ("'Unsaying His High Language,'" 70-72). To thus distinguish between the visual and verbal risks regarding this play's language as capable of being both phenomenal and also the means of perception into phenomena. Like the repetition of the curse it gives way to, the visual persists in this play as a language representing a thought it lacks the means to determine.

15. Shelley, *Prometheus Unbound*, 1.258–61.

16. Tilottama Rajan, in her essay "Deconstruction or Reconstruction: Reading Shelley's *Prometheus Unbound*" (*Studies in Romanticism* 23 [fall 1993]: 317–38), speaks of deconstruction in terms of this referential inconstancy which absolves all sin and guilt. Carol Jacobs remarks in a note on Rajan's essay (*Uncontainable Romanticism*, 207, n. 17) that this criticism may be traced to a restricted understanding of deconstruction (see Rajan 334–35). In order to evade this criticism, Rajan calls for "some form of reader-response theory which recognizes as personally and historically variable the response of an explicit reader to the intentionality and disunity of the text" (335). It can also be argued that in *Prometheus Unbound* such a reader is already dramatized in the figure of Earth who gives to Prometheus the very knowledge the play shows him to be unable to attain.

17. Shelley, *Prometheus Unbound*, 1.603–4.

18. Christine Berthin, in her essay "*Prometheus Unbound*, or Discourse and its Other" (*Keats-Shelley Journal* XLII [1993]), recognizes the role of failure in *Prometheus Unbound* when she observes, "something in *Prometheus Unbound* resists the failure of signification and, in fact, requires that failure in order to appear" (131). This something is dialectically bound to failure in Berthin's account and cannot therefore lead to language as a place of freedom, political or otherwise. The failure exemplified by Prometheus is not what is resisted but is itself the unavoidable means of resistance in Shelley's play. Given such a configuration, even failure is unable to coincide with itself since it is what it resists.

19. Shelley, *Prometheus Unbound*, 1.210–12.

20. Jerome Hogle, in "Unchaining Mythography: *Prometheus Unbound* and its Aftermath" (in his *Radical Transference and the Development of his Major Works* [New York: Oxford University Press, 1988], 167–82) resists such an argument when he claims a demythologizing of myth through Prometheus. In Hogle's account, this demythologizing produces a Promethean figure of continuous self-alteration through whom all previous myths are reconfigured. Such a Prometheus is, in Hogle's words, "transference incarnate" (172). In such a transference the freedom of Prometheus would have to be located by Hogle. That Shelley is working with the mythical in *Prometheus Unbound* is undoubtedly true, but restricting his unbinding to a reconfiguration that releases "a frame breaking en-

ergy" thematizes Prometheus as a figure for mutability and, in so doing, thematizes freedom as the experience of change. In a vein not so different from Hogle's, but without using myth as the object of her focus, Isobel Armstrong argues for a principle of constant change at work in *Prometheus Unbound*. Armstrong describes the movement of Shelley's text in terms of "substitutions that continually deconstruct and construct themselves" ("Shelley's Perplexity," in *Language as Living Form in Nineteenth Century Poetry* [Totowa, N.J.: Barnes and Noble, 1982], 122–40).

CHAPTER 6

1. Hölderlin, *Friedrich Hölderlin: Essays and Letters on Theory*, ed. and trans. Thomas Pfau (Albany: SUNY Press, 1988), 39; Hölderlin, *Sämtliche Werke* (Grosse Stuttgarter Ausgabe), ed. Friedrich Beissner (Stuttgart: Kohlhammer, 1943–1985), 4:221. (This edition will be subsequently referred to as *StA*.) The title of this essay ("Das Gesichtpunkt aus dem wir das Altertum anzusehen haben") reiterates the relation to antiquity explored by Keats in his sonnet "On First Looking into Chapman's Homer." In so doing, it emphasizes the way antiquity is first figured on the visual level, as an image. For a view of Hölderlin's relation to the modern across a broader range of his writings, see *Hölderlin und die Moderne: eine Bestandsaufnahme* (Tübingen: Attempto, 1995). A general account of Hölderlin's relation to Greece and its literature may be found in R. B. Harrison's *Hölderlin and Greek Literature* (Oxford, Eng.: Clarendon, 1975).

2. The most searching recent accounts of this relation and its significance for our modernity may be found in Philippe Lacoue-Labarthe's essays "The Caesura of the Speculative" and "Hölderlin and the Greeks" (both in *Typography: Mimesis, Philosophy, Politics* [Cambridge: Harvard University Press, 1989], 208–35, 236–47); and Françoise Dastur's *Hölderlin, tragédie et modernité* (Fougère: Encre Marine, 1992).

3. Benjamin's remarks on Hölderlin's translations are given in "The Task of the Translator." Benjamin notes, "[the]nineteenth century considered Hölderlin's translations of Sophocles as monstrous examples of . . . literalness" (*Gesammelte Schriften* [Frankfurt am Main: Suhrkamp, 1972–], 4.1.17). The close relation of modernity to translation is easily verifiable if one considers the kind of rhetoric accompanying a new translation of Homer, for example. Invariably, each translation may be called the exemplary translation of its age, and in this respect, each is thoroughly modern and thoroughly representative of its time. To the extent that these translations are representative (that is, perfect for their age), they do not, as Benjamin remarks later in "The Task of the Translator," come close to what Hölderlin achieved in his translations of Sophocles. Benjamin describes those translations as "prototypes of their kind, they are related to the most perfect trans-

lation of their text as the prototype is to its example" (4.1.21). More than the most perfect translation, Hölderlin's translations equal what they translate, because, as Benjamin also states, German is "powerfully affected by the foreign tongue" (4.1.20). On Hölderlin's translations, see Friedrich Beissner, *Hölderlins Übersetzungen aus dem Griechischen* (1933; reprint, Stuttgart: Metzler, 1961); W. Schadewalt, "Hölderlins Übersetzungen des Sophokles," in *Hellas und Hesperien* (1970); R. B. Harrison, *Hölderlin and Greek Literature* (Oxford: Oxford University Press, 1975); Philippe Lacoue-Labarthe, "The Caesura of the Speculative," *Glyph* 4 (Baltimore: Johns Hopkins University Press, 1978); Karl Reinhardt, "Hölderlin et Sophocle," in *Poésie* 23 (1982): 16–31; Jean Beaufret, *Hölderlin et Sophocle* (Paris: Monfort, 1983); Tom McCall, "The Case of the Missing Body," in *Le pauvre Holterling* 8 (Strömfeld: Roter Stern, 1988), 53–72; and Antoine Berman, "The National and the Foreign," in his *The Experience of the Foreign* (Albany: SUNY Press, 1992), 157–74.

4. Letter to Casimir Ulrich Böhlendorff [Letter 240], *Essays and Letters*, 152. This letter is presumed to have been written in November 1802, which places it just after his return from Bordeaux and at the beginning of the period marked by his mental derangement. The southern people are identified by Hölderlin as the people of the region that borders the Vendée.

5. Letter 240, *Essays and Letters*, 152; translation modified.

6. In pursuing such an understanding of individuality this reading of Hölderlin's letter to Böhlendorff is pursuing a sense of individuality quite different from that examined by Friedrich Beissner in his *Individualität in Hölderlins Dichtung* (1965), but which has been clearly seen by Peter Szondi in his "Überwindung des Klassizismus" (*Hölderlin-Studien*, [Frankfurt am Main: Suhrkamp, 1967], 110). A more recent volume of essays edited by Anselm Haverkamp and Manfred Frank is witness to the centrality of individuality to not just how to understand literature but also how it is produced (*Individualität* [Munich: Fink, 1988]).

7. Philippe Lacoue-Labarthe, in "Hölderlin and the Greeks" spells out what this means when he speaks of Hölderlin's engagement with Greece as a resistance to the "specter still haunting Europe: that of imitation" (236). Against this subordination to a Greece that one can only imitate, even if it is the failed imitation, from which modernity arises, Lacoue-Labarthe emphasizes in Hölderlin his understanding of a Greece divided and torn, that is, a tragic Greece whose inimitability begins with "the ruin of the imitable and the disappearance of models" (247). From this ruin emerges a Greece that, if imitated, will be nothing more than the exercise of a modernity caught within a mimesis it cannot relinquish. And this mimesis, as Lacoue-Labarthe's work has clearly shown, is precisely where its politics must be located (in this regard see his *La fiction du politique* [Paris: Bourgois, 1989]). On the dangers of restricting foreignness to the Greeks

234 Notes to Pages 162–67

alone and thereby ignoring the essential role of foreignness in the individuality of the modern (a sense that belongs to the modern and is not the exclusive property of the Greeks or of whatever is designated other in a like manner), see Andrzej Warminski's "Hölderlin in France," in his *Readings in Interpretation: Hölderlin, Hegel, Heidegger* (Minneapolis: University of Minnesota Press, 1986), 23–44. Warminski's remarks on the tendency to cling to categories of the mimetic (and as always where the mimetic is invoked, the tragic), even the most radical readings of what Greece means or meant, indicate the extent to which Greece does not cease to be silent whenever the self-representation of modernity is at stake.

8. The contradiction running through Winckelmann's account of a history originating with the Greeks is easily observed when we recall that Dresden, whose climate is markedly different, is considered the place where another Athens will arise. In Winckelmann's history, the logical link that governs the past and thus our sense of history is forgotten so that the future (and with it the present as the moment of transformation) may be given significance.

9. Letter 240, *Essays and Letters*, 153; translation modified.

10. Hölderlin's remark in this same letter that the reflexive power of the Greeks "becomes intelligible for us if we comprehend the heroic body of the Greeks" ("wenn wir den heroischen Körper der Griechen begreifen") does not contradict what he states at the end of this passage. What Hölderlin refers to here is glossed more precisely when he speaks of the "highest movement and phenomenalization of the concepts ['der Begriffe']." In contemplating the heroic bodies of the Greeks, the movement of phenomenalization and conceptualization takes place more explicitly than it would in the case of an ordinary body. What is rendered intelligible in this movement remains essential to Hölderlin.

11. *Essays and Letters*, 44. This text predates the letter to Böhlendorff by two years; and it is generally regarded as having been written in the summer of 1800.

12. "On Different Forms of Poetic Composition," *Essays and Letters*, 44.

13. Letter to Casimir Ulrich Böhlendorff (Letter 236, December 4, 1801), *Essays and Letters*, 150. While this letter figures prominently in many critical discussions of Hölderlin's relation to Greece, only Peter Szondi has submitted it to an essay-length interpretation ("Überwindung des Klassizismus," in his *Hölderlin-Studien*, 95–118).

14. Letter 236, *Essays and Letters*, 149–50; translation modified.

15. Letter 236, *Essays and Letters*, 149; translation modified.

16. The significance of what is at stake here can be gauged from a remark made by Jean-Luc Nancy at the beginning of *The Birth to Presence* ([Stanford, Calif.: Stanford University Press, 1993], 1): "West is precisely what designates itself as limit. This closure is named in many ways . . . in particular, it is named

representation." In Hölderlin's account, the Greeks put in place the possibility of this limit, leaving subsequent history to represent Greece as the event of this limit. Here, more than ever, it is instructive to distinguish between Greece and its historical fate (and above all, the systematic production of Greece as an example of historic destiny in Winckelmann).

17. Letter 236, *Essays and Letters*, 150; translation modified.

18. Although these poems are frequently discussed together, critical attention favors "Andenken," because it is without the difficult textual questions posed by the manuscripts of "Mnemosyne." For that reason it appears more accessible. This preference can be seen in the two of the most extensive readings of memory in Hölderlin, namely, Heidegger's "Andenken" (*Erläuterungen zu Hölderlins Dichtung* [Frankfurt am Main: Klosterman, 1981], 79–151); and Dieter Henrich's *The Course of Remembrance* (Stanford, Calif.: Stanford University Press, 1997). Only in the last pages of his book does Henrich address "Mnemosyne" and only then in the most general of terms (245–47). Heidegger refers to "Mnemosyne" on several occasions and clearly recognizes its importance, even though its interpretation is guided by "Andenken." Yet Heidegger only makes an interpretive gesture toward "Mnemosyne" despite reference to it (see, for example, "Das Gedicht," in *Erläuterungen*, 184, 190; and for an account of Heidegger's "reluctance" to read "Mnemosyne," see Véronique Fóti, *Heidegger and the Poets* [Atlantic Highlands: Humanities Press, 1992], 67–72). The most extensive reading of these two poems occurs in Roland Reuß's " . . . / *Die eigene Rede des andern*" *Hölderlins* Andenken *und* Mnemosyne (Strömfeld: Roter Stern, 1990). Yet, Reuß's achievement is less an interpretation of how these two poems intersect than an exhaustive line-by-line commentary of each poem. Anselm Haverkamp, in two related essays, "By the Figtree—Mnemosyne" and "Secluded Laurel—Andenken" (in *Leaves of Mourning* [Albany: SUNY Press, 1990], 37–77), takes up the questions posed by these two poems and, in particular, an element they both share: the fig tree. The sense of textual richness and theoretical questioning Haverkamp brings to the interpretation of this image as well as to the relation of these two poems distinguishes these two essays within Hölderlin criticism. Indeed, Haverkamp's reading of "Mnemosyne" clearly opens the necessity of facing interpretively the textual difficulties of this poem and above all its cruxes if it is to emerge from the shadow of "Andenken." In what follows, it is "Andenken" that will be read from the perspective of "Mnemosyne," rather than the other way round as has been the dominant tendency.

19. *Geschichte der Kunst der Altertums* (Vienna: Phaidon, 1934), 130.

20. The text of "Andenken" follows D. E. Sattler's edition in the *Frankfurter Ausgabe*. The translation is mine.

21. See "Andenken," in *Erläuterungen zu Hölderlins Dichtung* (Frankfurt am

Main: Klostermann, 1981), 151. Heidegger's emphasis falls upon the "jointure" signaled by such conjunctions. See also Adorno's "Parataxis—Zur späten Lyrik
Hölderlins," in *Gesammelte Schriften* (Frankfurt am Main: Suhrkamp, 1974). In
this essay, Adorno remarks, "In Hölderlin the poetic movement upsets for the
first time the category of meaning" (11:477). With this statement, Adorno opens
the question of the extent to which a linguistic work, and in particular poetry, can
pursue a path no longer recognizable to a criticism that merely begins and ends
with this category. In this context Derrida's essay "The Double Session" (*Dissemination* [Chicago: University of Chicago Press, 1981], 173–285), through its reading of syntax in Mallarmé, points to syntax as a poetic resource within which the
whole movement of referentiality and thus the category of meaning is opened.
That such an opening can only be recognized in its doubleness already locates on
the level of language the division, or caesura, through which Hölderlin sees the
Greeks, as Lacoue-Labarthe has argued in "The Caesura of the Speculative." Derrida's reading of Mallarmé takes up the question of such an opening within a sustained meditation on mimesis, thus reiterating the extent to which Hölderlin's
poetic thought also engages with the mimetic as he attempts to open a reflection
no longer subordinate to a modernity, whose only individuality and thus whose
only freedom will be determined negatively and dialectically by its failure to imitate Greece's self-representation as a political and aesthetic whole.

   22. Aristotle, *Poetics*, 56b38, 57a6.

   23. Here, this reading will depart strongly from Dieter Henrich, who insists
on a close acquaintance with the topography of the Bordeaux region. See *The
Course of Remembrance and Other Essays on Hölderlin* (Stanford, Calif.: Stanford
University Press, 1997), 143–210. For a more general treatment of landscape in
Hölderlin, see David J. Constantine, *The Significance of Locality in the Poetry of
Friedrich Hölderlin* (London: Modern Humanities Research Association, 1979).
Henrich's emphasis on the landscape and its two important evocations in the
poem stands in stark contrast to Heidegger's resolutely philosophical reading,
which Henrich faults for its inability to take into account how the difference be-
tween these evocations indicates the unity of this poem's thought. In this respect,
Henrich's reading, despite its ultimate recognition of the philosophical tenor of
Hölderlin's writing, reveals its own preconception in a unity that Hölderlin's
poem seeks to explore, rather than merely express. On such contradictions in
Henrich's interpretation of "Andenken," and in particular those involved in his
attempt to read the poem poetically, rather than philosophically, see Anselm
Haverkamp's "Secluded Laurel—Andenken," in *Leaves of Mourning*, 60–61.
Mention should also be made of Hent de Vries's insightful and philosophically
informed essay, "Monologisches Gesprach: Heideggers Vorlesung über Hölderlins Hymne 'Andenken'" (in *Zeitschrift für Germanistik* 2, no. 3 [1992]: 550–68).

24. In this respect, remember that no one departs in this poem for the Garonne. In the fifth stanza, only the sailors, we are told, have undertaken a voyage, presumably in the direction of the East Indies. The recall of the Bordeaux region, framed by reference to the conditions favoring a voyage at the beginning and then by the knowledge that such a voyage has already begun, emphasizes a structural aspect of the poem. This, in turn, poses the question of why the moment of departure, which in all respects can be recognized as an historical event, has no presence in the poem except as promise and remembrance. Such a question indicates that the topographical, so favored by Henrich as the resource of his reading, must be read for its role within the structure of the poem, and not as the source of that structure.

25. In this way, and more directly than the equinox, the relation of the conceptual to the phenomenal is posed by the word "noon." Indeed, to what does this word refer? Is it temporal and therefore accessible to experience? If there is such a moment, then it must belong within time. But for there to be a moment such as noon, different from both morning and afternoon, it must have a time all to itself and will therefore disrupt the orderly progression by requiring the day to be lengthened, however minutely. By insisting that this word have a time in which its meaning can be experienced, the logical inconsistency that arises whenever the conceptual is treated according to the demands of experience can be highlighted. For the treatment of the same relation using time and the clock as its examples, see Paul de Man's "Lyrical Voice in Contemporary Theory: Riffaterre and Jauss," in *Lyric Poetry: Beyond New Criticism*, ed. Chaviva Hošek and Patricia Parker (Ithaca, N.Y.: Cornell University Press, 1985), 62.

26. The translation used above is modified here in order to emphasize the word order. Likewise, in order to ensure that this word order still makes sense in English, "aber" has been retranslated as "however."

27. Beissner refers to a passage in Richard Chandler's *Travels in Asia Minor and Greece* (London, 1817), in which a burial mound associated with Achilles is described as being surrounded by trees and vineyards (*StA*, 2:828). Chandler specifically mentions fig trees among the trees he describes. However, without any other significant references, in particular ones that Hölderlin could have known, we are left to read this conjunction of a fig tree and the death of Achilles for its signification within the poem. As Böschenstein's concordance confirms, these are the only two references to a fig tree in Hölderlin's later poetry (*Konkordanz zu Hölderlins Gedichten nach 1800* [Göttingen: Vandenhoeck, 1964], 27). Heinz-Martin Dannhauer, in his *Wörterbuch zu Friedrich Hölderlin* (Tübingen: Niemeyer, 1985), verifies that these are the only two references to a fig tree in Hölderlin's oeuvre (165).

28. The text of "Mnemosyne" used here follows the choice and order of stan-

zas established by Sattler in his edition of Hölderlin' poetry (*Sämtliche Werke*, ed. D. E. Sattler and Wolfram Goddeck [Frankfurt am Main: Roter Stern, 1975–]). However, except for one variant noted below, the text followed here is the same as the text constituted for this stanza by Flemming Roland-Jensen in *Hölderlin's Muse: Edition und Interpretation der Hymne "Der Nymphe Mnemosyne* (Würzburg: Königshausen, 1989), 137.

29. Achilles is also the subject of an essay, "Über Achill" (*StA* 4:224–25) and an earlier poem from September 1798, "Achill" (*StA* 1:271). For a discussion of the more general question of the Greek hero in Hölderlin's poetry, see Jochen Schmidt, "Der Begriff des Zorns in Hölderlins Spätwerk," *Hölderlin-Jahrbuch* 15 (1967–1968): 128–57.

30. While this parallel is obvious, its significance to this poem has not been fully developed. One assumes this is largely so because "Andenken" offers no place to either Homeric heroes or other figures from Greek mythology. An exception to this assumption may be found in Bernd Witte's "Homerische Schatten: Ein historisch-kritischer Kommentar zu Hölderlins 'Andenken'" (in *Vorträge des Augsburger Germanstentags: Kultureller Wandel und die Germanistik in der Bundesrepublik*, 4 vols., ed. Johannes Janota (Tübingen: Niemeyer, 1993), 3:181–92. Still, in the case of "Andenken," its overwhelming national references are, as we have seen, to France. As a result, the reference in "Mnemosyne" to Achilles and the fig tree tends to offer nothing more than a footnote that draws our attention to an example of a lexical analogy between the two poems." In "By the Figtree," Anselm Haverkamp has opened up this image in a way that exploits its richness in the classical and the Christian literary tradition (*Leaves of Mourning*, 37–55). Yet, "Andenken" will still persist in questioning the role of such traditions, particularly their claim to remember what is meant by Hölderlin's own words.

31. Anselm Haverkamp reads the lyrical "I" implicit in this emphasis on "my" and "me" as representing an "identification through wrath" with the Greek heroes. As Haverkamp notes, Hölderlin's ode, "Thränen," characterizes heroes as wrathful ("zorn'gen Helden"). In the case of Achilles, his anger forms the subject of Homer's *Iliad*. Yet, it is more difficult to include Patroklos within this characterization, as Haverkamp indicates when he refers to Patroklos as the positive reflection of Achilles. Through such an identification and its failure, Haverkamp would account for the poet's inability to mourn as it is expressed in the famous closing lines of "Mnemosyne" ("By the Figtree—Mnemosyne," *Leaves of Mourning*, 41–42). The question posed by Patroklos will be taken up below in my discussion of the closing lines of "Mnemosyne."

32. In this respect, the armor functions in the same way as the clothing of Achilles does at the contests in honor of Patroklos. Recall what Hölderlin writes: "At the contests that are being held in honor of the dead Patroklos, almost all

other heroes of the Greek army wear more or less noticeably his color, and finally the old Priam in all his suffering appears to rejuvenate in front of the youth who, after all, was his enemy" (*Essays and Letters*, 44).

33. On Aeschylus's and later Shelley's use of the foreign as a means of defining a Greece no longer subordinate to another nation, see Chapter 4, "The History of Freedom: From Aeschylus to Shelley."

34. One aspect of the text cited here requires comment: the beginning of the second sentence, "Der auch." In Hölderlin's manuscript copy it is unclear whether "der" or "die" is intended. The word is corrected but in such a way that the persistent reading of "der" could result from the failure of "die" to obscure completely the first written word. Nevertheless the opposite could well be the case. (See the facsimile and transcription of Roland-Jensen, in *Hölderlin's Muse*; and those of D. E. Sattler, in *Sämtliche Werke* [Frankfurter Ausgabe], 1:61, 65. For an account of the issues and difficulties this raises, see Roland-Jensen, *Hölderlin's Muse*, 131, 135–36, and 186, as well as Roland Reuss's commentary in " . . . / *Die eigene Rede des andern*" [Strömfeld: Roter Stern, 1990], 655–56).

35. This context is emphasized by the sentence beginning "Die auch" ([She] also). Since within this sentence the who "also" referred to is not specified, we are left to consider the preceding sentences of this stanza for its antecedent. One should not overlook that these sentences all refer to those who have died—Achilles, Ajax, Patroklos, and many others—even if we cannot agree with Beissner's interpretation of the loosening of Mnemosyne's hair as if it were the cutting of a lock signifying death (see note 34 above). On the necessity of distinguishing Mnemosyne from the death of the other heroes, see Hans-Dieter Jung, "Ist Mnemosyne gestorben?" in *Mnemosyne und die Musen* (Würzburg: Königshausen und Neumann, 1993), 264–72. This book also contains an extensive account of the development of the Mnemosyne figure in the thought and myth of antiquity (see 124–92).

36. Hölderlin's syntax does not exclude the possibility that Mnemosyne is the subject of the phrase "ablegte den Mantel" and that subsequently "Gott" should be read as the appositional subject of "löste." The difficulty of deciphering whether Hölderlin writes "der" or "das abendliche" (as well as why the "a" of "abendlich" is not capitalized) contributes to the syntactic ambiguity present in this stanza. On this ambiguity, see Roland-Jensen, *Hölderlin's Muse*, especially 125–37.

37. Here, Hölderlin use of "lösen" recalls Homer's frequently used euphemism for the death of heroes in the *Iliad*—when they die their sinews are loosened, untied, or unstrung.

38. Nancy reflects on this birth in a passage whose relevance to both Hölderlin's relation to the Greeks and the argument being developed here requires little

comment: "It is different for whoever comes after the subject, whoever succeeds to the West. He *comes*, does nothing but come, and for him, presence in its entirety is coming. . . . Presence is what is born, and does not cease being born. Of it and to it there is birth and only birth. This is the presence of whoever, for whomever *comes*: who succeeds the 'subject' of the West, who succeeds the West—this coming of another that the West always demands, and always forecloses" (*The Birth to Presence* [Stanford, Calif.: Stanford University Press, 1993], 2).

39. In this respect, the error of Hölderlin's mourning is to be distinguished from Haverkamp's reading of this ending in "By the Figtree" (*Leaves of Mourning*, 42). For Haverkamp, such a mourning becomes, after Freud, the faulty mourning of melancholia. It remains to be seen to what extent Hölderlin's understanding of mourning would render Freud's distinction between mourning and melancholia impossible to sustain, unless this distinction is itself an example of melancholia—in the sense developed by Haverkamp. Haverkamp also emphasizes the sense of *fehlgehen* present in *fehlen* (41) and does so in order to argue that mourning is itself absent (therefore only melancholia can be present). In either case, Hölderlin is explicit: mourning takes place, and only by taking place its erring can occur. This aspect of mourning informs my discussion here.

40. On errancy in Hölderlin's writing, see also Hans-Jost Frey, *Der unendliche Text* (Frankfurt am Main: Suhrkamp, 1990); Thomas Schestag, *Parerga* (Munich: Klaus Boer, 1991), 17ff; and Patrick Greaney, "Language and Form: Hölderlin's Errancy," *MLN* 113, no. 3 (1998): 537–60.

41. In the case of Mnemosyne, this going astray can also be perceived in the poem through the way in which Hölderlin introduces her. She does not appear directly but through her association with the city of Eleutherai ("Am Kithäron aber lag / Elevtherä, der Mnemosyne Stadt" ["But near Kithairon lay / Eleutherai, city of Mnemosyne"]). Since Mnemosyne appears by means of a city that holds her name as an epithet, her presence in the poem is initially metonymic. The subsequent sentence of this stanza continues as if this metonymy was a metaphorical relation—the name Mnemosyne being understood as the meaning of "Stadt" and "Elevtherä." Through this transformation, Mnemosyne appears as if she had actually been introduced by the sentence beginning, "Am Kithairon. . . . " But as Hölderlin's writing makes clear, Mnemosyne is already amiss. We are only given a place for her name; and this place, as the Greek name used here indicates, is not merely a place-name but the name of freedom.

42. This is the difference against which the topographical emphasis of Henrich's reading of "Andenken" is directed. Henrich's emphasis on what is to be recalled indicates the extent to which his interpretation of this poem is guided by the necessity of such a gathering together: *aber er muß doch*.

43. On this aspect of the title to Hölderlin's poem, see Heidegger's essay "An-

denken," in *Erläuterungen zu Hölderlins Dichtung* (Frankfurt am Main: Klostermann, 1981), 150.

44. This distinction is borne out by Hölderlin's persistent use of the present tense in the passages that could most easily be read as the recall of past scenes. The tense makes clear: what is described is what is present to the poet in thought.

45. Of the symbolic meanings that can be attached to the fig tree, the most insistent is that of fertility and reproduction. The frequent appearance of the fig and fig tree in the Christian Bible invokes this sense—as Roland-Jensen notes there are more than sixty occurrences (*Hölderlin's Muse*, 115). Since the fig tree simply marks the place of a death in "Mnemosyne," no development of this sense appears to be intended by Hölderlin. However, if the appropriation of this tree by Christianity is considered, then the death of Achilles could be read as taking place beside a symbol of the era which took the place of the classical. But to sustain this reading, the poem would have to be reduced to an understanding of antiquity that remains trapped within a simple opposition of the Christian to the classical.

46. Beissner lists three references to the fig tree in the *Iliad* (*StA* 2:828); Roland-Jensen adds a fourth omitted by Beissner. In each case, the fig tree signifies nothing for Achilles. In its first occurrence, it simply marks, as Andromache tells us, the place where Troy is most open to attack (6.433). The second occurrence functions as a marker recording the progress of the Trojans' flight back to the safety of the city (11.167). In the third, it specifies the place where Achilles comes across Lykaon (21.38), and, in the last, it is mentioned as a feature of the landscape Achilles and Hektor run past in the scene leading to Hektor's death (22.145).

47. As stated earlier, the fig tree marks the place in which the passage of a time is described. In "Andenken," the time in question, the equinox, has no temporal existence of its own; it is only known by association with the women who walk there during the time in which the equinox is to occur. In order to have a sign of its occurrence, this time is thus figured in the action of these women: "An Feiertagen gehn / Die braunen Frauen daselbst . . . Zur Märzenzeit,' / Wenn gleich ist Nacht und Tag" ("On festive days walk / The brown women in that very place . . . In time of March / when equal is night and day"). In this way the visual image of the women walking is both the sign and substitute for a difference that takes neither space nor time.

48. Structurally, this is made clear in the poem when Hölderlin repeats in the final stanza his use of "dort" in the opening stanza. The first occurrence of "dort" specifies the place in the landscape to which we are to go; the second specifies the place at which the landscape evoked by the first use is taken by the sea. In this

way, the poem unfolds between what is given (a command to greet what is re-membered) and a taking away of what one is commanded to greet.

49. On the inversion present in these two moments, see Timothy Bahti's fine reading of the rhetorical organization of "Andenken" in his *Ends of the Lyric: Direction and Consequence in Western Poetry* (Baltimore: Johns Hopkins University Press, 1996), 127–45.

50. These lines have not been discussed above, but their consequences have been traced through the lines dealing with dialogue. This command is expressed as follows: "Es reiche aber, / Des dunkeln Lichtes voll, / Mir einer den duften-den Becher, / Damit ich ruhen möge" ("But pass to me, / Someone, the fragrant cup / Full of dark light / So that I may rest").

51. The whole structure of this memory as a metonymy of names can be read in just one sentence in "Mnemosyne": "Am Kithäron aber lag / Elevtherä, der Mnemosyne Stadt" ("But near Kithairon lay / Eleutherai, city of Mnemosyne").

52. The general tendency to privilege this moment in the poem does not it-self err. It only does so when, through a kind of critical mourning, the met-onymical progression of Hölderlin's thought is transformed into a series of meta-phors whose meaning establishes a course to which the poem is subsequently subordinated.

Index

In this index an "f" after a number indicates a separate reference on the next page, and an "ff" indicates separate references on the next two pages. A continuous discussion over two or more pages is indicated by a span of page numbers, e.g., "57–59." *Passim* is used for a cluster of references in close but not consecutive sequence.

Cultural Memory | *in the Present*

Library of Congress Cataloging-in-Publication Data

Ferris, David S.
  Silent urns : romanticism, Hellenism, modernity / David S. Ferris
    p.   cm. — (Cultural memory in the present)
  Includes bibliographical references (p.) and index.
  ISBN 0-8047-2942-5 (alk. paper) — ISBN 0-8047-2943-3 (pbk. : alk. paper)
    1. English poetry—19th century—History and criticism.   2. Keats, John,
  1795–1821—Knowledge—Greece.   3. Shelley, Percy Bysshe, 1792–1822—
  Knowledge—Greece.   4. Winckelmann, Johann Joachim, 1717–1768—
  Knowledge—Greece.   5. Hölderlin, Friedrich, 1770–1843—Knowledge—
  Greece.   6. Schelling, Friedrich Wilhelm Joseph von, 1775–1854.   7. Greek
  literature—History and criticism—Theory, etc.   8. German literature—
  Greek influences.   9. English poetry—Greek influences.   10. Mythology,
  Greek, in literature.   11. Greece—In literature.   12. Modernism (Literature).
  13. Romanticism.   14. Hellenism.   I. Title.   II. Series.
  PR127.F47   2000
  821'.7093238—dc21   99-086877

  ∞ This book is printed on acid-free, archival quality paper.

  Original printing 2000

  Last figure below indicates the year of this printing:
  09   08   07   06   05   04   03   02   01   00

  Typeset by James P. Brommer in 11/13.5 Garamond